CULTURALLY DIVERSE AND UNDERSERVED POPULATIONS OF GIFTED STUDENTS

Essential Readings in Gifted Education

Series Editor
Sally M. Reis

Alexinia Y. Baldwin
EDITOR

CULTURALLY DIVERSE AND UNDERSERVED POPULATIONS OF GIFTED STUDENTS

A Joint Publication of Corwin Press and the National Association for Gifted Children

ESSENTIAL READINGS IN GIFTED EDUCATION
Sally M. Reis, SERIES EDITOR

CORWIN PRESS
A Sage Publications Company
Thousand Oaks, California

For information:

Corwin Press
A Sage Publications Company
2455 Teller Road
Thousand Oaks, California 91320
www.corwinpress.com

Sage Publications Ltd
1 Oliver's Yard
55 City Road
London EC1Y 1SP
United Kingdom

Sage Publications India Pvt. Ltd.
B-42, Panchsheel Enclave
Post Box 4109
New Delhi 110 017 India

Printed in the United States of America

Library of Congress Cataloging-in-Publication Data

Culturally diverse and underserved populations of gifted students / Alexinia Y. Baldwin, editor.
    p. cm. — (Essential readings in gifted education; 6)
"A joint publication of Corwin Press and the National Association for Gifted Children."
Includes bibliographical references and index.
ISBN 1-4129-0431-5 (pbk.)
    1. Gifted children—Education—United States. 2. Children of minorities—Education—United States. 3. Children with social disabilities—Education—United States. 4. Multicultural education—United States. I. Baldwin, Alexinia Y. II. National Association for Gifted Children (U.S.) III. Series.
LC3993.9.C85 2004
371.95—dc22

                                              2004001091

This book is printed on acid-free paper.

04   05   06   07   08   10   9   8   7   6   5   4   3   2   1

Acquisitions Editor:	Kylee Liegl
Editorial Assistant:	Jaime Cuvier
Production Editor:	Sanford Robinson
Typesetter:	C&M Digitals (P) Ltd.
Cover Designer:	Tracy E. Miller
NAGC Publications Coordinator:	Jane Clarenbach

Contents

About the Editors

Sally M. Reis is a professor and the department head of the Educational Psychology Department at the University of Connecticut where she also serves as principal investigator of the National Research Center on the Gifted and Talented. She was a teacher for 15 years, 11 of which were spent working with gifted students on the elementary, junior high, and high school levels. She has authored more than 130 articles, 9 books, 40 book chapters, and numerous monographs and technical reports.

Her research interests are related to special populations of gifted and talented students, including: students with learning disabilities, gifted females, and diverse groups of talented students. She is also interested in extensions of the Schoolwide Enrichment Model for both gifted and talented students and as a way to expand offerings and provide general enrichment to identify talents and potentials in students who have not been previously identified as gifted.

She has traveled extensively conducting workshops and providing professional development for school districts on gifted education, enrichment programs, and talent development programs. She is co-author of *The Schoolwide Enrichment Model*, *The Secondary Triad Model*, *Dilemmas in Talent Development in the Middle Years*, and a book published in 1998 about women's talent development titled *Work Left Undone: Choices and Compromises of Talented Females*. Sally serves on several editorial boards, including the *Gifted Child Quarterly*, and is a past president of the National Association for Gifted Children.

Alexinia Y. Baldwin is a professor emeritus in the Department of Curriculum and Instruction at the University of Connecticut, Storrs. She is a specialist in Education of the Gifted with emphasis on the minority gifted child. Her articles and chapters on this topic appear in many journals and textbooks. She developed the Baldwin Identification Matrix, which is used by many school districts and has co-edited a text titled *The Many Faces of Giftedness: Lifting the Masks*.

Her professional background and some of her many activities are B. S., Tuskegee University; M.A., University of Michigan; Ph.D., University of Connecticut; classroom teacher of music, physical education, teacher of the gifted; Associate Professor, State University of New York, Albany; Director of International Teacher Education Program with University of Manchester, England; professor and department head, Department of Curriculum and Instruction, University of Connecticut; President, The Association for Gifted (TAG) 1978-1979; U.S. Delegate to the World Council for Gifted and Talented, 1981-2003; board member, National Association for Gifted Children; associate editor, *Journal for Exceptional Children*; International President of Altrusa International Inc. 1999-1997; Teacher of the Year award for the Association for Gifted and Talented in the State of New York (AGATE) given in her name.

Series Introduction

Sally M. Reis

The accomplishments of the last 50 years in the education of gifted students should not be underestimated: the field of education of the gifted and talented has emerged as strong and visible. In many states, a policy or position statement from the state board of education supports the education of the gifted and talented, and specific legislation generally recognizes the special needs of this group. Growth in our field has not been constant, however, and researchers and scholars have discussed the various high and low points of national interest and commitment to educating the gifted and talented (Gallagher, 1979; Renzulli, 1980; Tannenbaum, 1983). Gallagher described the struggle between support and apathy for special programs for gifted and talented students as having roots in historical tradition—the battle between an aristocratic elite and our concomitant belief in egalitarianism. Tannenbaum suggested the existence of two peak periods of interest in the gifted as the five years following *Sputnik* in 1957 and the last half of the decade of the 1970s, describing a valley of neglect between the peaks in which the public focused its attention on the disadvantaged and the handicapped. "The cyclical nature of interest in the gifted is probably unique in American education. No other special group of children has been alternately embraced and repelled with so much vigor by educators and laypersons alike" (Tannenbaum, 1983, p. 16). Many wonder if the cyclical nature to which Tannenbaum referred is not somewhat prophetic, as it appears that our field may be experiencing another downward spiral in interest as a result of current governmental initiatives and an increasing emphasis on testing and standardization of curriculum. Tannenbaum's description of a valley of neglect may describe current conditions. During the late 1980s, programming flourished during a peak of interest and a textbook on systems and models for gifted programs included 15 models for elementary and secondary programs (Renzulli, 1986). The Jacob Javits Gifted and Talented Students Education Act passed by Congress in 1988 resulted in the creation of the National Research Center on the Gifted and Talented, and dozens of model programs were added to the collective knowledge in the field in areas related to underrepresented populations and successful practices. In the 1990s, reduction or elimination of gifted programs occurred, as budget pressures exacerbated by the lingering recession in the late 1990s resulted in the reduction of services mandated by fewer than half of the states in our country.

Even during times in which more activity focused on the needs of gifted and talented students, concerns were still raised about the limited services provided to these students. In the second federal report on the status of education for our nation's most talented students entitled *National Excellence: A Case for Developing America's Talent* (Ross, 1993), "a quiet crisis" was described in the absence of attention paid to this population: "Despite sporadic attention over the years to the needs of bright students, most of them continue to spend time in school working well below their capabilities. The belief espoused in school reform that children from all economic and cultural backgrounds must reach their full potential has not been extended to America's most talented students. They are underchallenged and therefore underachieve" (p. 5). The report further indicates that our nation's gifted and talented students have a less rigorous curriculum, read fewer demanding books, and are less prepared for work or postsecondary education than the most talented students in many other industrialized countries. Talented children who come from economically disadvantaged homes or are members of minority groups are especially neglected, the report also indicates, and many of them will not realize their potential without some type of intervention.

In this anniversary series of volumes celebrating the evolution of our field, noted scholars introduce a collection of the most frequently cited articles from the premier journal in our field, *Gifted Child Quarterly*. Each volume includes a collection of thoughtful, and in some cases, provocative articles that honor our past, acknowledge the challenges we face in the present, and provide hopeful guidance for the future as we seek the optimal educational experiences for all talented students. These influential articles, published after a rigorous peer review, were selected because they are frequently cited and considered seminal in our field. Considered in their entirety, the articles show that we have learned a great deal from the volume of work represented by this series. Our knowledge has expanded over several decades of work, and progress has been made toward reaching consensus about what is known. As several of the noted scholars who introduce separate areas explain in their introductions, this series helps us to understand that some questions have been answered, while others remain. While we still search for these answers, we are now better prepared to ask questions that continue and evolve. The seminal articles in this series help us to resolve some issues, while they highlight other questions that simply refuse to go away. Finally, the articles help us to identify new challenges that continue to emerge in our field. Carol Tomlinson suggests, for example, that the area of curriculum differentiation in the field of gifted education is, in her words, an issue born in the field of gifted education, and one that continues to experience rebirth.

Some of the earliest questions in our field have been answered and time has enabled those answers to be considered part of our common core of knowledge. For example, it is widely acknowledged that both school and home experiences can help to develop giftedness in persons with high potential and that a continuum of services in and out of school can provide the greatest likelihood that this development will occur. Debates over other "hot" issues such as grouping and acceleration that took place in the gifted education community 30 years ago are now largely unnecessary, as Linda Brody points out in her introduction to a series of articles in this area. General agreement seems to have been reached, for example, that grouping, enrichment, and acceleration are all necessary to provide appropriate educational opportunities for gifted and talented learners. These healthy debates of the past helped to strengthen our field but visionary and reflective work remains to be done. In this series, section editors summarize what has been learned and raise provocative questions about the future. The questions alone are some of the most thoughtful in our field, providing enough research opportunities for scholars for the next decade. The brief introductions below provide some highlights about the series.

DEFINITIONS OF GIFTEDNESS (VOLUME 1)

In Volume 1, Robert Sternberg introduces us to seminal articles about definitions of giftedness and the types of talents and gifts exhibited by children and youth. The most widely used definitions of gifts and talents utilized by educators generally follow those proposed in federal reports. For example, the Marland Report (Marland, 1972) commissioned by the Congress included the first federal definition of giftedness, which was widely adopted or adapted by the states.

The selection of a definition of giftedness has been and continues to be the major policy decision made at state and local levels. It is interesting to note that policy decisions are often either unrelated or marginally related to actual procedures or to research findings about a definition of giftedness or identification of the gifted, a fact well documented by the many ineffective, incorrect, and downright ridiculous methods of identification used to find students who meet the criteria in the federal definition. This gap between policy and practice may be caused by many variables. Unfortunately, although the federal definition was written to be inclusive, it is, instead, rather vague, and problems caused by this definition have been recognized by experts in the field (Renzulli, 1978). In the most recent federal report on the status of gifted and talented programs entitled *National Excellence* (Ross, 1993), a newer federal definition is proposed based on new insights provided by neuroscience and cognitive psychology. Arguing that the term *gifted* connotes a mature power rather than a developing ability and, therefore, is antithetic to recent research findings about children, the new definition "reflects today's knowledge and thinking" (p. 26) by emphasizing talent development, stating that gifted and talented children are children and youth with outstanding talent performance or show the potential for performing at remarkably high levels of accomplishment when compared with others of their age, experience, or environment. These children and youth exhibit high performance capability in intellectual, creative, and/or artistic areas, possess an unusual leadership capacity, or excel in specific academic fields. They require services or activities not ordinarily provided by the schools. Outstanding talents are present in children and youth from all cultural groups, across all economic strata, and in all areas of human endeavor. (p. 26)

Fair identification systems use a variety of multiple assessment measures that respect diversity, accommodate students who develop at different rates, and identify potential as well as demonstrated talent. In the introduction to the volume, Sternberg admits that just as people have bad habits, so do academic fields, explaining, "a bad habit of much of the gifted field is to do research on giftedness, or worse, identify children as gifted or not gifted, without having a clear conception of what it means to be gifted." Sternberg summarizes major themes from the seminal articles about definitions by asking key questions about the nature of giftedness and talent, the ways in which we should study giftedness, whether we should expand conventional notions of giftedness, and if so, how that can be accomplished; whether differences exist between giftedness and talent; the validity of available assessments; and perhaps most importantly, how do we and can we develop giftedness and talent. Sternberg succinctly summarizes points of broad agreement from the many scholars who have contributed to this section, concluding that giftedness involves more than just high IQ, that it has noncognitive and cognitive components, that the environment is crucial in terms of whether potentials for gifted performance will be realized, and that giftedness is not a single thing. He further cautions that the ways we conceptualize giftedness greatly influence who will have opportunities to develop their gifts and reminds readers of our responsibilities as educators. He also asks one of the most critical questions in our field: whether gifted and talented individuals will use their knowledge to benefit or harm our world.

IDENTIFICATION OF HIGH-ABILITY STUDENTS (VOLUME 2)

In Volume 2, Joseph Renzulli introduces what is perhaps the most critical question still facing practitioners and researchers in our field, that is, how, when, and why should we identify gifted and talented students. Renzulli believes that conceptions of giftedness exist along a continuum ranging from a very conservative or restricted view of giftedness to a more flexible or multidimensional approach. What many seem not to understand is that the first step in identification should always be to ask: identification for what? For what type of program or experience is the youngster being identified? If, for example, an arts program is being developed for talented artists, the resulting identification system must be structured to identify youngsters with either demonstrated or potential talent in art.

Renzulli's introductory chapter summarizes seminal articles about identification, and summarizes emerging consensus. For example, most suggest, that while intelligence tests and other cognitive ability tests provide one very important form of information about one dimension of a young person's potential, mainly in the areas of verbal and analytic skills, they do not tell us all that we need to know about who should be identified. These authors do not argue that cognitive ability tests should be dropped from the identification process. Rather, most believe that (a) other indicators of potential should be used for identification, (b) these indicators should be given equal consideration when it comes to making final decisions about which students will be candidates for special services, and (c) in the final analysis, it is the thoughtful judgment of knowledgeable professionals rather than instruments and cutoff scores that should guide selection decisions.

Another issue addressed by the authors of the seminal articles about identification is what has been referred to as the distinction between (a) convergent and divergent thinking (Guilford, 1967; Torrance, 1984), (b) entrenchment and non-entrenchment (Sternberg, 1982), and (c) schoolhouse giftedness versus creative/productive giftedness (Renzulli, 1982; Renzulli & Delcourt, 1986). It is easier to identify schoolhouse giftedness than it is to identify students with the potential for creative productive giftedness. Renzulli believes that progress has been made in the identification of gifted students, especially during the past quarter century, and that new approaches address the equity issue, policies, and practices that respect new theories about human potential and conceptions of giftedness. He also believes, however, that continuous commitment to research-based identification practices is still needed, for "it is important to keep in mind that some of the characteristics that have led to the recognition of history's most gifted contributors are not always as measurable as others. We need to continue our search for those elusive things that are left over after everything explainable has been explained, to realize that giftedness is culturally and contextually imbedded in all human activity, and most of all, to value the value of even those things that we cannot yet explain."

ACCELERATION AND GROUPING, CURRICULUM, AND CURRICULUM DIFFERENTIATION (VOLUMES 3, 4, 5)

Three volumes in this series address curricular and grouping issues in gifted programs, and it is in this area, perhaps, that some of the most promising practices have been implemented for gifted and talented students. Grouping and curriculum interact with each other, as various forms of grouping patterns have enabled students to work on advanced curricular opportunities with other talented students. And, as is commonly known now about instructional and ability grouping, it is not the way students are grouped that matters most, but rather, it is what happens within the groups that makes the most difference.

In too many school settings, little differentiation of curriculum and instruction for gifted students is provided during the school day, and minimal opportunities are offered. Occasionally, after-school enrichment programs or Saturday programs offered by museums, science centers, or local universities take the place of comprehensive school programs, and too many academically talented students attend school in classrooms across the country in which they are bored, unmotivated, and unchallenged. Acceleration, once a frequently used educational practice in our country, is often dismissed by teachers and administrators as an inappropriate practice for a variety of reasons, including scheduling problems, concerns about the social effects of grade skipping, and others. Various forms of acceleration, including enabling precocious students to enter kindergarten or first grade early, grade skipping, and early entrance to college are not commonly used by most school districts.

Unfortunately, major alternative grouping strategies involve the reorganization of school structures, and these have been too slow in coming, perhaps due to the difficulty of making major educational changes, because of scheduling, finances, and other issues that have caused schools to substantially delay major change patterns. Because of this delay, gifted students too often fail to receive classroom instruction based on their unique needs that place them far ahead of their chronological peers in basic skills and verbal abilities and enable them to learn much more rapidly and tackle much more complex materials than their peers. Our most able students need appropriately paced, rich, and challenging instruction, and curriculum that varies significantly from what is being taught in regular classrooms across America. Too often, academically talented students are "left behind" in school.

Linda Brody introduces the question of how to group students optimally for instructional purposes and pays particular concern to the degree to which the typical age-in-grade instructional program can meet the needs of gifted students—those students with advanced cognitive abilities and achievement that may already have mastered the curriculum designed for their age peers. The articles about grouping emphasize the importance of responding to the learning needs of individual students with curricular flexibility, the need for educators to be flexible when assigning students to instructional groups, and the need to modify those groups when necessary. Brody's introduction points out that the debate about grouping gifted and talented learners together was one area that brought the field together, as every researcher in the field supports some type of grouping option, and few would disagree with the need to use grouping and accelerated learning as tools that allow us to differentiate content for students with different learning needs. When utilized as a way to offer a more advanced educational program to students with advanced cognitive abilities and achievement levels, these practices can help achieve the goal of an appropriate education for all students.

Joyce VanTassel-Baska introduces the seminal articles in curriculum, by explaining that they represent several big ideas that emphasize the values and relevant factors of a curriculum for the gifted, the technology of curriculum development, aspects of differentiation of a curriculum for the gifted within core subject areas and without, and the research-based efficacy of such curriculum and related instructional pedagogy in use. She also reminds readers of Harry Passow's concerns about curriculum balance, suggesting that an imbalance exists, as little evidence suggests that the affective development of gifted students is occurring through special curricula for the gifted. Moreover, interdisciplinary efforts at curriculum frequently exclude the arts and foreign language. Only through acknowledging and applying curriculum balance in these areas are we likely to be producing the type of humane individual Passow envisioned. To achieve balance, VanTassel-Baska recommends a full set of curriculum options across domains, as well as the need to nurture the social-emotional needs of diverse gifted and talented learners.

Carol Tomlinson introduces the critical area of differentiation in the field of gifted education that has only emerged in the last 13 years. She believes the diverse nature of the articles and their relatively recent publication suggests that this area is indeed, in her words, "an issue born in the field of gifted education, and one that continues to experience rebirth." She suggests that one helpful way of thinking about the articles in this volume is that their approach varies, as some approach the topic of differentiation of curriculum with a greater emphasis on the distinctive mission of gifted education. Others look at differentiation with a greater emphasis on the goals, issues, and missions shared between general education and gifted education. Drawing from an analogy with anthropology, Tomlinson suggests that "splitters" in that field focus on differences among cultures while "lumpers" have a greater interest in what cultures share in common. Splitters ask the question of what happens for high-ability students in mixed-ability settings, while lumpers question what common issues and solutions exist for multiple populations in mixed-ability settings.

Tomlinson suggests that the most compelling feature of the collection of articles in this section—and certainly its key unifying feature—is the linkage between the two areas of educational practice in attempting to address an issue likely to be seminal to the success of both over the coming quarter century and beyond, and this collection may serve as a catalyst for next steps in those directions for the field of gifted education as it continues collaboration with general education and other educational specialties while simultaneously addressing those missions uniquely its own.

UNDERREPRESENTED AND TWICE-EXCEPTIONAL POPULATIONS AND SOCIAL AND EMOTIONAL ISSUES (VOLUMES 6, 7, 8)

The majority of young people participating in gifted and talented programs across the country continue to represent the majority culture in our society. Few doubts exist regarding the reasons that economically disadvantaged, twice-exceptional, and culturally diverse students are underrepresented in gifted programs. One reason may be the ineffective and inappropriate identification and selection procedures used for the identification of these young people that limits referrals and nominations and eventual placement. Research summarized in this series indicates that groups that have been traditionally underrepresented in gifted programs could be better served if some of the following elements are considered: new constructs of giftedness, attention to cultural and contextual variability, the use of more varied and authentic assessments, performance-based identification, and identification opportunities through rich and varied learning opportunities.

Alexinia Baldwin discusses the lower participation of culturally diverse and underserved populations in programs for the gifted as a major concern that has forged dialogues and discussion in *Gifted Child Quarterly* over the past five decades. She classifies these concerns in three major themes: *identification/selection, programming,* and *staff assignment and development.* Calling the first theme **Identification/Selection**, she indicates that it has always been the Achilles' heel of educators' efforts to ensure that giftedness can be expressed in many ways through broad identification techniques. Citing favorable early work by Renzulli and Hartman (1971) and Baldwin (1977) that expanded options for identification, Baldwin cautions that much remains to be done. The second theme, **Programming**, recognizes the abilities of students who are culturally diverse but often forces them to exist in programs designed "for one size fits all." Her third theme relates to **Staffing and Research,** as she voices concerns about the diversity of teachers in these programs as well as the attitudes or mindsets of researchers who develop theories and conduct the research that addresses these concerns.

Susan Baum traces the historical roots of gifted and talented individuals with special needs, summarizing Terman's early work that suggested the gifted were healthier, more popular, and better adjusted than their less able peers. More importantly, gifted individuals were regarded as those who could perform at high levels in all areas with little or no support. Baum suggests that acceptance of these stereotypical characteristics diminished the possibility that there could be special populations of gifted students with special needs. Baum believes that the seminal articles in this collection address one or more of the critical issues that face gifted students at risk and suggest strategies for overcoming the barriers that prevent them from realizing their promise. The articles focus on three populations of students: twice-exceptional students—gifted students who are at risk for poor development due to difficulties in learning and attention, gifted students who face gender issues that inhibit their ability to achieve or develop socially and emotionally, and students who are economically disadvantaged and at risk for dropping out of school. Baum summarizes research indicating that each of these groups of youngsters is affected by one or more barriers to development, and the most poignant of these barriers are identification strategies, lack of awareness of consequences of co-morbidity, deficit thinking in program design, and lack of appropriate social and emotional support. She ends her introduction with a series of thoughtful questions focusing on future directions in this critical area.

Sidney Moon introduces the seminal articles on the social and emotional development of and counseling for gifted children by acknowledging the contributions of the National Association for Gifted Children's task forces that have examined social/emotional issues. The first task force, formed in 2000 and called the Social and Emotional Issues Task Force, completed its work in 2002 by publishing an edited book, *The Social and Emotional Development of Gifted Children: What Do We Know?* This volume provides an extensive review of the literature on the social and emotional development of gifted children (Neihart, Reis, Robinson, & Moon, 2002). Moon believes that the seminal studies in the area of social and emotional development and counseling illustrate both the strengths and the weaknesses of the current literature on social and emotional issues in the field of gifted education. These articles bring increased attention to the affective needs of special populations of gifted students, such as underachievers, who are at risk for failure to achieve their potential, but also point to the need for more empirical studies on "what works" with these students, both in terms of preventative strategies and more intensive interventions. She acknowledges that although good counseling models have been developed, they need to be rigorously evaluated to determine their effectiveness under disparate conditions, and calls for additional research on the affective and counseling interventions with specific subtypes of gifted students such as Asian Americans, African Americans, and twice-exceptional students. Moon also strongly encourages researchers in the field of gifted education to collaborate with researchers from affective fields such as personal and social psychology, counseling psychology, family therapy, and psychiatry to learn to intervene most effectively with gifted individuals with problems and to learn better how to help all gifted persons achieve optimal social, emotional, and personal development.

ARTISTICALLY AND CREATIVELY TALENTED STUDENTS (VOLUMES 9, 10)

Enid Zimmerman introduces the volume on talent development in the visual and performing arts with a summary of articles about students who are talented in music, dance, visual arts, and spatial, kinesthetic, and expressive areas. Major themes that appear in the articles include perceptions by parents, students, and teachers that often focus on concerns related to nature versus nurture in arts talent development; research about the crystallizing experiences of artistically talented students; collaboration between school and community members about identification of talented art students from diverse backgrounds; and leadership issues related to empowering teachers of talented arts students. They all are concerned to some extent with teacher, parent, and student views about educating artistically talented students. Included also are discussions about identification of talented students from urban, suburban, and rural environments. Zimmerman believes that in this particular area, a critical need exists for research about the impact of educational opportunities, educational settings, and the role of art teachers on the development of artistically talented students. The impact of the standards and testing movement and its relationship to the education of talented students in the visual and performing arts is an area greatly in need of investigation. Research also is needed about students' backgrounds, personalities, gender orientations, skill development, and cognitive and affective abilities as well as cross-cultural contexts and the impact of global and popular culture on the education of artistically talented students. The compelling case study with which she introduces this volume sets the stage for the need for this research.

Donald Treffinger introduces reflections on articles about creativity by discussing the following five core themes that express the collective efforts of researchers to grasp common conceptual and theoretical challenges associated with creativity. The themes include **Definitions** (how we define giftedness, talent, or creativity), **Characteristics** (the indicators of giftedness and creativity in people), **Justification** (Why is creativity important in education?), **Assessment** of creativity, and the ways we **Nurture** creativity. Treffinger also discusses the expansion of knowledge, the changes that have occurred, the search for answers, and the questions that still remain. In the early years of interest of creativity research, Treffinger believed that considerable discussion existed about whether it was possible to foster creativity through training or instruction. He reports that over the last 50 years, educators have learned that deliberate efforts to nurture creativity are possible (e.g., Torrance, 1987), and further extends this line of inquiry by asking the key question, "What works best, for whom, and under what conditions?" Treffinger summarizes the challenges faced by educators who try to nurture the development of creativity through effective teaching and to ask which experiences will have the greatest impact, as these will help to determine our ongoing lines of research, development, and training initiatives.

EVALUATION AND PUBLIC POLICY (VOLUMES 11, 12)

Carolyn Callahan introduces the seminal articles on evaluation and suggests that this important component neglected by experts in the field of gifted education for at least the last three decades can be a plea for important work by both evaluators and practitioners. She divides the seminal literature on evaluation, and in particular the literature on the evaluation of gifted programs into four categories, those which (a) provide theory and/or practical guidelines, (b) describe or report on specific program evaluations, (c) provide stimuli for the discussion of issues surrounding the evaluation process, and (d) suggest new research on the evaluation process. Callahan concludes with a challenge indicating work to be done and the opportunity for experts to make valuable contributions to increased effectiveness and efficiency of programs for the gifted.

James Gallagher provides a call-to-arms in the seminal articles he introduces on public policy by raising some of the most challenging questions in the field. Gallagher suggests that as a field, we need to come to some consensus about stronger interventions and consider how we react to accusations of elitism. He believes that our field could be doing a great deal more with additional targeted resources supporting the general education teacher and the development of specialists in gifted education, and summarizes that our failure to fight in the public arena for scarce resources may raise again the question posed two decades ago by Renzulli (1980), looking toward 1990: "Will the gifted child movement be alive and well in 2010?"

CONCLUSION

What can we learn from an examination of our field and the seminal articles that have emerged over the last few decades? First, we must **respect the past** by acknowledging the times in which articles were written and the shoulders of those persons upon whom we stand as we continue to create and develop our field. An old proverb tells us that when we drink from the well, we must remember to acknowledge those who dug the well, and in our field the early articles represent the seeds that grew our field. Next, we must **celebrate the present** and the exciting work and new directions in our field and the knowledge that is now accepted as a common core. Last, we must **embrace the future** by understanding that there is no finished product when it comes to research on gifted and talented children and how we are best able to meet their unique needs. Opportunities abound in the work reported in this series, but many questions remain. A few things seem clear. Action in the future should be based on both qualitative and quantitative research as well as longitudinal studies, and what we have completed only scratches the surface regarding the many variables and issues that still need to be explored. Research is needed that suggests positive changes that will lead to more inclusive programs that recognize the talents and gifts of diverse students in our country. When this occurs, future teachers and researchers in gifted education will find answers that can be embraced by educators, communities, and families, and the needs of all talented and gifted students will be more effectively met in their classrooms by teachers who have been trained to develop their students' gifts and talents.

We also need to consider carefully how we work with the field of education in general. As technology emerges and improves, new opportunities will become available to us. Soon, all students should be able to have their curricular needs preassessed before they begin any new curriculum unit. Soon, the issue of keeping students on grade-level material when they are many grades ahead should disappear as technology enables us to pinpoint students' strengths. Will chronological grades be eliminated? The choices we have when technology enables us to learn better what students already know presents exciting scenarios for the future, and it is imperative that we advocate carefully for multiple opportunities for these students, based on their strengths and interests, as well as a challenging core curriculum. Parents, educators, and professionals who care about these special populations need to become politically active to draw attention to the unique needs of these students, and researchers need to conduct the experimental studies that can prove the efficacy of providing talent development options as well as opportunities for healthy social and emotional growth.

For any field to continue to be vibrant and to grow, new voices must be heard, and new players sought. A great opportunity is available in our field; for as we continue to advocate for gifted and talented students, we can also play important roles in the changing educational reform movement. We can continue to work to achieve more challenging opportunities for all students while we fight to maintain gifted, talented, and enrichment programs. We can continue our advocacy for differentiation through acceleration, individual curriculum opportunities, and a continuum of advanced curriculum and personal support opportunities. The questions answered and those raised in this volume of seminal articles can help us to move forward as a field. We hope those who read the series will join us in this exciting journey.

REFERENCES

Baldwin, A.Y. (1977). Tests do underpredict: A case study. *Phi Delta Kappan, 58,* 620-621.

Gallagher, J. J. (1979). Issues in education for the gifted. In A. H. Passow (Ed.), *The gifted and the talented: Their education and development* (pp. 28-44). Chicago: University of Chicago Press.

Guilford, J. E. (1967). *The nature of human intelligence.* New York: McGraw-Hill.

Marland, S. P., Jr. (1972). *Education of the gifted and talented: Vol. 1. Report to the Congress of the United States by the U.S. Commissioner of Education.* Washington, DC: U.S. Government Printing Office.

Neihart, M., Reis, S., Robinson, N., & Moon, S. M. (Eds.). (2002). *The social and emotional development of gifted children: What do we know?* Waco, TX: Prufrock.

Renzulli, J. S. (1978). What makes giftedness? Reexamining a definition. *Phi Delta Kappan, 60*(5), 180-184.

Renzulli, J. S. (1980). Will the gifted child movement be alive and well in 1990? *Gifted Child Quarterly, 24*(1), 3-9. **[See Vol. 12.]**

Renzulli, J. (1982). Dear Mr. and Mrs. Copernicus: We regret to inform you . . . *Gifted Child Quarterly, 26*(1), 11-14. **[See Vol. 2.]**

Renzulli, J. S. (Ed.). (1986). *Systems and models for developing programs for the gifted and talented.* Mansfield Center, CT: Creative Learning Press.

Renzulli, J. S., & Delcourt, M. A. B. (1986). The legacy and logic of research on the identification of gifted persons. *Gifted Child Quarterly, 30*(1), 20-23. **[See Vol. 2.]**

Renzulli J., & Hartman, R. (1971). Scale for rating behavioral characteristics of superior students. *Exceptional Children, 38*, 243-248.

Ross, P. (1993). *National excellence: A case for developing America's talent.* Washington, DC: U.S. Department of Education, Government Printing Office.

Sternberg, R. J. (1982). Nonentrenchment in the assessment of intellectual giftedness. *Gifted Child Quarterly, 26*(2), 63-67. **[See Vol. 2.]**

Tannenbaum, A. J. (1983). *Gifted children: Psychological and educational perspectives.* New York: Macmillan.

Torrance, E. P. (1984). The role of creativity in identification of the gifted and talented. *Gifted Child Quarterly, 28*(4), 153-156. **[See Vols. 2 and 10.]**

Torrance, E. P. (1987). Recent trends in teaching children and adults to think creatively. In S. G. Isaksen (Ed.), *Frontiers of creativity research: Beyond the basics* (pp. 204-215). Buffalo, NY: Bearly Limited.

Introduction to Culturally Diverse and Underserved Populations of Gifted Students

Alexinia Y. Baldwin

University of Connecticut, Storrs

The issues related to the absence of representative numbers of culturally diverse populations of gifted students in programs for the gifted are highlighted in the twelve seminal journal articles from *Gifted Child Quarterly* during the last two decades. Recommendations for addressing these problems have emerged in the research of several authors, yet lingering concerns remain about the continuing absence of these students in programs for the gifted. The concerns focus on testing strategies, societal pressures, attitudes of teachers, researchers who continue to cite heritability causes, and persons in the community who view programs for the gifted as elitist. To address this continuing concern in the field, recommendations for future action should be based on qualitative and quantitative research as well as longitudinal studies.

The lack of culturally diverse and underserved populations in programs for the gifted is a major concern that has forged dialogues and discussion in *Gifted Child Quarterly* over the past five decades. Although the articles referenced under this topic underscore a basic concern, they barely scratch the surface regarding the many variables and issues that still need to be explored. These issues can be classified in three major themes: *identification/selection, programming and staff assignment,* and *development.*

The process of **Identification/Selection** has been the Achilles' heel of efforts to show that gifted programs recognize that giftedness can be expressed in many ways. Early efforts to create identification processes that would allow trained teachers or staff to locate gifted children who might not have scored high on the regular IQ or achievement tests proved very beneficial. Early work by Renzulli and Hartman (1971) and Baldwin (1977) to broaden the process for identifying gifted students gave school districts a much needed alternative to using only IQ or achievement tests to select students thus giving minority students a better chance of being selected. Clarke (1988) organized identification processes used in school districts classifying them as either used for screening or for identification. She designed an identification matrix, but placed the majority of the processes in the matrix under screening techniques. Few of the alternative forms were placed under identification, which narrowed the choices used to *identify* giftedness. Although procedures outside of the usual academic or IQ testing are still being suggested as alternatives, a strong dependence remains on the use of IQ tests, as does a belief that they are more relevant for identification techniques.

Programming should offer a continuum of services that recognize the abilities of students who are culturally diverse, as opposed to limited program offerings designed for "one-size-fits-all." Little attention has been given to using students' strengths in the screening or identification process as a catalyst to help students succeed in the areas of their weaknesses. Most of the programming was based on a deficit model where expectations were low or content was "dumbed down." Appropriate curriculum models and scheduling have been used more as an organizational imperative rather than a theoretically sound strategy for meeting the needs of these students. This inappropriate approach to programming placed the minority student at a double disadvantage.

Staffing for classes of the gifted has constituted another issue related to the inclusion of this population, but an even more important variable is the attitude or mindset of the researcher who develops theories and conducts the research that addresses these concerns. Gifted programs, as a whole, have a low percentage of minority staff members that ironically coincides with the low percentage of minority students in programs for the gifted. The attitudes of both minority as well as the usual majority staff members influence all aspects of programming for students. Minority staff might consider such programs "elitist," whereas majority staff members believe that giftedness rests in the ability to succeed in specific academic courses singularly or in combination. Teacher education programs have been slow to include courses and requirements about the education of gifted students. This has been the source of misunderstandings or preconceived notions about the existence of giftedness in minority students.

Politically correct terminology has evolved over the years in these seminal articles, using words such as disadvantaged, minority, black, African American, culturally diverse, underserved, culturally deprived, and ethnic minority. Although the use of "African American" is currently popular, the term "black" was used when the article titled "I am black but look at me, I am also gifted" (Baldwin, 1987) was written. Reissman (1962) posited a definition of "culturally deprived," defining it as a group of cultural and racial minorities; however, as the nomenclature changes, the use of the term culturally deprived changed its original intent and became a term that implied a deprived culture for these groups. Although a variety of these terms are used interchangeably in this introductory chapter, they all refer to students who are underserved and/or unrepresented in classes for the gifted.

INCLUSION

Scott, Deuel, Jean-Francois, and Urbano (1996) point out that "in the United States of America, children from culturally different and/or low socioeconomic environments constitute a growing percentage of all students, yet assessment tools that effectively evaluate their academic potential are lacking" (p. 147).

One strong theme that continues to surface is that heritability is one reason for the lack of success among African Americans to score well on IQ tests. However, recent evidence suggests that scores on tests often do not indicate the potential of these students. Jensen (1998), in his most recent book, *The G factor: The science of mental ability*, has provided a detailed review of the role that heredity plays in the abilities of various racial or ethic groups. He stated that, "Individual differences in mental test scores have a substantial genetic component indexed by the coefficient of heritability (in the broad sense)" (p. 169, suggesting a hierarchical list of the mental abilities among various ethnic and racial groups. Baldwin and Start (1987) studied 57 inner city minority students using methods suggested by Jensen and had different findings. Unlike other Jensen research projects showing a high correlation between the button box results, the academic achievement tests, and the Standard Progressive Matrices (SPM), a correlation was not found with these students. Jensen had posited that correlations with the SPM, a non-verbal test, would bolster his argument that the depressed scores on various intelligence tests were not related to lack of background in school-related subjects or other societal concerns but in fact were related to heredity. Although the findings of this research cannot be generalized to a larger population, the use of the SPM did help to identify some students in this population who had not been selected for the gifted program due to lower test scores but who should have been considered for selection in programs for the gifted.

PROGRAMMING

A case study conducted by Baldwin (1977) shows the effects of a stimulating classroom on the success of an all-black class of students who did not fit the IQ profile of gifted students. The research contradicts the validity of IQ scores determining whether or not students of this ethnic group are gifted. She cited the case study of 24 fourth-grade black students who would not have been admitted to a program for the gifted without an advocate who saw potential in them, and developed a stimulating environment in which the innate abilities of these students could flourish. The original IQ scores on the Slosson test, which ranged from 100–180, did not indicate the potential of these students; however, a six-year follow-up study revealed that all of the students were in college with substantial scholarship awards in various parts of the country. A follow-up study (Baldwin, 2003) with these students as adults indicated that they perceived that success in their chosen careers resulted from the extended opportunities that further developed their abilities through challenges and high expectations as members of this class for the gifted. One adult male student indicated that this class resolved the lack of challenge in his original placement in school, and changed his peer groups. He also indicated that this class even kept him from joining a gang.

The students in the case study were given an opportunity to design experiments, challenge ideas, conduct research, and challenge their own skills and abilities. The unique ability of each student was viewed as a strength and used as a catalyst for developing or enhancing individual areas of weaknesses. The teacher acted as a facilitator, and worked with the students to develop their skills. One student, who is now a political advisor, indicated that in his writing class he wrote to various embassies around the world for information on aspects of the particular country. He was required to give an oral report to the class on his findings and this helped him overcome his shyness and provided him with additional knowledge about how to secure resources of information that he still finds useful today. It also gave him an opportunity to reflect and assess how he had learned. "Recent research in cognitive psychology applied to education has supported the notion that children benefit from instructional approaches that help them reflect upon their own learning processes" (Marzano, 1988, as cited in Armstrong, 1994).

ATTITUDES

Attitudes about conceptions of intelligence must be changed as Baldwin (1987) has suggested. Research in this volume verified the need for attitude adjustments for a wider view of intelligence by teachers and administrators who develop criteria and procedures for inclusion of students in programs for the gifted. According to the research by Tomlinson, Callahan, and Lelli (1997), this attitude adjustment includes involvement of parents, mentors, and the need for curricula that are flexible and bring attention to the many ways intelligence can be exhibited. In the district in which this research was completed, a high percentage of minorities were not included in the gifted program. This research was designed to help teachers understand this problem and find ways to support gifted students in this district through Project START (Support To Affirm Rising Talent). The case studies presented discuss what recognition of worth and potential can achieve for minority group children. As the authors explained:

When a teacher begins to think about a child in more positive than negative ways, when a classroom becomes more flexible, when a parent hears a message from school that a child is worth special investment, when the doors to school seem open and inviting, when someone from outside the school comes and spends time with a child, important transformations occur. . . . Students who may face life "with their dukes up" because of the tensions which surround them find school a more inviting place and home a bit more hopeful (p. 17).

Following this idea, Baldwin (1984) discussed some assumptions that should be considered as an important part of attitude adjustments, including that

- Giftedness expressed in one dimension is just as important as giftedness expressed in another.
- Giftedness can be expressed through a variety of behaviors.
- Giftedness in any area can be a clue to the presence of potential giftedness in another area, or a catalyst for the development of giftedness in another area.
- A total ability profile is crucial in the educational planning for the gifted child.
- Carefully planned subjective assessment techniques can be used effectively in combination with objective assessment techniques.
- All populations have gifted children who exhibit behaviors that are indicative of giftedness.
- Behaviors classified as gifted should be above and beyond the average of a broad spectrum of individuals. (p. 3)

The process for changing attitudes and recognizing potential in minority students should begin in kindergarten. In this volume, an article written by Scott, et al. (1996) discussed research conducted with four hundred regular education kindergarten students and thirty-one kindergarten students selected for gifted programs. Using a battery of nine cognitive tasks, the researchers showed that this method could be used to identify more ethnic minority children. The authors demonstrated an unusual philosophical perspective regarding the development of a new type of test to identify children from ethnic minority groups, suggesting that

although the current trend is to consider giftedness to reflect multiple characteristics and to define it, therefore, in terms of multiple criteria . . . it is not necessarily the case that one would want to develop a new test that attempts to identify all children falling under such an inclusive concept. Rather, one may attempt to develop a new test that more effectively identifies a subgroup of gifted children . . . those who will excel in the academic domain. To find this type of gifted student, one must assess cognitive processes since cognitive competency can be expected to relate to academic performance (p. 148).

These researchers used a more effective method to select minority students who had the potential for academic excellence as a result of effective and stimulating classroom activities. The findings of this study were preliminary but showed that gifted, minority children could be identified in kindergarten using a brief battery of cognitive tasks. Early identification could place children on the track toward academic success in school.

Kirschenbaum (1998) used dynamic assessment as a diagnostic procedure for finding the potential of students who might not have had educational opportunities due to poor schooling or societal handicaps. According to Vygotsky's (1978) philosophy, stimulating cognitive ability by instructing students on how to perform certain tasks, measuring their progress, and then solidifying what they have learned by solving similar problems reflects the underlying zone of proximal development that encourages teachers to continue to assist the child to move beyond his present ability level. The test-intervention retest process provides support and helps students move to a higher "zone" that is indicative of their potential.

COMMUNITY AND PEER EXPECTATIONS

Another area of concern in research centers around the dilemmas in which male minorities often find themselves when living within their ethnic communities. The attitude of the community may put pressure on black males in gifted classes or programs, causing them to deny their giftedness and refuse to take advantage of the opportunity to delve into more challenging material. This community pressure, however, is not limited to males. Fordham and Ogbu (1986) discovered in their research that black girls also felt pressure to hide their giftedness. Minority gifted students may feel pressured to reject any attempts to develop their intellectual skills because these are the "white man's" activities that should not be followed. Ogbu (1995) has written about ". . . psychological pressures against 'acting white' that are just as effective in discouraging involuntary minority students from striving for academic success. . . . The dilemma of involuntary minority students is that they may have to choose between 'acting white' . . . and 'acting black'" (p. 588). Ogbu defines involuntary minorities as those "who were originally brought to the United States or any other society against their will" (p. 585).

Hébert (2000) has shown in his study of urban males that participating in activities outside of the ethnic group, a strong belief in self and the development of friends of all ethnic groups, and strong family support provided them the inner strength to resist the pressure to reject attempts to develop their intellectual ability. Additionally, Hébert and Beardsley (2001) conducted a case study research to review the role that teachers, parents, and community members played in the development of abilities of rural students. This case study of a rural black male who overcame the inhibiting factors in his environment indicated that rural poverty could have a debilitating influence on students. In spite of these obstacles, students who grow up in impoverished backgrounds often display the ability to rise above these circumstances and exude self-confidence when their families, teachers, and communities give them emotional support. Poverty can deny a student some material things but an active mind and heart can be nourished creatively. Mentors can also be very important in the development of the abilities of children in similar circumstances.

LIMITING CIRCUMSTANCES

In Patton, Prillaman, and VanTassel-Baska's 1990 article, the philosophical underpinnings of the processes used to select students for gifted and talented classes were discussed. Interestingly enough, the propositions regarding diversity were evident in written program documents, but decisions regarding the funding and the structural processes often resulted in the use of traditional methods for selecting minority students. The sample in this national study included documents from fifty states and territories. With the latest national push for "no child left behind," many state educators felt compelled to use more traditional test procedures to ensure continued funding. This hampers the creative process needed to alleviate the problem to ensure that no **gifted** child is being left behind.

Gardner's *Frames of Mind* (1983) featuring his Seven-Plus intelligences (presently including 2 more) has become a vehicle by which multiple criteria are used to create more inclusive identification and programming processes. Although efforts to design assessment techniques and classroom activities representing these intelligences are currently widely used, this concept should first help change the theories and philosophies regarding intelligence rather than to change the design of classroom activities.

In my own work in this area (1994), I investigated the work of teachers who explored a wide range of abilities and interests using Gardner's concept of multiple intelligences. These teachers increased the number of minority primary-grade students who were included in gifted classes; however, problems emerged for these students at the fourth-grade level when more traditional methods of selection were used. Some students assessed by the standard IQ test were denied admission due to their evaluation scores. As an evaluator of the program, I found that in spite of this let down, changes occurred with parents, teachers, and students as a result of this experimental program. There were perceptible changes in the students who entered the fourth grade whether in gifted classes or the regular classes. The changes were seen in self-assurance, task commitment, and skill levels for the students. Teachers became more sensitive to the qualities that indicated giftedness and the processes advocating for those students. Parents became more active in advocating for their students as well and are becoming more involved with their schoolwork. These student changes were similar to those found by Díaz (1998) whose research emphasized the critical importance of early curricular enrichment and talent development. Her research found that the underachievement of gifted and talented culturally diverse students stemmed from low self-efficacy (which may have been an outcome of family situations), school counseling procedures, teachers who lack awareness of the needs of these students, hostile community environments, language differences, and prejudice. These variables led to disruptive behaviors, defensive attitudes, and ultimately, the underachievement of high school students.

FUTURE WORK

Addressing issues related to the population of underserved students requires an in-depth examination of the intervening variables that play an important role in understanding and solving the problems. Much work remains in each of the areas discussed in this introduction, and the questions that emerge call for both qualitative and quantitative research.

- How effective is the identification and placement of minority students in classes in which expectations of success are based on experiences that the majority students have had? Are preparatory classes needed to increase the likelihood for the success of these students? Would this be a politically correct procedure to embrace?
- What curriculum design and teaching strategies are most effective in working with students from different racial and ethnic groups?
- What role does or should the community play in supporting the minority students who show exceptional ability?
- Does current brain research help answer some of the questions about ability and learning potential?
- How can creativity be used as an assessment tool for identification? What role does creativity play in the intellectual quotient?
- Is it possible to, and should we, eliminate IQ tests as an indicator of giftedness?

These questions, and many others, must be asked to more adequately meet the needs of diverse students. Hopefully, future teachers and researchers in gifted education will find answers that can be embraced by educators, communities, and families, and that the needs of these students will be more effectively met in their classrooms.

REFERENCES

Armstrong, T. (1994). *Multiple intelligences in the classroom.* Alexandria, VA: Association for Supervision and Curriculum Development.

Baldwin, A.Y. (1977). Tests do underpredict: A case study. *Phi Delta Kappan, 58,* 620-621.

Baldwin, A. Y. (1984). *Baldwin identification matrix for the identification of gifted and talented.* New York: Royal Fireworks.

Baldwin, A.Y. (1987). I am black but look at me, I am also gifted. *Gifted Child Quarterly,* 31(4), 180-185. **[See Vol. 6, p. 1.]**

Baldwin, A. Y., & Start, K. B. (1987). *Raven matrices scores and educational achievement of black underprivileged children.* Paper presented at the biennial meeting of the World Council for Gifted and Talented, Salt Lake City, UT.

Baldwin, A. Y. (1994). The seven plus story: Developing hidden talent among students in socioeconomically disadvantaged environments. *Gifted Child Quarterly, 38*(2), 80-84. **[See Vol. 6, p. 149.]**

Baldwin, A. Y. (2003). *1967-2003 Reflections of gifted African American students.* Unpublished manuscript.

Clark, B. (1988). *Growing up gifted (3rd. ed.).* Columbus, OH: Merrill Publishing Company.

Díaz, E. I. (1998). Perceived factors influencing academic underachievement of talented students of Puerto Rican descent. *Gifted Child Quarterly, 42*(2), 105-122. **[See Vol. 6, p. 161.]**

Fordham, S., & Ogbu, J. U. (1986). African American students' school success: Coping with the "burden of acting white." *Urban Review, 18,* 176-206.

Gardner, H. (1983). *Frames of mind: The theory of multiple intelligences.* New York: Basic Books.

Hébert, T. P. (2000). Defining belief in self: Intelligent young men in an urban high school. *Gifted Child Quarterly, 44*(2), 91-114. **[See Vol. 6, p. 63.]**

Hébert, T. P., & Beardsley, T. M. (2001). Jermaine: A critical case study of a gifted black child living in rural poverty. *Gifted Child Quarterly, 45*(2), 85-103. **[See Vol. 6, p. 107.]**

Jensen, A. (1998). *The g factor: The science of mental ability.* Westport, CT: Praeger.

Kirschenbaum, R. J. (1998). Dynamic assessment and its use with underserved gifted and talented populations. *Gifted Child Quarterly, 42*(3), 140-147. **[See Vol. 6, p. 49.]**

Marzano, R. J., Brandt, R., Hughes, C., Jones, B., Presseisen, B., and Rankin, C. (1988). *Dimensions of thinking: A framework for curriculum and instruction.* Alexandria, VA: Association for Supervision and Curriculum Development.

Ogbu, J. U. (1995). Understanding cultural diversity and learning. In J. A. Banks & C. A. Banks (Eds.), *Handbook of research on multicultural education* (pp. 582-593). New York: Macmillan Publishing Co.

Patton, J. M., Prillaman, D., & VanTassel-Baska, J. (1990). The nature and extent of programs for the disadvantaged gifted in the United States and Territories. *Gifted Child Quarterly, 34*(3), 94-101. **[See Vol. 6, p. 141.]**

Renzulli J., & Hartman, R. (1971). Scale for rating behavioral characteristics of superior students. *Exceptional Children, 38,* 243-248.

Reissman, F. (1962). *The culturally deprived Child.* New York: Harper Row Publishers.

Scott, M. S., Deuel, L. S., Jean-Francois, B., & Urbano, R. C. (1996). Identifying cognitively gifted ethnic minority children. *Gifted Child Quarterly, 40*(3),147-153. **[See Vol. 6, p. 35.]**

Tomlinson, C. A., Callahan, C. M., & Lelli, K. M. (1997). Challenging expectations: Case studies of high potential, culturally diverse young children. *Gifted Child Quarterly, 41*(2), 5-18. **[See Vol. 6, p. 11.]**

Vygotsky, L. S. (1978). *Mind in society: The development of higher mental processes.* Cambridge, MA: Harvard University Press.

1

I'm Black But Look at Me, I Am Also Gifted

Alexinia Y. Baldwin

State University of New York at Albany

The lack of representation of black gifted children in educational programs for the gifted is a cause for great concern. Historical precedents and lack of empirical data on appropriate identification processes and educational planning techniques have been noted as part of the reason for the lack. A discussion of research data to date indicates that observation techniques, community involvement, and peer, parent, and teacher nominations are viable techniques to use in identifying the black gifted child. The data also show that leadership skills, creativity, and mental processing abilities, are good indicators of giftedness among the black students. Identification, curriculum, the instructional environment (teacher, setting, strategies), and evaluation are discussed as important aspects of a total plan for the black gifted child. Alternatives for program planning are recommended.

Editor's Note: From Baldwin, A.Y. (1987). I'm black but look at me, I am also gifted. *Gifted Child Quarterly*, *31*(4), 180-185. © 1987 National Association for Gifted Children. Reprinted with permission.

PROBLEM IN PERSPECTIVE

The low representation of black children in programs for the gifted is a frustrating phenomenon. Heritability reasons for this condition have been alluded to by persons such as Jensen (1969) and Eysenck (1973). However, research by Baldwin (1977), Hilliard (1976), and Torrance (1971) shows that IQ and achievement tests cannot be depended upon to assess the capabilities of these children. There are many intervening variables which are rooted in historical and environmental precursors. Variables such as socioeconomic deprivation, cultural diversity, social and geographic isolation, and a relative perception of powerlessness, require assessment or identification techniques which cut across these variables to locate the hidden talents of the black child.

According to a report on poverty (one of the intervening variables) Malcolm (1985) indicates that 48 percent of all black children live in poverty and they represent 32 percent of all poor children. This startling statistic highlights the importance of using restructured processes for locating and developing abilities of gifted black children. The task is not an easy one because a single answer regarding characteristics or required curriculum cannot be generalized to all black students. The experiential groupings within the black ethnic structure are quite diverse although the common ingredients of parentage or physical features identify the individual as black. These common ingredients have compounded the effects of the intervening variables listed above.

Historically, giftedness among black students has been a long-standing concern. The need to recognize and develop the giftedness of blacks was a concern of black leaders who were early agents of change. During the late 19th and early 20th centuries, Booker T. Washington and W.E.B. DuBois epoused philosophies which placed emphases on developing the talents and gifts of black students. DuBois (1903) talked about the "talented tenth" and strongly urged that identification and development of this talent be pursued with vigor. His philosophy reflected a concern for the development of academic abilities; whereas Washington's (1900) often repeated statement, "Cast down your buckets where you are," reflected his philosophical approach highlighting the need to develop academic as well as creative and other non-academic specific talents. Historians have tried to draw sharp distinctions between these two educators, but while they differed in their philosophical emphases, their common concern was the recognition and nurturance of the potential or evidenced ability of black people—a group of Americans who were struggling to develop and overcome the indignities that had been imposed upon them through the centuries.

RELATED RESEARCH

During the first half of the twentieth century, concern for or interest in the black gifted child within institutions of public education was practically non-existent. Although studies by Witty and Jenkins (1934–36) and by Proctor (1929) indicated

Figure 1   Profile of Intelligence Test Scores for Screening for Gifted Class Entry

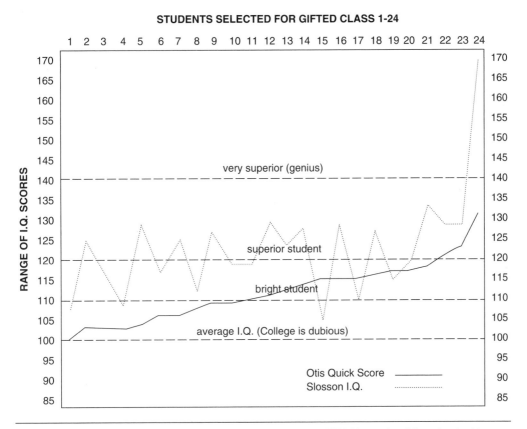

NOTE: From "Study shows tests can underpredict success," April 1976. *National and State Leadership Training Institute for Gifted and Talented Bulletin.* Reprinted by permission.

that giftedness existed among black students, very little systematic planning or research to include these children in gifted programs occurred whether they were housed in segregated or integrated school systems. Theories and concepts regarding the identification of gifted black students have been proposed, but there is a dearth of empirical studies from which to draw for decision-making purposes. Studies that are cited in this article represent a cross-section of reported data regarding identification and educational planning for gifted students.

Federal funds that became available during the mid-sixties for innovative educational programming provided an opportunity for the development of a program for gifted black elementary students (Baldwin, 1977). Longitudinal data from this program highlight the importance of alternative approaches to locating and providing educational experiences for gifted black children.

Figure 1 shows a profile of the IQ scores of 24 fifth grade boys and girls who were selected from a pool of 100 black children representing six schools within

Figure 2   Profile of Achievement Scores in Paragraph Meaning for Years
1966-1969

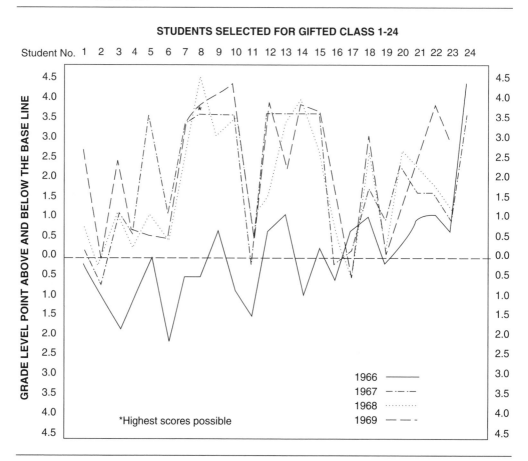

STUDENTS SELECTED FOR GIFTED CLASS 1-24

NOTE: From "Study shows tests can underpredict success," April 1976. *National and State Leadership Training Institute for Gifted and Talented Bulletin.* Reprinted by permission.

a large southern city in 1966. The Otis Quick Scoring Mental Abilities Test was the first source of IQ scores. Paragraph meaning, arithmetic, and word meaning scores of the Stanford Achievement tests taken at the end of the fourth grade were used. Those students scoring 100 IQ or above on the Otis-Lennon Quick Score IQ Test plus those showing grade equivalent scores (GE) of 3.5 or above on the achievement tests were placed in the identification pool. The Slosson Intelligence Test was administered to the entire pool of nominees, and with the data collected from each of these sources, 24 students were selected. The age range was 9.5–10.7. The IQ scores ranged from 100 to 160+ with a GE range from 2.5–4.0. Strict adherence to the scores, which are represented in Figure 1, would have eliminated all but two or three of the students because the city-wide cut-off IQ score for programs for the gifted was 132.

Figure 2 shows the achievement scores in paragraph meaning which were used as part of the identification process in 1966. It is obvious by the line representation for 1966 that many of these children were working far below grade level. Lines on the graph representing subsequent years indicate the outstanding change in achievement of approximately 19 out of the 24 students and the evidence of improved achievement for all of them. The original IQ scores did not indicate this type of potential. A six-year follow-up study indicated that all of the students were in college in various parts of the country with some on substantial scholarships. The educational awards earned by this group included a first place award in a national science competition, a senior year scholarship to study in France, and National Merit Award first and second place winners.

As has been illustrated in the preceding case study, the use of designated score ranges on the IQ or achievement tests as the only criteria for giftedness can significantly affect the black child's ranking for inclusion in programs for the gifted. In this case the use of criteria other than IQ scores proved to be effective.

Hilliard (1976) proposed the use of behavioral styles found in music, religion, and language as vehicles through which intelligence among black children can be discovered. The theoretical framework for his proposition was taken from the behavioral styles research of Cohen (1971) and Shapiro (1965). The item answers on the prescreening test which Hilliard designed clustered around behavioral characteristics usually associated with giftedness. Among these characteristics were alertness, confidence, sense of humor, expressiveness, verbal creativity, and risk-taking. Hilliard's research suggests that these characteristics can be significant indicators of high level ability.

Another attempt to identify black students was done by Davis (1978). Although longitudinal data to verify the effectiveness of this technique are not yet available, Davis has presented a strong argument for community-based identification. A development framework for nomination was designed for black and white community persons to use as one aspect of the identification process. Fifteen students were nominated by this process and placed in programs for the gifted. The areas of giftedness identified for these children included psychosocial ability; talent in specific areas such as math, science, or music; and general cognitive processing ability separately or in combination with other abilities. The report of the study indicated that these students were quite successful in the educational experiences which were planned for them. Davis' small study capitalized on the importance of a significant identification strategy which is often overlooked in school; that is, using community recommendations regarding the giftedness of students,

Analysis of data gathered on an identification process used for 205 black students in the Washington, DC area was reported by Blackshear (1979). She found that nominations from peers, parents, and teachers were most predictive of selection for the program. Of those who were successful and continued in the program after one year, the strongest predictor variable was creative thinking. Items used on the identification matrix for this group of students included informal creative thinking tests, reading and math tests, school grades, and peer, parent, and teacher nominations.

Along these same lines, Dabney (1980) reported in a four year study of black adolescents, that among those children identified as gifted, high level leadership skills appeared to be most predictive of success in the program for the gifted and in their ability to meet college entry requirements at prestigious colleges.

The role of observation strategies for identifying gifted black students has not been fully explored; however, observation of everyday performances as these children interact with their peer group or environment in school and outside of school, can play an important role in the identification process of black gifted children. This assumption has not been verified by controlled research techniques; however, corroborating information from black teachers who have observed black students in class and an analysis of the relationship of these sample behaviors in relation to existing intelligence models, lend credence to the assumption.

An indication of intellectual acuity, for example, can be demonstrated in the child's ability to understand and explain relationships using content common to the child's environment An elaborate story told in non-standard English might not be acceptable as evidence of ability; unfortunately, the focus becomes the English usage, not the detailed plot or figurative language ability displayed. High levels of intellectual processing abilities such as divergent production, transformation of a variety of content, and flexibility of thought can, for example, be displayed through the ability to use commonplace items for purposes other than those for which they were invented. The ability to recall and accurately report detailed information on events which occurred in the community can be a sign of high levels of memory skills and the ability to organize and classify information. These are just a few examples of observable performances that can be used as indicators of exceptional ability. A table of common descriptors (Baldwin, 1985) and a supplemental checklist (Baldwin, 1984) have been designed to help observers recognize behaviors that can be indicative of intellectual acuity.

The black gifted child might bring to the learning environment many skill weaknesses, but he or she might also have strengths which could be used to develop the skills necessary for continued development of all of their abilities. The use of familiar experiences to encourage the growth of abilities in order to accomplish the goals of the curriculum will be crucial.

Music or graphic arts might be the child's area of interest or strength. Cognitive skills in area such as math, science, language development, or history, and skills in research techniques, or synthesis of information can be generated through music or the arts. For junior high students, for instance, parallels in politics and the changing characteristics of jazz can afford a great motivation for the development of basic skills. Students can be challenged to find connections or parallels between the type of political or economic atmosphere (conservative or liberal; depression or boom) and "raw or cool jazz." They can be encouraged to listen to recordings of jazz to determine differences and to search the literature for historical landmarks in politics and economics. As was stated in a previous article (Baldwin, Gear, and Lucito, 1978),

> I think it is important to explain that our goals for the population concerned here are both cognitive and affective in nature. It is imperative

that we plan precisely for these children because we have assumed that there are gaps in their previous school training, and new plans should involve them in a vertical movement in acquiring knowledge while involving them in a horizontal movement where they increase depth of knowledge. (p. 19)

The teaching strategies, the teacher, and the environment are important aspects of the program for the black gifted child. The attitude of the teacher is a crucial element in the child's development. This attitude must be one which is free of prejudice or preconceived stereotypes. There must be acceptance of the child as person who is potentially capable of high achievement. Teachers will need training in recognizing and interpreting these behavioral patterns and the relationship of these patterns to giftedness.

EDUCATIONAL PLANNING

The discussion in this article is not intended to suggest that there is a distinct and totally different program which should be designed for black gifted students. It is intended to show how important it is that program planning, from identification through evaluation of the student, integrate those aspects that are necessary to recognize and enhance the abilities of the black gifted child.

After the process of identification has taken place, developing the appropriate educational plan for the black gifted child that includes the same elements of a design for all children is crucial. To operationalize a plan, attention must be given to each element of the total program framework and the relationship of this plan to the needs of this population. This framework includes: (1) Defining the Population — identification; (2) Deciding the Goals — curriculum; (3) Instructional System — teaching strategies, the teacher, the environment; (4) Evaluation — quality of program, processes, and products.

The first concern in developing curriculum for the gifted black child is that it must be differentiated as for all gifted students. Within this context the curriculum and instructional system which are designed to meet the needs of the black gifted child will be reflected in the plans designed for all gifted students. Differentiation will focus upon more depth and breadth in content, process, product, and teaching strategies. Further ideas for differentiation can be found in Maker (1982a, 1982b) and Kaplan (1986).

The integration of personal development goals such as improved self-concept is important for a program for the gifted. Exum and Colangelo (1979) have recommended the use of a Black Identity Facilitation (BIF) model which includes several components which other programs often ignore. The model includes a cognitive portion which represents a psycho-historical examination of the black experience, a developmental reading portion which includes readings which refer to black gifted children, and laboratory experiences which examine cross-cutural interactions. Along these lines, Frasier and McCannon

(1981) have recommended the use of bibliotherapy which involves children in reading about characters much like themselves in race and socioeconomic levels, who have made significant accomplishments.

The next important aspect of teacher behavior is the ability to understand and to have a higher level of tolerance for behavioral characteristics which don't fit the usual conception of giftedness. The teacher must also play a leadership role in developing harmony and acceptance among the children within the classroom. The teacher must be accepting but must also plan with the students to set criteria and expectancies for cognitive and non-cognitive behaviors.

The evaluation of the success of activities and student development must, in the case of the black gifted child, be primarily formative. Formative evaluation will give the teacher a chance to adjust or alter procedures to meet the needs of the black child. This evaluation must not be solely dependent upon grades achieved but on a combination of behaviors which are important in the total development of the child. It is important that the children themselves become contributors to the evaluation process.

CONCLUSION

The problem of finding and meeting the needs of the black gifted child, as discussed in the preceding paragraphs, has highlighted the importance of additional research and application of appropriate processes for identifying gifted black children. The importance of the role of the teacher and the environment in which the black child will be placed has also been stressed. Although it is important that generalizations not be made for all black children who might be gifted, a good understanding of the variables which might intervene in the process of providing the appropriate educational environment for these children is important. The experience of black gifted students within the total grouping of gifted students should be one where aspects of the black culture will be a part of the lesson explored by all of the children. When ethnic groups have knowledge and understanding of another cultural group, the self-concept and sphere of experience for all groups is broadened and enriched. It is clear that there is a need for an increased understanding of the large pool of gifted or potentially gifted black children who need encouragement and guidance in the development of their abilities.

REFERENCES

Baldwin, A.Y. (1977). Tests do underpredict: A case study. *Phi Delta Kappan, 58*(8), 620–621.

Baldwin, A.Y. (1984). *The Baldwin Identification Matrix 2 for the identification of the gifted and talented: A handbook for its use.* New York: Trillium Press.

Baldwin, A.Y. (1985). Programs for the gifted and talented: Issues concerning minority populations. In F. D. Horowitz & M. O'Brien (Eds.), *The gifted and talented:*

Developmental perspectives (pp. 223–247). Washington, DC: American Psychological Association.

Baldwin, A. Y., Gear, G., & Lucito, L. (Eds.). (1978). *Educational planning for the gifted: Overcoming cultural, geographic, and socio-economic barriers.* Reston, VA: Council for Exceptional Children.

Blackshear, P. (1979). *A comparison of peer nomination and teacher nomination in the identification of the academically gifted, black, primary level student.* Unpublished doctoral dissertation, University of Maryland, College Park.

Cohen, R. (1971). *The influence of conceptual role-sets on measures of learning ability. Race and intelligence.* Washington, DC: American Anthropological Association.

Dabney, M. (1980). *The Black adolescent: Focus upon the creative positives.* Paper presented at the annual meeting of the Council for Exceptional Children. Philadelphia, PA. (ERIC Document Reproduction Service No. ED 189 767).

Davis, P. (1978). *Community-based efforts to increase the identification of the number of gifted minority children.* Ypsilanti, MI: Eastern Michigan College of Education. (ERIC Document Reproduction Service No. ED 176 487).

DuBois, W. E. B. (1903). The talented tenth. In *The Negro problem.* New York: James Port Company.

Eysenck, H. L. (1973). *Measurement of intelligence.* Lancaster, England: Medical and Technical Publishing Company Ltd.

Exum, H., & Colangelo, N. (1979). Enhancing self-concept with gifted black students. *Roeper Review, 1,* 5–6.

Frasier, M. & McCannon, C. (1981). Using bibliotherapy with gifted children. *Gifted Child Quarterly, 25,* 81–85.

Hilliard, A. G. (1976). *Alternative to IQ testing: An approach to the identification of the gifted "minority" children* (Report No. 75 175). San Francisco, CA: San Francisco State University. (ERIC Document Reproduction Service No. ED 147 009).

Jensen, A. (1969). How much can we boost IQ and scholastic achievement? *Harvard Educational Review, 39,* 1–123.

Kaplan, S. (1986). Qualitatively differentiated curricula. In C. J. Maker (Ed.), *Critical issues in gifted education: Defensible programs for the gifted* (pp. 121–134). Rockville, MD: Aspen Publishers.

Maker, C. J. (1982a). *Curriculum development for the gifted.* Rockville, MD: Aspen Publishers.

Maker, C. J. (1982b). *Teaching models in education of the gifted.* Rockville, MD: Aspen Publishers.

Meeker, M. & Meeker, R. (1979). *SOI Learning Abilities Test* (rev. ed.). El Segundo, CA: SOI Institute.

Malcolm, A. (1985, October 20). Poverty: New class of youthful poor, less educated, politically silent. *New York Times,* p. B5.

Proctor, L. (1929). *A case study of thirty superior colored children of Washington, D.C.* Unpublished master's thesis, University of Chicago, IL.

Shapiro, D. (1965). *Neurotic styles.* New York: Basic Books.

Torrance, E. P. (1971). Are the Torrance tests of creative thinking biased against or in favor "of disadvantaged groups?" *Gifted Child Quarterly, 15,* 75–80.

Washington, B. T. (1971). Up from slavery: An autobiography (rev. ed.). Willlamstown, MA: Corner House Publishers.

Witty, P. & Jenkins, M. (1934). The educational achievement of a group of gifted Negro children. *Journal of Educational Psychology, 25,* 585–597.

2

Challenging Expectations: Case Studies of High-Potential, Culturally Diverse Young Children

Carol Ann Tomlinson

Carolyn M. Callahan

Karen M. Lelli

University of Virginia

For an array of complex reasons, minority students and students from low-income backgrounds are typically underrepresented in programs for learners identified as gifted. Project START, a university/school district collaboration, identified and served high-potential, low-income and/or

Editor's Note: From Tomlinson, C. A., Callahan, C. M., & Lelli, K. M. (1997). Challenging expectations: Case studies of high-potential, culturally diverse young children. *Gifted Child Quarterly, 41*(2), 5-17. © 1997 National Association for Gifted Children. Reprinted with permission.

minority, primary age students based on multiple intelligence theory. Instructional and programmatic interventions also included multicultural emphases, language immersion, use of manipulatives, participation in mentorships, and a family outreach program. This article reports findings from eight case studies of START learners, and provides insights into factors that promoted success and discouraged success for these learners, both in the regular classroom and in transition to special services for gifted learners.

Minority students, particularly those from low-income backgrounds, are typically underrepresented in programs for gifted learners (Baldwin, 1994; Frasier & Passow, 1994; U.S. Department of Education, 1993). This is the case for an array of reasons, including: limited and limiting definitions of giftedness, lack of culturally sensitive means of assessing potential, inadequate preparation of teachers in issues and practices related to an increasingly multicultural school population, and lack of awareness among teachers about ways in which potential in culturally diverse populations may be manifested (Ford, 1994; Frasier, Garcia & Passow, 1995). Further, once identified for services provided for gifted learners, students from minority cultures may fare poorly in programs that overlook cultural differences in learning (Ford, 1994). Classrooms and cultures are incompatible when content, methods of teaching, teacher/student interactions, learning styles, and classroom environment are premised solely or largely on majority views and modes of learning (Banks & Banks, 1993; Tharp, 1989). While there is much diversity within any single cultural or economic group, and it is thus important not to overgeneralize about individuals within such groups, researchers have found patterns of learning in varied cultural and economic groups that illuminate the reason many minority students are less successful. Their experience may mitigate against meeting the expectations for learning in traditional classroom environments (Banks, 1993). For example, students from Black and Hispanic groups, as well as learners from low-income backgrounds are likely to use more external clues to solve problems and to have difficulty with abstract learning situations; African-American students are likely to prefer physical and affective engagement in tasks rather than predominantly cognitive engagement; students from low-income backgrounds have difficulty seeing relationships between their behavior and its consequences; students from several minority groups as well as from low-income backgrounds prefer cooperative rather than competitive classrooms, and loosely structured rather than tightly structured environments; and African-American students often prefer spoken rather than written communication, and dramatic rather than direct approaches to communication (Banks, 1993; Shade, 1994). Moreover, students from minority and low-income backgrounds may become quickly disengaged from learning if they fail to see relevance between their own experiences and language, and the school curriculum (Cummings, 1986). Further, the importance of school and its relevance are enhanced for students from minority and low-income backgrounds when representatives of their community, including but not limited to parents, play an active role in school and its endeavors (Cummins, 1986; Vadasy & Maddox, 1992). Research also indicates clearly that classrooms which send implicit or explicit messages that a child (or his/her culture) is somehow inferior or deficient damage self-perceptions and subsequently are detrimental to achievement and success (Bennett, 1990; Baruth & Manning, 1992; Ford, 1996).

Putting the Research to Use

Case studies of high-potential, low-economic primary-age learners reported here suggest a need for educators to understand with specificity the environments from which such students individually come to school. Classroom environments and concepts such as "success" and "failure" should bridge home and school so that educators are focusing on individual possibilities rather than norm-defined "shortcomings." The studies also suggest that schools can be effective in helping parents of such students develop skills of parenting for talent development, and that multi-faceted school interventions (including such elements as classroom modifications, family outreach, and mentorships) may be important in addressing the complexities of student and family profiles.

Despite a proliferation of interest in identification of minority students for programs for gifted learners and their nurturance in gifted programs, few in-depth studies have been undertaken to provide insight about the relative efficacy of alternative identification methods or about the experiences of culturally diverse youngsters identified and served as gifted.

THE STUDY

Project START (Support To Affirm Rising Talent) was a three-year collaborative research project conducted jointly by the University of Virginia and the Charlotte-Mecklenburg (NC) Public Schools. Whereas approximately 40% of Charlotte-Mecklenburg students are minority, fewer than 10% of enrollment in programs for gifted learners was minority. Approximately 69% of African-American students in the district's elementary schools were from low-income backgrounds. The purposes of Project START were to: (a) develop identification procedures based upon Howard Gardner's (1983) multiple intelligence theory,

(b) identify high-potential primary age students from culturally diverse and/or low economic backgrounds through use of this framework, (c) investigate the reliability and validity of the procedures, and (d) test the efficacy of specific interventions on achievement and attitudes about school of identified students. Combinations of interventions varied across experimental sites and included classroom interventions (instruction based on multiple intelligences, a multicultural environment, manipulative-based instruction, and language immersion), mentorships provided by community members, and a family outreach program. Classroom teachers involved in the project either volunteered to participate or responded affirmatively to a principal request to do so. Staff development for classroom interventions took place during week-long institutes during each summer of the project, monthly afternoon meetings throughout each school year of the project, and debriefing sessions following classroom observations of participating teachers by the project coordinator and/or project consultant.

The larger study included both quantitative and qualitative design. (For information on Project START as a whole, see Callahan, Tomlinson, Plucker, & Tomchin, 1996.) One component of Project START research was a series of case studies of students identified and participating at least two years in Project START classrooms. This article reports on the case study component of the larger project.

PURPOSE OF THE CASE STUDIES

High-risk, high-potential learners, such as those in Project START, often seem to fare poorly when assessed only via "traditional" standardized measures. Further, those measures do not allow a glimpse into connections between home and school which are important in any child's life, but which may have particular bearing on lives of children for whom poverty and/or cultural minority status are complicating factors.

Qualitative study (Merriam, 1988; Yin, 1989), utilizing observation and interview, allowed home-school connections to be explored, enabled researchers to look for indicators of success or lack of success not likely to be reflected on standardized measures, and provided a mechanism for examining the impact of varied program components (singly and together) on the lives of students and families. Further, they enabled researchers to determine factors which may inhibit or promote success of these learners in the project.

THE SAMPLE

At the end of the second year of Project START, all participating teachers were asked to nominate in writing a student in their class who appeared "successful" in START and one who appeared "unsuccessful." Further, they were asked to explain their reasoning in making the nominations. Teachers were told that four students from the "successful" category and four from the "unsuccessful" category would be selected by researchers for case studies to take place in the final year of the project. University of Virginia researchers selected eight students for case study based first on teacher comments and then on first year test score growth which seemed to corroborate the teachers' impression of success (that is, a student who showed marked growth on the Iowa Test of Basic Skills during the first year of START) or non-success (that is, a student who made little, no, or negative growth on the ITBS during year one of START).

Four of the students selected were in third grade during the case study year, and four were in second. Selected students attended six different elementary schools, some suburban and some urban.

The case study project coordinator was a University faculty member who also served as a consultant for Project START. Other researchers for the project were graduate students with advanced training in gifted education and qualitative research methods. Each researcher had primary responsibility for developing case studies on two students. Researchers were blind to the successful/unsuccessful rating of students on whom they developed case studies.

DATA COLLECTION

Researchers each spent a minimum of six days onsite in the students' classrooms, and conducting interviews with parents. Three site visits spread over three months allowed researchers to follow up with questions raised in early analysis of data and allowed for observation of students over time. Parents were notified of the case study project (they had given consent earlier in START for student participation in research related to the project) and their cooperation was sought. All parents contacted were supportive of the research and agreed to being interviewed for the case studies.

Triangulation of method and sources was employed in the research (Patton, 1990). Initially, researchers observed their subjects in their educational surroundings, including full-day observations, initial classroom teacher interviews, principal interviews, and interviews with the child's START teacher from the previous school year. Second round visits included interviews with target students, parent interviews, mentor interviews, family outreach coordinator interviews, classroom observation, and additional teacher interviews. Third round site visits included classroom observation and follow-up interviews based on data analysis to that point. At some point in the site visits, researchers also had an opportunity to observe mentorship orientation meetings, faculty meetings, special classes (e.g., English as a Second Language, resource classes for students identified as gifted), and school events (e.g., Christmas programs). Supporting documents (e.g., lesson plans, student work, project handbooks) also served as data sources when available.

Initially, observations were made based loosely on project elements (e.g., multiple intelligences, language immersion, multiculturalism, and use of manipulatives in learning) as well as to determine a general profile of the learner as reflected in the class. Interviews began with a "grand tour" question (Spradley, 1979). Later, semi-structured interview protocols (Bogdan & Biklen, 1982) were developed and used, based on key project goals and questions which arose from first round interviews.

Researchers made extensive observation and field notes (Merriam, 1988) in the course of each site visit, and kept reflective journals (Bogdan & Biklen, 1982) throughout the case study period. All interviews were tape recorded, transcribed for analysis, and checked for accuracy and completeness by the researcher.

DATA ANALYSIS

Following each field visit, researchers paired to debrief on field notes, observation notes, and transcripts. Researchers used a constant comparison method of data analysis (Bogdan & Biklen, 1982), coding notes for recurrent patterns and, ultimately, themes. In addition, notes and transcripts were reviewed by a research coordinator to probe for additional questions, ambiguities, and themes. Each child's case was individually constructed by its primary researcher according to a case study analysis protocol developed to promote categorical consistency across cases. Categories included a description of school and home settings, a vignette of a typical school experience, the child's involvement in START (from observation as well as perspectives of parent, child, family outreach coordinator, mentor coordinator, principal, and other key players), curricular modifications observed and/or reported, evidence of the child's talent (strength) areas, and additional themes and impressions. Group debriefing sessions were held between each site visit to look for emergent common and disparate themes among the cases. An audit trail of data collection and analysis (Lincoln & Guba, 1985) is available.

The eight cases themselves are lengthy, and are thus not included in toto in this article. They are available upon request. Included here are digests of two "successful" and two "unsuccessful" students to provide readers with some insight into both the students involved and the case studies themselves. The synopses are followed by a discussion of key themes from all eight cases.

TWO "SUCCESSFUL" START STUDENTS

Charelle

Charelle is an African-American student in the third grade, on free lunch, homeless for much of the year, and much loved and supported by both parents. Her mother is a housekeeper in a local hospital. Her father "flips burgers" (her words) at a fast-food restaurant. Now in housing in a different school zone,

Charelle still attends the school in which she began, because her mother makes the long bus ride with Charelle, continuing on to her own job via public transportation. Charelle is often as much as an hour late for class because of the extended bus ride, but when she arrives in her classroom, she becomes immediately absorbed in her school work. Charelle's teacher feels the long ride seems worthwhile to Charelle's parents because the school has been nurturing to the family, and that Project START "may have been the icing on the cake (that kept them coming)."

Charelle seems to be hungry, not so much for food as for knowledge. She often asks for extra schoolwork to do at home. Her current teacher calls her " . . . a joy. I feel lucky to have her in my class. There are few children intrinsically motivated like Charelle . . . She's a real big ham. She would act out anything. She's just kind of bright and bubbly and effervescent and gregarious . . . She writes. She loves to tell stories. She's a good leader in a group . . . not as a forceful leader, but she coaches, like, 'Well, maybe we should do this.' She's blown the doors off math in here. I have her well into fourth grade math." Charelle's second grade teacher echoes, "She's very talented in writing and reading. She is very creative, good in art, good in all subjects . . . " The teacher points out a piece of Charelle's art work which is permanently displayed in the school corridor.

The researcher who observed and interviewed for Charelle's case study calls her "a ray of sunshine undimmed by her circumstances." Her mother, who seems quite aware of ideas underlying this multiple-intelligence-based program, explains that "(Charelle) has very good writing skills. I'd say literature is a pretty smart area for her." Her father says, "She does what she sets out to do, and then when she's finished, she'll show us what she's done."

In her school, there is no START mentorship. Her parents say they have had difficulty coming to Family Outreach activities, but talked with enthusiasm about plans to attend an upcoming START activity which would include bowling. The Family Outreach Coordinator, however, says, "I think START has had an impact on Charelle and her family because they have been to most of our meetings."

Charelle's second grade teacher appeared to be a subscriber to the instructional methods central to START. Her classroom is flexible, center-based, and gives evidence of a multiple intelligence emphasis. "I knew that Charelle was a good writer, so I really used her a lot in a lot of linguistic activities . . . I was making sure the children were in the seven intelligences, and this was in the lessons we did, and because of that, I think Charelle was able to choose activities that were very good (for her)."

Her third grade teacher, a first-year teacher who became both a teacher and a START teacher just prior to the opening of school, seemed less clear about the nature of START instruction, "I keep my START students with my assistant during math because they are fasterpaced. They do problem-solving with multiplication, single and double digits, while my other students are figuring out how much a quarter is." Nonetheless, this teacher, too, establishes a flexible environment. "I think (Charelle) loves, enjoys, feels comfortable being in this environment as opposed to an environment that says, 'Sit straight up, speak only when you are spoken to, school is not fun' type of environment." Students in this third grade room were allowed to investigate and speak freely. "That's what I want her to do, is be able to take a risk in an environment were she knows I won't crush her. So I feel like this is a little bit of a START environment, where (students) are able to do things they wouldn't be able to do in the normal classroom environment, where the learning is self-directed."

The school principal seemed less than effusive about START, noting that it "seems to be of benefit to the children." She added that being asked by program administrators to keep a log of contacts with parents was "a little much."

Throughout the duration of the case studies, Charelle's attitude and work remained sterling. However, absenteeism became more of a factor with each month. Teachers expressed doubt about whether she would finish the school year.

William

William is a third grade African-American student whose observer called him "verbally calm, cool and collected, and behaviorally explosive." He does not receive free lunch at school. His mother works hard—extra hours around Christmas "to buy presents for me," he says. William is very attuned to his mother's work schedule and whether she will be home when he is. His father appears to be largely absent from his life. William's current teacher reports that his two key male role models are uncles—one who plays basketball in Europe, and one recently incarcerated. He has no siblings. On the other hand, the school's Family Outreach Coordinator reports that, "His parents always come to our Family Outreach meetings. I mean, when they can . . . You can't always expect that they drop whatever (they are doing) and come have lunch with the kids all the time . . . They are very supportive of him and Project START."

Sometimes when William's mother comes to school, however, she is defensive and accusatory with his teachers. On one occasion, she became verbally abusive with his third grade teacher. The teacher asked her to bring her son to school the next morning so they could all talk about the issue at hand. She didn't show up. She wrote a note and said she couldn't make it. She apologized and made a total turnaround." Earlier, a similar incident happened with William's second grade teacher, who asked William's mother to come the following day to talk with the principal about the confrontation. During that meeting, his mother was "the picture of support and understanding." During the case study interviews, she was supportive, cooperative, and complimentary of his teachers and the school.

William plays pranks on adults and peers alike in ways which are humorous and generally well received. For instance, he and a friend used fake blood to stage a series of "cuts" which resulted in a series of students being sent to the nurse, until she became wise to the origin of the injuries. He introduced the interviewer to his cousin, telling her about the things they did together as relatives.

Later, of course, the interviewer discovered the two boys were not related. In her field notes, she commented, "William can be very convincing."

His third grade teacher suggests, "He's very good at relating to children and adults. His verbal expression skills are incredible. I'm sure you've talked with him, and you know that. He's not intimidated in any way by adults, and with questions, he's very free to give his response, his feelings, and his opinions." "He's sensitive to the feelings of the other students. He's careful not to be pompous about being identified for START. Some students let the others know when they get to do something special. He doesn't brag or anything like that." At another point, however, the teacher notes (and observer confirms) that he has trouble with peer relationships. "I've had to move several students (away from William) . . . He's getting into trouble more often . . . I've even had a phone call from a mother requesting that (her daughter) be moved away from him."

William does not like to be touched. "When students bump into him in the busy classroom, he takes it as a challenge and defends himself." At the end of the case study observations, when the observer told him she would not be coming back to his class again, William became combative and would not make eye contact or verbal contact with her for the rest of the day.

William has had a mentor for each of his two years in START. Both mentors report enjoying him. Last year's mentor tells of being sure to gauge his mood before she began a session with him, "I would hang back and let him take the initiative when he was ready." She says this helped their working relationship and that she tried communicating this strategy to his teacher, "to help smooth whatever was happening in his life at the time." His third grade mentor says he was "forewarned" about William by last year's mentor. He gives his two protégés "a little time to goof around, but they don't take advantage of it." William likes working on the stage in the cafeteria, so his third grade mentor often plans activities that can be done there.

Both William's second and third grade teachers lead classrooms which seem immersed in kindness. Both use center-based classrooms, with his third grade teacher appearing to emphasize a multiple intelligence approach more than his second grade teacher, who seems to stress affect over content and process. William's second grade teacher uses puppets to help the students express themselves, ensures that dioramas on the wall represent many cultures, and talks about channeling his potential "bossiness to good use" by naming him director of a play the class was going to perform. "It was a time he really shined in class," she explains.

His third grade teacher has many learning centers around the room which reflect a variety of "intelligences," although she says she does not consciously plan for every intelligence on a daily basis. She has even moved out her teacher's desk so there will be more space for student exploration. She talks in terms of William's strength areas. "He's very good about communicating his needs. He doesn't stumble over his words or anything . . . He drew the three-dimensional figures (in the geometry mural) himself. I didn't help him with that . . . He was extremely fluid and adept with this (spatial) activity. He knows how to make three-dimensional rectangles, prisms, cubes and things like that . . . A lot of the students have no idea how to make a cube using toothpicks." This teacher also works to use a concept-based approach to teaching her third graders—for example, geometry lessons based on congruence and non-congruence.

William sees himself in terms of academic strengths, too, although he seems unaware of a vocabulary directly related to multiple intelligences. "I really like math. (We were working with) congruent figures . . . I drew a figure (a castle) and then had to make my space figures congruent . . . and I had a pyramid, rectangular prism, and a cube in my castle." William does not refer to his behavior problems.

His observer called him "a complicated little individual with an exceptional mind . . . a man of many faces."

TWO "UNSUCCESSFUL" START STUDENTS

Tev

Tev's family immigrated to the United States from Cambodia 10 years ago, with the aid of a sponsor in this country—a relationship which has been maintained for their decade of residence here. Tev is a second grader with two working parents and a sister born the year after Tev's parents arrived in Charlotte. He is not on free lunch, and the school's mentor coordinator reports that while she did not know where the parents worked, she felt the family was "financially sound." The school psychologist says both children appear well adjusted and that the school has received no requests from the family for any sort of assistance. Tev has an extended family in the immediate area—uncles who are also immigrants from Cambodia. His grandmother comes to this country for extended visits from time to time.

At home, the telephone is answered in English. All other family communication is conducted in Cambodian. Tev's father is very attentive to his son and Tev reads to his father every evening. There is an active Family Outreach program at Tev's school, and his parents have attended every activity which it has sponsored. However, his father struggles with English, seems to have little idea about the meaning of Project START, and expresses a concern to know from the interviewer whether his son is doing well in school. He knows his son is good with computers and hopes someday to be able to buy one for him to use at home. School personnel see Tev's father as a "silent partner." No one in the school appears to have attempted to use a translator to facilitate communication with the family.

Tev's school is 78% African-American and 10% ESL (English as a Second Language). There is a strong administrative effort to have a teaching staff which reflects the ethnic majority. Tev's first and second grade teachers use extensive multi-ethnic literature and talk with students about cultures. Nonetheless, there are racial slurs on the walls of the school, and a teacher's assistant gave advice to a child about, "not letting a White girl beat you." In a culture circles activity, Tev did not draw a circle representing his Cambodian heritage.

Tev's second grade teacher describes him as "not really below grade level. He's not one of my best. But he's really not below grade level. He tries. I can read enough of his stories that he's sounding stuff out."

In listing him as an example of an unsuccessful student, his first grade teacher wrote that he was "extremely shy" and that she had been unsuccessful "in bringing him outward through activities" in class. She explained that he loves math and is very good in it, but that "he does not communicate." She added that his first grade mentor "had been frustrated because she cannot get him to talk." During the Christmas concert at school, Tev knew none of the words to the songs, but stood on stage smiling broadly and moved his lips to the rhythm of the music.

In school, Tev seems bothered by little and bothers no one. He is said by his teachers to be "non-verbal" and "a very quiet child." At lunch, he eats little and talks little, but on the playground, he plays with a number of the boys.

During a typical second grade morning of drill-based work with writing and math, he is meticulous with the math. Observer field notes describe his "making sure that his double digit numbers fit neatly under each other with long, straight black lines under them, and proper spacing for the total," and indicate that he is generally ahead of his classmates in his math work. The observer also notes that when he copies sentences from the board, "his letters are neat and meticulous as his numbers, but his sentences come slowly and he often lifts his eyes from the paper to the board to copy the correct letters."

There are two places at school when Tev's voice is released—with his ESL teacher and with his mentor. Tev leaves and re-enters his regular classroom with virtually no notice from anyone. In his ESL room, the teacher suggests, "He gets his work done, raises his hand, and verbalizes more than in his regular class." The observer concurred. In a picture-based exercise designed to help ESL students develop categories and contents of the categories, Tev named nearly all the objects accurately.

Not surprisingly, Tev viewed his first grade mentor with an "Uh-oh, here she comes again" attitude. His second grade mentor, however, is a freeing and affirming influence for Tev. When the graduate student in economics arrives, Tev is demonstrably excited. The mentor feels Tev "is not as timid as everyone else has characterized . . . We had an automatic bond, so that's why I say, you know, he feels comfortable around me, and I feel comfortable around him. So it wasn't where we had to sit there and pull teeth, you know." This mentor sees Tev's achievement as being "advanced." "I was surprised with his reading. He could read really well, and his math was pretty good too . . . He's just a quick learner." In this setting, when he works with other students, he "talks and giggles." The mentor also sees Tev's strengths with the computer. "He knows how to go from menu to menu, how to use the mouse, even using the number pad and to click from one story to another."

Both Tev's first and second grade teachers say Project START has made them "more aware." His first grade teacher says, "I feel like I was doing a lot of things already, but I wasn't really thinking about them or writing them down in categories like linguistic and logical-math, and it's made me do a lot of research too. I'm constantly searching for new activities to do for spatial . . . So I order a lot of manipulatives and things for building and gears and things like that to really tap into the spatial intelligence."

She has also worked to do some concept-based instruction—generally separate from her centers which remain skill based. She sees Project START lessons as apart from other teaching, but says, "With my Project START lessons, I just think it was more appealing to them, and they weren't tuning me out so much because they were doing (work) in a way that they liked to do it. It's hard. It's a lot of planning. But it's definitely beneficial . . . It really has to be thought out in advance." She also says that this year, there's little time for spatial activities— one of Tev's strengths.

The principal of the school, a strong supporter of Project START, reads about, studies, and attends conferences related to multiple intelligences and multiculturalism. "We as a society need to do a better job with understanding other cultures," she says.

Tev seems to be "coming out" of his shyness a bit, according to his second grade teacher. He doesn't appear to be unhappy about any of his classroom activities, but with the exception of time spent with his mentor, he doesn't seem to be excited about them either.

Denisha

Denisha is an African-American third grader on free lunch. She is one of two children of a single mother, but often interacts with members of her extended family. Her mother works as a graphic artist and has had some college education. They live in a government housing project. Denisha saw her uncle shot and killed in front of her house. This event seems to have shaped her life in palpable ways.

At night, she fears the darkness, and calls to her mother to sing to her so she won't be afraid. She likes being in control of events, which makes people (including her mother and teacher) talk about her capacity to be bossy. She has a strong sense of justice and a need to protect people to whom she feels injustice is being done. "One day, this boy had to stay inside from recess because he had one red check (for misbehavior) and I had one red check (but I could go outside). And that wasn't fair. So I said, 'I'm gonna stay inside because she wouldn't let him go outside.'"

Denisha wants to be a lawyer when she grows up so she "can protect people." Her mother worries that she will be judged by her very dark skin or because she lives in the projects. "I want her to be judged by what she knows. She worries that Denisha is not getting as much support at school as she should be getting. She has attended all of the Family Outreach activities and says they have helped her understand her daughter better. The Family Outreach Coordinator (also a fourth grade teacher) for the school, however, is resentful of her START duties, saying she feels as though she's been "made to do someone else's work for them," and that she can't plan too many family outreach activities because of the busy schedules of parents. Nonetheless, Denisha seems to admire her and says she wants her for her fourth grade teacher. The coordinator is "amazed" by this, and does not suggest that Denisha may identify with her, at least in part, because she is one of the few African-American teachers in the school.

Denisha's mother keeps in touch with the teachers to encourage them to "push" Denisha in school. Denisha's current teacher also believes that this mother has very high goals for her child. They have had extended telephone conversations on a couple of occasions. "She expects (Denisha) to be doing her best and has always been very supportive if I needed that."

Mother and teacher also agree that Denisha is a compulsive talker. "She talks too much," says her mother. "(When she was little) the only way we could keep her quiet in church was to give her pencil and paper, and that's how she learned to write. Started at the age of one. She's been writing her alphabet ever since." Her third grade teacher notes, "She will tell you what she thinks, and she means it. If she hurts your feelings, she'll say she's sorry, but that's what she meant. If she's not happy with someone, she's a little more difficult to manage. But she's forthright in any case."

Denisha is also sensitive. Her mother explains, "She's like an angel. She senses my problems and my fear, my hate, or whatever. She like, 'Momma, are you all right?' I'm like, 'Yeah, I'm fine,' you know, and it irritates me sometimes because it scares me. I'm like, 'Oh God, this child. I don't get her. I don't understand her, and every day she's like a new challenge.'" Her teacher reports that if she gets caught misbehaving, "that really upsets her." The class has a procedure through which any student can place a problem on the class roundtable agenda. The group meets weekly to discuss problems the students cannot resolve on their own. "When a problem involving her is submitted, "that upsets her. She doesn't want that."

In Denisha's third grade class, the observer reports, "more time and energy are spent disciplining and threatening the kids into line than actually teaching and guiding them." The atmosphere is "tight" for this child who seems to need a looser fit. She seems to daydream a lot, although her teacher realizes she knows the answers even when she appears detached. At one point, Denisha leans back and says to no one in particular, "I was just thinking that I've been here 40 days. I wonder what it will feel like when I have been here for 60 days."

During a science lesson, Denisha tries to engineer a group project, but her two teammates become weary of her suggestions and begin a glue gun war. When time is called, her group is the only one which has not finished the work. "Only her simple drawing adorns the collage." She tells her mother, "I don't have any friends at school, don't nobody want to play with me." Her mother asks, "Well, are you trying to boss all the games and be controlling?" Denisha responds, "No. I just be me." I'm like, 'Oh, God! (chuckle) 'cause I know he, and she'll tell you. If there's something wrong, she's gonna let you know . . . She's bossy. I'd say she's a bossy little kid."

In second grade, her teacher responded to Denisha's "attitude problem and impatience" by assigning her to an aide for special work. The observer concluded that the extra attention and focus may have been a positive for Denisha who, this year, "appears to be floundering alone in an atmosphere where discipline and order are the cornerstone of the class, even at the expense of the lesson. Accompanying this dynamic is the feeling that they never quite get down to the lesson." Denisha tells her mother she is bored in class. That Denisha is an excellent writer is the only way her third grade teacher speaks of her in a purely positive way.

Denisha, her mother, and second grade teacher talk about how much she enjoyed her mentor in grade two. Her mother recalls, "I know she loved (the mentor). They were so much alike. Their birthdays were a day apart. They liked the same subjects, and after her visit, (Denisha) would talk about her for the rest of the week." Denisha herself says, "I liked leaving my classroom and working on projects with her." During third grade, mentorships began late. By December, she had only met with her new mentor once.

Denisha's second grade teacher appeared "extremely committed to curriculum recommendations from START." She explained in detail how she used multiple intelligences as a way to organize her planning, how it brought out the creativity in her students, and re-energized her as a teacher. She accumulated a private library of books with a multicultural emphasis, which she encouraged students to read in the room or to check out.

Her third grade teacher reported that, "Project START is probably more in line with what I personally would prefer doing the majority of the time. But the (district mandated) testing we are put through . . . sort of inhibits me from doing as much of it as I would like . . . so I'm just putting my toes in the water, so to speak, and seeing what fits best for me right now."

While Denisha talks of boredom in her regular classroom, she tells her mother she loves going to the special class for gifted learners for which she was recently identified. The teacher of this class, however, sees her as having potential above performance. Commenting on a field trip related to architecture, the teacher noted that Denisha was visibly disengaged throughout the visit and did not function as a part of the group. He commented that if she lives in an environment where she simply appreciates shelter and safely, "this type of subject matter may seem superfluous and irrelevant to her." The teacher did not suggest making modifications in the subject matter to address the issue of relevance for Denisha.

Denisha does not seem to understand the concept of varied intelligences, but rather talks about strengths in discrete subjects or areas. "Most time I'm good in math, reading, social studies, and basketball . . . singing, 'cause I used to sing in children's choir, or praying."

Her mother says her daughter's strengths probably lie in spelling or math, "because she loves to spell and she loves numbers as well. She'll say, 'Well, I can't do this,' and I'm like, 'Okay, explain it to me, what you have to do.' And by the time she finishes explaining it to me, I'm lost and she knows how to do it . . . I think in one way she's bright, but (Denisha) herself, she's like an angel."

DISCUSSION

Qualitative research does not claim generalizability, and it is not the intent of this discussion to generalize either to the entire START population or to other populations. Nonetheless, taking a look at the four "successful" and four "unsuccessful" START students points to some positive elements in this program, as well as hinting at some cautions and considerations which may be of use to other program developers and implementers in similar settings.

Recurrent Themes

Several themes emerged as important from the 8 case studies, individually and collectively.

1) Without exception, these 8 students had at least one parent who staunchly and consistently supported them and were proud of them. Said one mother, "There was one extra sparkling star out there that shined on my baby and made her go. She reached up there and took her star. It was hers to have, she took it, she kept it, and now it's hers for life, and it's not going anywhere."

Despite barriers of language, poverty, fear, and distance (which were factors in the lives of all eight families), these parents believed in their children and wanted to be a part of making their lives better. Such parents may be especially wise sources of investment for schools with meager resources. They did not always know how to parent well, but they wanted to know. They did not always know how to help their children with schooling, but they wanted to know. They were appreciative of even modest efforts, were active learners themselves, and were ready partners with school personnel. Without exception—whether their children were judged to be "successful" or "unsuccessful" in START—they defied the stereotype of uninvolved and unreachable parents.

2) Without exception, the eight START students and their parents felt the program made a positive and important difference to the student involved and/or to the family. While many of the students and parents were unclear about the meaning (or existence) of multiple intelligences, they were quite clear that the school was sending them a message that the child was important, smart, and worthy of attention. The message was not lost on parental self-esteem either. As one parent noted, "The school thinks my kid is smart. That must mean I'm okay too—that I'm doing something right." For many of these parents, a formal communication from the school indicating that a child had great potential which the school wanted proactively to develop was a first. For one parent, it was frightening. She didn't show her child the letter because she feared it would turn out to be a mistake—a letter not about her child at all.

3) For the teachers, the concept of multiple intelligences served as a "boundary breaking" metaphor. That is, talking in specific and concrete terms about a range of intelligences affirmed for the teacher—at least intellectually—the possibilities of children whose capacities seemed "unorthodox" or beyond the traditional schoolhouse conception of "smart." The teachers seemed to buy in, with relative ease, to the notion that START students had potential which teachers could build upon, making the teachers believers rather than doubters where these children were concerned. Early in the first year of START, a teacher reflected, "Once I would have seen these children as different with problems. Now I see them as different with potential." That attitude, albeit subtle, may well have immense power to communicate positively to students (and parents) whose lives are cluttered with problems.

4) The team approach—or at least multi-avenue approach—to serving students used by Project START turned out to be powerful in an unanticipated way. The Project assumption that teachers can have a positive impact on young learners through the classroom, mentors from the community, and that families can be strengthened through family outreach appears generally sound as reflected in these 8 students. However, in no instance did all components of the program work well for a given child. Sometimes a teacher was a strong advocate for the child, the mentor a real encouragement, and family outreach worked less well. In other instances, the mentor and family outreach components were effective, and one or more of the child's teachers appeared less effective with the START learner. Having involvement by several key adults and program components means that if one element is weak, the capacity of the program to have a positive impact is not extinguished.

WHAT ABOUT "SUCCESSFUL" VS. "UNSUCCESSFUL"?

These students make a compelling case for the semantic complexities of a construct like "success." Most of the parents appeared to judge their children to be successful—they were "smart," "hanging on," even in the face of stunning difficulty. Two students judged successful by their teachers at the end of year one in Project START were reported to be "talented in many areas." Both students were female, compliant, and unobtrusive. The other two nominated as successful (and selected for the case studies) were listed by their teachers because of progress in self-esteem and behavior. The male was said to engage in "less fighting" at the end of the year than at the beginning, and to have "checked his attitude." The female was noted to have "a better attitude," and "more complete work."

Nominating comments on students deemed by their teachers to be "unsuccessful," and selected for the case studies, were more mixed. Tev was said to be uncommunicative (no sense in the nominating comments or interviews that the language barrier might be the cause). A male was said to be unsuccessful because he talked a lot, but in unproductive ways, and because he had behavior problems which were not channeled in positive ways. A female (Denisha) was said to be unsuccessful because she had "become more demanding of attention," seemed "to feel she deserved special consideration," and was "not putting forth her best effort." The fourth "unsuccessful" student selected for the case study was said to have "demonstrated minimal talent."

Test scores (Iowa Test of Basic Skills), not likely to best reflect growth in nontraditional student populations, did affirm teacher conceptions of success in one instance (that is, showed marked growth during the course of year 1 of the project), and non-success in one instance (that is, showed little growth, no growth, or negative growth during year 1 of the project). In two cases, the teacher judged a child unsuccessful when the ITBS indicated marked growth. In two instances, the teacher judged a child successful when the ITBS indicated little, no, or negative growth.

In general, among these students and teachers, a child was more likely to be judged successful by a teacher if he/she (1) demonstrated outstanding ability in "traditional" areas (e.g., writing, reading, spelling, math) and/or (2) was a "low maintenance" student (e.g., was compliant and had few or no behavior problems). Also in general among these students, a child was likely to be judged unsuccessful if he/she (1) demonstrated talent predominantly in nontraditional areas (e.g., spatial, intrapersonal) and/or (2) was a "high maintenance" student (e.g., required considerable intervention from the teacher to deal with complications caused by language or behavior). The former pattern suggests that, not surprisingly, teachers were unable to rapidly change their conceptions of intelligence. The latter pattern suggests that in classrooms where teachers must deal with so many students, problems, and decisions, a child who challenges the system becomes a stressor and simply doesn't measure up to the prevailing norms for success.

It is important to note, however, that in at least three instances, students deemed to be successful or unsuccessful by their first year teachers were viewed as opposite by their second year teachers. In these instances, case study observers felt the reversal of judgment was more a product of teacher differences than changes in the children.

In actuality, the case studies indicate that all eight of the START students "succeeded" in one or more noteworthy ways: increased attendance, escalating enthusiasm for schoolwork, growing self-esteem, developing language skills, identification for participation in the districtwide program for students identified as academically gifted, developing talent, and even burgeoning test scores on traditional measures of achievement. All of the eight succeeded in several of these categories during the two-year duration of the project.

What Worked for These START Students

Mentorships. For the eight case study students, the most overt enthusiasm—from students, parents, and even teachers—was for the mentorship component of Project START. While the mentorship program was relatively modest (e.g., sometimes starting later in the year, typically meeting no more than once a week, meetings generally in the school rather than outside school, inconsistent linkage with classroom activities), it was concrete, visible, and positive. Students often indicated that they liked being singled out to leave the class for something peers would like to have the chance to do. It seemed to be a signal read by the protégés and other students that participants were important in the eyes of the school. For many, if not most, of these students, this may have been their first such school experience.

In addition, the mentors themselves were often dedicated to and effective with their protégés. Tev's mentor gave him a voice. Belinda (a case study student not described above) was paired for two years with a local television meteorologist who was devoted to her young charge. Hungry for attention, Belinda responded eagerly. On Tuesdays (mentor days), unlike other days, she was never late or absent. She dressed up and wore a special perfume. She worked hard in her classroom on those days to ensure that her group got no "misconduct points." Belinda's second grade teacher, the mentor coordinator, and Belinda's mother all attribute a positive transformation in her behavior and interest in school to "the TV weather lady." "She is able to zone in on (Belinda's) interests. There has been a big change in her attendance and tardiness." Prior to the mentor relationship, Belinda consistently refused to take part in physical education. The mentor encouraged her. "Now (Belinda) is walking the mile, running it, skipping around it, hopping around it, and just a lot of different things. She's developed coordination, which she should have developed a long time ago." Her mother also explains that Belinda used to become frustrated when she could not do things quickly and flawlessly. "(The mentor) taught her, it's not 'I'm gonna die if it's not done.' I can take my time and do this. (Belinda) was rushing through everything and nothing was getting done right . . . Then she slowed down and took her time." She says the mentor has also taught her daughter, "the importance of when you tell somebody you're gonna be there, be there. Okay. Don't come up with excuses. Just be there." Belinda's mother also believes her daughter is better in math because of strategies taught her by the meteorologist.

And the mentorship for Belinda tapped into her curiosity. "She loves to learn things she doesn't know, that she never even knew existed. (Belinda) didn't even know what a meteorologist was, and now she's all about learning about what a meteorologist is, what is the weather gonna be, how does (the mentor) get her information? What tools do they use? How do they know this is right?"

Belinda is allowed to stay up at night to watch her mentor on the late news so she can learn more about the profession. The power of knowledge has translated into family power as well. "When a seven year old can sit there and tell a twelve year old something she doesn't know, tell me they don't feel special. Very!"

Family outreach. While the quality and consistency of the family outreach program varied from school to school, and while different parents had differing participation records, all of the case study students' parents knew about, appreciated, and attended at least some of the family outreach functions. In every instance, the parents were open to learning what was shared with them at the meetings. They also liked it when their children performed during those events. "The children really shine. It makes me feel good."

For most of these parents, family outreach activities were the only school activities they attended. Transportation provided by the school to these functions was a help. The lure of pizza suppers and door prizes was interesting. But the parents mentioned these elements only casually. What they talked about was the chance family outreach provided to take part in activities with their children, and the chance it gave them to be more effective parents.

Belinda's mother, for example, suggests that through family outreach, she learned about agencies she could call when she needed help for her children. "They (also) taught me it's okay to get angry. It doesn't make me a bad person, doesn't make me an abnormal parent. It makes me a very normal parent. And then (they taught me) to release my anger in a positive way. (They taught me) how to sit down and talk to the kids, put myself on their level and to talk to them like, 'We can work this out together.' They taught me it's okay to say you're sorry to your children, that is doesn't make you less of a parent, doesn't make you littler in their eyes . . . Also how to deal with peer pressure, how to use positive punishment and discipline . . . If it hadn't been for Project START, I just don't know (what would have happened to us). A specific strategy shared through family outreach which this single mother of four, who works two jobs, now uses to lessen tensions at home is an "attitude box." When anyone walks in the house with a problem, they write it on paper, drop it in a box, and literally leave it at the door. Later, they sit down together, look at the problems in the box, and find solutions together. The family also uses "time out" as a strategy which they learned through family outreach to calm tensions. When someone is frustrated and negative tensions are mounting, a family member will suggest that person take a time out so they can regroup. This mom talks about "things we've gathered and learned and nestled for hibernation out of Project START . . . (things) nobody can take away from us."

Classroom modifications. Instructional adaptations advocated by START are the least consistently positive element of the Project for the eight case study students. This should not be surprising in that teachers were being asked to change attitudes and practices in ways which caused major dissonance for many of them, with modest staff development, and in a shorter period of time than literature suggests is feasible. Further, teachers in this district are under heavy mandates to raise student test scores on skills-based competency tests. This particular pressure made it even more difficult for many START teachers to depart from a drill-and-skill approach to teaching in favor of a more concept-based, sense-making approach advocated by START.

Some of the 16 teachers whose students were studied were eager subscribers to START instruction. One teacher found that START provided her with models and strategies to create the student-centered classroom she had always wanted but didn't know how to achieve. One day when a researcher was in her classroom and students were working intently in several groups around the room on tasks of their own design, she talked about a child who had brought in materials from home as a result of earlier study and who had then organized peers to work with him on the materials, about a boy reading contentedly in a rocking chair, and then commented, "I've always dreamed of having a classroom that looks like this, but until this year, I never knew how to make it happen. I am so happy with my teaching now." This veteran teacher of 15 years made major changes in her instructional routines, using not only multiple intelligences but also concept-based instruction in her planning and teaching. Several of the other teachers of case study students also expended concerted and consistent effort to plan lessons which were accessible via varied intelligence strengths, used learning centers more consistently, and learned to offer students more choices in their learning. Principals, researchers, and school resource teachers (e.g., support teachers for students identified as gifted) all commented repeatedly that START classrooms in general were more active, student-centered, and engaging than non-START classrooms. One support teacher conjectured that participation in START gave teachers "justification for trying new things . . . or loosening up their teaching style."

On the other hand, many of the 16 "case study" teachers made few consistently observable adaptations in regard to START instruction. Some came to understand how they might change and to develop a sense that making adaptations could benefit their students, but only "got their toes in the water" when in came to translating understandings into action. Others remained resistant to even the idea of change, suggesting that such changes took too much time, were counter to the district's testing mandates, or even that they did not understand what START was about. (This latter assertion was most defensible for third grade teachers who only entered the project during its last year, and who did receive considerably less guidance and coaching in the instructional components of START than did first and second grade teachers.)

For most of the teachers whose students were in the case study group, "language immersion" remained "letting the kids talk a lot," manipulatives remained the property of math instruction, and multiculturalism was largely reflected in diversification of literature and study of holidays. These practices often had less to do with teacher rejection of principles than lack of time to become comfortable and conversant with extensive changes indicated by a student-centered, multiple intelligence, concept-based, multicultural, language-immersion, manipulative-oriented classroom!

Most of the "low maintenance" case study students had two START teachers who championed them. Most of the "high maintenance" students had at least one.

Looking to the Future: Lessons Learned

While not claiming generalizability, the START cases suggest several themes for future researchers on related projects to consider.

1. Educators must develop images of high-potential, high-risk learners which extend well beyond the classroom. These students and their families have complex lives which—positively or negatively—profoundly affect relationships at school and engagement in learning. For example, Tev is seen by many at school as non-communicative and shy. Strange as it seems, little, if any, connection was articulated by school personnel between his family's lack of comfort with English and his own reticence. Similarly, little attention seemed to be paid to his growth from ground-zero to his current developing fluency. Judged on an absolute standard, he becomes a non-entity. Judged on personal development, he is anything but unsuccessful.

Likewise, Denisha is seen as combative by many adults in her school setting. While that may, in fact, be the case, dealing with her combativeness as a somewhat volitional behavior versus as the result of a terrible fear born of early violence in her life might well make the difference in adults who resent her behaviors and address negativity with negativity, rather than adults who understand her need for control and justice, and thus work with her in more positive ways.

One mother, not minding her language, understood. "You know, they can lash out in anger because they're all pissed off because daddy got up and left years ago, and it's just affecting them." In spite of family outreach programs which were a plus, case study researchers got little indication that school personnel were aware of and addressing the specific, "loaded" circumstances of these children's lives.

Merely developing pre-project case studies, such as the ones completed later in START for this report, could provide sensitive educators with powerful insights into learners' lives and help teachers craft environments which ameliorate rather than ignore or complicate already challenging circumstances. In any case, linking knowledge of the child at home to knowledge of the child at school is important. Certainly a rich interpretation of a multicultural curriculum would be enhanced by educators extending their understanding of the cultures from which their learners actually come.

2. In project design as it relates to teacher change powerful enough to predict substantial impact on the learning of high-risk, high-potential learners, at least two themes recurred among teachers of the case study children. First, if such teacher change is to occur, substantial time and consistent coaching are required. That notable modification did occur in some START classrooms has been addressed earlier. However, many teachers were just beginning to enact change as the funding cycle ended. One teacher said as the project ended, "I think I'm beginning to catch on here, but now you're going away." District support beyond the grant funding cycle seems imperative in order to be fair to teachers who risk change, and in order to avoid a prevalent sense of revolving door mandates which come and go with little impact other than disruption in teachers' lives. Further, examination of case study teachers suggests a need for consistent, ongoing, on-site coaching of teachers toward desired change throughout the funding cycle. Staff development which is

concentrated in a week in the summer and monthly after school meetings is likely to be more effective in developing "knowledge about" than translation into action.

A second theme among teachers of case study students is the need to select sites for funding where district and/or school initiatives are in harmony with goals of the grant being funded. Project START goals encouraged teachers to develop student-centered classrooms in which students have an opportunity to construct meaning via high relevance content and activities, to use nontraditional assessment mechanisms, and to provide numerous avenues to learning so that children with strong talent in nontraditional areas recognize themselves and their potential through the curriculum. On the contrary, the district in this setting had a heavy emphasis on raising student test scores on traditional, skill-based tests—to the degree that teacher salaries are linked to ascending test scores, and as one teacher noted, "principals disappear overnight if the test scores don't go up." START teachers found it confusing and difficult to embrace these competing approaches simultaneously. One noted, "What START is telling us to do makes sense to me. It feels right. But I'm afraid for my job if I try it and (students') scores fall." Not only were teachers compromised by being pulled in what they continued to perceive as opposite directions, but the issue of time to bring about teacher change was compounded due to the fact that the almost total emphasis on drill and skill found in primary classrooms was so far removed from a more concept and meaning based approach desired by Project START.

3. Several of the case study students were identified for and participated in the district's program for gifted learners, a major goal of Project START. Generally, support staff in the program for the gifted appear enthusiastic about working with these students, interested in their progress, and aware of adjustment issues which face these students as they enter such a program. For example, several support teachers discussed pressure on African-American males by peers to conform to group norms rather than be a part of academic success. Several also talked about disparity in START students' projects in comparison with projects completed by more affluent students who have a broader range of support mechanisms at home. Less evident is a specific plan for undergirding START student success in academically advanced programs and classes (e.g., peer support groups, after school work sessions for project work with transportation home provided, additional during-school time for project work with support teachers, etc.). There was also less evidence of differentiation of instruction in special classes for START learners (and others who might benefit from it) to address experiential gaps, learning styles, issues of content relevance, and so on. When programs such as START are created, at least in part to promote equity of identification for and participation in programs for students identified as gifted, it appears important to emphasize success-building for students who participate in the services which open to them as a result of the initiatives.

A FINAL THOUGHT

In Project START, as reflected in the eight case study students, time and support for teacher change was limited, mentorships were only loosely linked with classrooms, family outreach tended to make parents feel valued in special project activities but seemed to stop short of involving parents in "mainstream" school events, and the notion of multiple intelligences served more as a metaphor for student possibilities than a robustly translated approach to extending student intelligences toward expert levels. Said in that way, Project START seems a less than complete effort at making a difference in the lives of Tev, Denisha, William, Charelle, and the other four case study students. Studying these students in some depth and over several months, however, led to a different impression. Certainly given extended time and resources, more could be accomplished with each facet of the project, and thus for the students. However, what appears evident in these children's lives—and those of their families—is that even modest affirmation and intervention such as the type inaugurated by Project START makes a real difference. When a teacher begins to think about a child in more positive than negative ways, when a classroom becomes more flexible, when a parent hears a message from school that a child is worth special investment, when the doors to school seem open and inviting, when someone from outside the school comes and spends time with a child, important transformations occur. Teachers emphasize what is right with a child rather than what is wrong. Parents who feel oppressed by what doesn't work in their lives begin to see something that does work. Students who may face life "with their dukes up" because of the tensions which surround them find school a more inviting place and home a bit more hopeful. In these ways, there was success in varying degrees for all of the case study students which appeared directly linked to Project START initiatives. A clear message from the START case studies is the necessity to challenge expectations of educators *about* talent in culturally diverse and low economic learners before those educators can begin to understand how to provide appropriately challenging expectations *for* those learners.

REFERENCES

Baldwin, A. (1994). The seven plus story: Developing hidden talent among students in socioeconomically disadvantaged environments. *Gifted Child Quarterly, 38,* 80–84.

Banks, J. (1993). Approaches to multicultural curriculum reform. In J. A. Banks and C. A. M. Banks, *Multicultural education: Issues and perspectives* (2nd ed.) (pp. 195–214). Boston: Allyn & Bacon.

Banks, J., & Banks, C. (1993). *Multicultural education: Issues and perspectives.* Boston: Allyn & Bacon.

Baruth, L., & Manning, M. (1992). *Multicultural education of children and adolescents.* Bacon: Allyn & Bacon.

Bennett, C. (1990). *Comprehensive multicultural education: Theory and practice.* (2nd ed.). Boston: Allyn & Bacon.

Bogdan, R., & Biklen, S. (1982). *Qualitative research for education. An introduction to theory and methods.* Boston: Allyn & Bacon.

Callahan, C., Tomlinson, C., Plucker, J., & Tomchin, E. (1996). *Support to affirm rising talent: A collaborative project between the University of Virginia and the Charlotte-Mecklenburg Schools.* Storrs, CT: National Research Center on the Gifted and Talented.

Cummins, J. (1986). Empowering minority students: A framework for intervention. *Harvard Educational Review, 56,* 18–36.

Ford, D. (1994). *The recruitment and retention of Black students in gifted programs.* Research-Based Decision Making Series, The National Research Center on the Gifted and Talented. Storrs: The University of Connecticut.

Ford, D. (1996). *Reversing underachievement among gifted Black students: Promising practices and programs.* New York: Teachers College Press.

Frasier, M., & Passow, A. (1994). *Toward a new paradigm for identifying talent potential.* Storrs, CT: The National Research Center on the Gifted and Talented.

Frasier, M., Garcia, J., & Passow, A. (1995). *A review of assessment issues in gifted education and their implications for identifying gifted minority students.* Storrs, CT: The National Research Center on the Gifted and Talented.

Gardner, H. (1993). *Multiple intelligences: The theory in practice.* New York: Basic Books.

Lincoln, Y., & Guba, E. (1985). *Naturalistic inquiry.* Beverly Hills, CA: Sage.

Merriam, S. (1988). *Case study research in education: A qualitative approach.* San Francisco: Jossey Bass.

Patton, M. (1990). *Qualitative evaluation and research methods.* Newbury Park, CA: Sage.

Shade, B. (1994). Understanding the African American learner. In E. R. Hollins, J. E. King, & W. C. Hayman (Eds.), *Teaching diverse populations: Formulating a knowledge base* (pp. 175–189). New York: State University of New York Press.

Spradley, J. (1979). *The ethnographic interview.* New York: Holt, Rinehart and Winston.

Tharp, R. (1989). Psychosocial variables and constants: Effects on teaching and learning in schools. *American Psychologist, 44,* 349–359.

U.S. Department of Education (1993). *National excellence: A case for developing America's talent.* Washington, DC: Office of Educational Research and Improvement.

Vadasy, P. & Maddox, M (1992). *Yakima equity study: The conditions of success for migrant, Hispanic, and Native American students in the Yakima Valley.* Washington Research Institute.

Yin, R. (1989). *Case study research: Design and methods.* Newbury Park, CA: Sage.

3

Identifying Cognitively Gifted Ethnic Minority Children

Marcia Strong Scott

Lois-Lynn Stoyko Deuel

Beda Jean-Francois

Richard C. Urbano

University of Miami

Four hundred kindergarten children in regular education and 31 kindergarten children identified as gifted were presented a cognitive battery consisting of nine different tasks. Five measures representing the three open-ended tasks were associated with both a significant group difference and the presence of high-performing outliers from the regular education sample.

Editor's Note: From Scott, M. S., Deuel, L. S., Jean-Francois, B., & Urbano, R. C. (1996). Identifying cognitively gifted ethnic minority children. *Gifted Child Quarterly*, 40(3), 147-153. © 1996 National Association for Gifted Children. Reprinted with permission.

When frequency distributions for the two groups were computed based on a total score summed over the five measures, seven of the eight regular education students with the highest score, the upper 2%, were either Black/Non Hispanic or White/Hispanic. The upper 2% of the regular education sample performed at a level above 81% of the gifted sample. The data suggest that using a child's performance on a cognitive battery may prove to be effective for identifying gifted minority children who have not previously been identified as having superior cognitive abilities.

In the United States, children from culturally different and/or low income backgrounds constitute a growing percentage of all school children, yet assessment tools that effectively evaluate their academic potential are lacking. Consequently, children from culturally different and/or low income families are less likely (Chinn & Hughes, 1987) to be identified as gifted. They have been, and remain, underrepresented in programs for the gifted and talented (e.g., Borland & Wright, 1994; Harris & Ford, 1991; Klausmeier, Mishra, & Maker, 1987; Maker, 1996; Mills, & Tissot, 1995; Ortiz & Gonzalez, 1989; Richert, 1987; Rycraft, 1990). As Passow and Frasier (1996) have stated, "Even with the significant and constant increases in both number and proportions of racial/ethnic minority and economically disadvantaged students in the public school population that have occurred in recent decades, underrepresentation of these students in programs for the gifted seems not to have changed substantially (p. 198)."

The issue of differential identification is not simply one of academic fairness. It may have real socioeconomic impact, contributing to the gulf between mainstream and minority cultures and causing this gap to widen (Borland, 1996). Eligible for gifted, but unplaced, ethnic minority students, when compared to a similar group of eligible students who were placed in a gifted program, were more likely to have dropped out of school and less likely to have gone on to college (Smith, LeRose, & Clasen, 1991). Such data clearly point out the necessity of finding a more effective means to identify minority and/or low income gifted children.

Although the current trend is to consider giftedness to reflect multiple characteristics and to define it, therefore, in terms of multiple criteria (e.g., Clasen, Middleton, & Connell, 1994; Passow & Frasier, 1996), it is not necessarily the case that one would want to develop a new test that attempts to identify all children falling under such an inclusive concept. Rather, one may attempt to develop a new test that more effectively identifies a subgroup of gifted children. That is the position we have taken. The subgroup we wish to identify consists of those who have been called "schoolhouse gifted" by Passow and Frasier

(1996). These are the students most likely to advance to a level of collegiate or graduate education. What then should one evaluate or assess if one wishes to identify gifted children who might demonstrate superior academic performance if provided with enriched educational programs? Because of an absence of sufficient and appropriate experiences, many ethnic minority and low income children may not have the requisite skills to perform academically in a manner that reflects their untrained abilities (Mills & Tissot, 1995). Therefore, one must find measures which identify those minority children with the *potential* for academic excellence because their demonstrated academic performance may not reflect what they might do under improved educational circumstances.

Putting the Research to Use

The identification of ethnic minority students for programs is a persistent concern in the field of gifted education. This study presents encouraging results for school districts implementing broad screening programs for young children. Using tasks from a kindergarten screening test for children with disabilities, gifted children from culturally diverse backgrounds are found among a regular education sample. The tasks which show the most promise for identifying ethnic minority and low income gifted students are open-ended items with maximum ceiling. In contrast to frequent reports of test bias, the most successful tasks in this study are verbal. Practitioners will find three useful messages from the results. First, ethnic minority gifted students can be located through kindergarten screening programs which involve large numbers of children. Second, open-ended tasks which encourage fluency are the most promising. These kinds of tasks are familiar to educators of the gifted. Third, verbal tasks which use familiar concepts and vocabulary do not necessarily discriminate against young ethnic minority gifted students.

Assessing such alternate characteristics as visual performing arts ability or psychomotor ability (e.g., Masten, 1985) is unlikely to identify the type of gifted children this study targets, i.e., those who will excel in the academic domain. To find this type of gifted student, one must assess cognitive processes since cognitive competency can be expected to relate to academic performance. What evidence is there that assessing cognitive capability will lead one to the identification of gifted ethnic minority students? Borland and Wright (1994), successfully identified a small sample of young potentially academically gifted low income minority children using both traditional and non-traditional assessments that relied heavily on cognitive evaluations. In addition, when arguments are made to shift to, or include, nonverbal assessments in order to better identify gifted minority children, the measures suggested typically assess cognitive capabilities (e.g., Matthews, 1988; Mills & Tissot, 1995; Tyler-Wood & Carri, 1993). Cognition, therefore, is a good candidate to serve as the basis of a new test to identify minority students with the potential for superior academic performance.

In the study to be described, cognitive ability was assessed through the administration of a battery of nine cognitive tasks, most of which were nonverbal (e.g., Tyler-Wood & Carri, 1993). The battery had been developed to identify children with mild learning problems who would be at risk for academic failure (e.g., Scott, Deuel, Claussen, & Sanchez, 1993; Scott et al., 1996). If these cognitive tasks were effective in identifying *low* performing outliers, it was reasoned, some of them might also prove effective in identifying *high* performing outliers. This hypothesis was tested in the current study.

The battery was presented to a large multi-ethnic sample of kindergarten children, some of whom had been identified as gifted by their school district. The actual administration proceeded in a game-like manner that should produce a child-friendly, nonthreatening instrument (Clasen, Middleton, & Connell, 1994). This mode of presentation is more likely to encourage optimal responding from ethnic minority children who may be less experienced or comfortable with administration procedures associated with typical standardized instruments.

The gifted and regular education groups were compared to determine if the cognitive performance of the top 2% of regular education children overlapped the performance levels of the gifted sample. If it did, then it could be determined if any of these high performing regular education outliers belonged to ethnic minority populations. If some were, then the use of this particular method of cognitive evaluation to identify potential high academic achievers would be demonstrated. Further research and development would then be warranted (Passow, 1989), in order, for example, to select the best set of measures.

METHOD

Participants

A total of 431 kindergarten children enrolled in public schools participated in this study. Of these, 31 children were classified as gifted. In the Dade County Public School System (DCPS), a child is eligible for the gifted program if he or she demonstrates 1) a need for a special program, 2) a majority of characteristics of gifted students according to a standard scale or checklist, and 3) superior intellectual development as measured by an intelligence quotient of two (2) or greater standard deviations above the mean on an individually administered intelligence test. If the student is a member of an underrepresented group, he/she will be eligible if he/she demonstrates 1 and 2 above, and obtains a score equal to or greater than the 98th percentile on a) an intelligence test, or b) achievement test, or c) Torrance Test of Creativity, or 4) a score of 9 or higher on a matrix that includes assessments of intellectual abilities, achievement skills (reading comprehension or math application), creativity (Torrance) and a teacher rating scale.

The mean chronological age of the gifted sample was 73 months (range = 66–82 mos) and the mean IQ score was 135 (range = 127–150). Only two children had IQ scores below 130. This mean is based on 28 of 31 gifted children for whom IQ scores were available. Of the 31 kindergarten children already identified as gifted, three were Black/NonHispanic (B/NH), two were White/Hispanic (W/H) and 26 were White/NonHispanic (W/NH). Nineteen of the gifted sample were female and 12 were male.

The 400 regular education children were all those kindergarten children out of a sample of 459 who were not receiving any special education services, were not identified as gifted, and whose chronological age fell within the age range of the gifted sample. The mean chronological age for this regular education group was also 73 mos, range = 66–82. There were 150 B/NH children, 147 W/H children and 103 W/NH children in the regular education sample. Of these, 159 were female and 241 were male. The Dade County Public School System, from which the sample was drawn, is an urban school system that serves more than 300,000 children from a multi-ethnic, multi-racial population. It is the fourth largest school district in the country. For administrative purposes, DCPS is divided into six regions. The public school children in this study were enrolled in 28 different public schools with at least three and as many as seven schools located within each of the six regions. Thus, the sample in this study is representative of the children served in this school district.

As a rough estimate of socioeconomic status, we used the percentage of children in each of the participating public schools who were on reduced-price or free lunch. This percentage ranged from a low of 20 to a high of 92. Socioeconomic status was widely represented in the sample.

Instrument

For all but the word task, colored photographs of meaningful pictures appeared on white paper placed in a four-hole legal size black binder. The word task was presented verbally, and required no visual aids. The tasks are described below in the same order as they appeared in the battery. All tasks are listed and all the dependent measures are numbered in Table 1.

For the *picture pointing task*, six unrelated meaningful pictures were displayed on each of four pages. The quality of the child's pointing sequence on each of the four arrays was scored. Based on previous data (Scott, et al., 1996), two dependent measures were evaluated: a quality score which was the sum of the scores assigned to each of the four sequences (possible range = 0 to 12); and a penalty score which was defined as the quality score minus the total number of repetitions and omissions.

A *picture recognition task* came next in the series. There was a training page (picture of sun glasses) and a test page (pictures of identical sunglasses, a bow,

Table 1   The Mean Scores and *SD*s for Each of the Dependent Measures for Both Educational Groups

Tasks/Measures	Gifted Education (N = 31)		Regular Education (N = 400)		Significance
	Mean	SD	Mean	SD	
Picture Pointing					
1. Quality Score	8.6	3.3	9.0	2.9	ns
2. Penalty Score	8.5	3.3	8.6	3.4	ns
Picture Recognition					
3. Penalty Score	15.1	1.0	14.0	2.4	$p < .02$
Word Meaning					
4. Airplane	7.4	3.2	6.0	2.9	$p < .02$
5. Banana	6.5	2.2	4.9	2.5	$p < .01$
Standard Oddity					
6. Number Correct	8.9	0.2	8.8	0.8	ns
Dot Matrix Oddity					
7. Number Correct	6.4	1.1	5.4	1.5	$p < .001$
Animal and Dot Sequencing					
8. Number Correct	3.7	0.4	3.5	0.8	ns
Rhyming					
9. Number Correct	1.9	0.2	1.7	0.5	$p < .04$
Unstructured Information					
10. Cats	9.8	4.0	8.1	4.4	$p < .05$
11. Fruits	4.9	2.0	3.5	1.9	$p < .001$
Structured Information					
12. People Diffs	6.0	3.6	2.5	1.8	$p < .001$

a lady bug and a calculator) to illustrate the task requirements. This was followed by two sets, each set consisting of one memory array of eight pictures and two test arrays of eight pictures each. Four of the pictures in each recognition test array were identical to pictures in the memory array and four were new pictures. The seen-before pictures appeared in the same position as they had on the memory page. The dependent measure was the number of correct recognition choices out of 16 minus the number of incorrect selections summed over the two sets.

For the *word meaning task*, the children were first asked to tell what the word *airplane* meant and then what *banana* meant. The most abstract or categorical definitions were given a score of 3, e.g., "They go to other countries," or "It's a fruit." More specific or functional descriptions were given a score of 2, e.g., "It flies," or "You eat it." Specific descriptors were given a score of 1, e.g., "Has bathrooms in it," or "It's shaped like a rainbow." Statements with several components in them, were given a score equal to the sum of the component scores, e.g., "It has wings (1) that help it fly" (2) = 3 points. Only true statements were scored. Children were prompted, e.g., "What else can you tell me about airplanes?" until the child could offer no more descriptors. The dependent measures were the total number of points awarded to each word.

The fourth task consisted of nine unique *standard oddity arrays*, each consisting of two identical and one different picture. The dependent measure was the number of correct selections out of nine.

The fifth task consisted of seven *dot matrix oddity problems* where same and different were defined by the number of orange dots in the matrices. The dependent measure for this task was the number of correct selections out of seven.

The sixth task was a *sequencing* or *ordering task*. There were two pages of animal picture sequences and two pages of colored dots in sequence. For the animal sequences, animal pictures were placed across the top of each page, each picture appearing above a black line. At the end of the row, there was another black line with nothing above it (a missing picture). On the bottom of the page, were three choice pictures. For the dot sequence problems, different colored dots were used in the same manner as were the animals. The dependent measure was the number of correct selections out of four.

A *picture rhyme task* was the seventh in the series. There was one training and two test pages. On each there were two pictures on the top and two pictures on the bottom separated by a thick black line that bisected the page horizontally. One of the picture pairs had names that rhymed and the other pair did not. The dependent measure was the number of correct choices out of two.

For the eighth task, an *unstructured semantic information task*, 15 cats were displayed on the first page and fruit (apples, pears, grapes and oranges), gathered together within a cotton cloth, was displayed on the second. The child was asked first to tell everything he or she knew about cats, and then what he or she knew about fruit. Everything that was true for all or most exemplars of that concept, was given one point. The child was prompted, e.g., "What else can you tell me about cats?" until he or she could provide no further descriptions. The dependent measures were the total number of points awarded to each of the two concepts.

For the ninth and last task, a *structured information task*, the child was shown four people who varied over age, race and gender. The children were asked to tell how people *differed* from one another. They were given one point for every difference mentioned that was true, e.g., "Some are girls," "Have different names." The dependent measure was the total number of points awarded.

Administration and Instructions

The children were seen individually by a male or female tester and told that they would play some picture games. Seated next to the child, the tester opened the binder and showed the page relevant to each task. A standardized protocol accompanied each task.[1]

For the three open-ended generating tasks, word meaning, unstructured information and structured information, probes were used liberally to encourage the child to give as much as he or she could and receive the highest score possible. When the child had completed the battery, the tester gave him or her an "award certificate" and, in addition, the child selected two stickers to put on it.

Of the 147 W/H regular education kindergarten children participating in this study, 120 were tested in English, 21 in Spanish and for 6 the directions were provided in both English and Spanish. The two W/H children in the gifted group were both tested in English. Testing language was determined based on information from the child's teacher, the child's stated preference and the child's ability to comprehend instructions in the language of his or her choice. If the child did not appear to understand the initial language used, the tester, who was fluent in both English and Spanish, presented the instructions in both languages to ensure that the child understood the task. Responses in either English or Spanish were accepted.

RESULTS

Because we were evaluating the usefulness of a child's performance on a set of cognitive tasks to identify academic giftedness, there were two parts to the evaluation process. The validity of the tasks was first determined by identifying those associated with a significantly superior performance by the identified gifted *group* when compared to the regular education *group*. If a task was associated with group differences, it could be identified as validly differentiating cognitive capability. The second criterion applied was a pragmatic one. A task would also have to be associated with the presence of a few high performing outliers from the regular education sample.

To determine which tasks and/or measures were associated with group differences, we first contrasted the two groups using separate analyses of variance (ANOVAs) for measures 3, 6, 7, 8, 9, and 12 (see Table 1) and three multivariate analyses of variance (MANOVAs) to assess measures 1 and 2 of the picture pointing task, 4 and 5 of the word meaning task, and 10 and 11 of the unstructured information task. Shown in Table 1 are the means and SDs for both the regular education and gifted groups on each of the 12 measures as well as the p values. The mean performance of the two groups on the picture pointing task was nearly identical for both measures 1 and 2. Surprisingly, when the groups were compared using a MANOVA, with quality score and penalty score as two dependent measures, the overall MANOVA was significant, $F(2,428) = 3.10$, $p < .05$. However, neither of the univariate follow-up tests was significant, $F(1,429) = < 1.0$, both $ps > .10$.

On the picture recognition task, the gifted group correctly recognized about one more picture on average (measure 3). This small difference was significant when the groups were compared on a simple ANOVA, $F(1,429) = 6.33$, $p < .02$.

These young gifted children generated verbal descriptions of the meaning of airplane and banana that were awarded higher scores than those generated by the regular education group on both measures 4 and 5 (see Table 1). This performance difference was associated with a significant overall MANOVA, $F(2,428)=6.16$, $p < .01$. On the univariate follow-up analyses, both airplane and banana were associated with a significant group difference, $F(1,429) = 6.46$, $p < .02$ and $F(1,429)=10.99$, $p < .01$, respectively.

As can be seen in Table 1, the groups were at ceiling level on the standard oddity task (measure 6). Not unexpectedly, the groups did not differ significantly on this measure, $F(1,429) = < 1.0$, $p > .10$. However, a group mean difference reflecting about 1 more correct response for the gifted group on the dot matrix oddity problem (measure 7) was significant, $F(1,429) = 15.65$, $p < .001$.

The two groups had similar mean scores on the sequencing task and not surprisingly, the performance of the groups was not significantly different, $F(1,429) = 3.39$, $p > .05$. A similar slight mean difference favoring the gifted group on the rhyme task (measure 9) was significant, $F(1,429) = 4.37$, $p < .04$.

For the unstructured task, the gifted students generated more information (see Table 1). This difference was reflected in a significant overall MANOVA, $F(2,428) = 7.16$, $p < .01$, and significant group differences for both cats, $F(1,429) = 3.92$, $p < .05$, and fruit, $F(1,429)=14.33$, $p < .001$.

The final measure, knowledge of differences among people (measure 12), was associated with a large mean difference and a significant ANOVA, $F(1,429)=90.29$, $p < .001$, reflecting the greater knowledge of differences displayed by the young children already identified as gifted.

To summarize, although the gifted kindergarten sample displayed a superior level of performance on 10 of the 12 cognitive measures, these differences reached significance only for measures 3 (picture recognition), 4 and 5 (word meaning-airplane, banana), 7 (dot matrix oddity), 9 (rhyming), 10 and 11 (unstructured information -cats, fruits), and 12 (structured information -people differences). These eight measures can be considered valid indicators of giftedness.

Frequency distributions of the number of children from the regular education sample who achieved each of the scores obtained by at least one child were computed for each of the eight measures whose validity as a measure reflecting cognitive giftedness had been demonstrated. Shown in Table 2 are frequency distributions for measures 3 and 11. The two distributions demonstrate the difference between a task which is too easy and one which locates high performing outliers. It can be seen that on the picture recognition task 30% (120 of 400) of the regular education sample achieved a perfect score. There were no outliers on this task. However, for the unstructured information task measure 11, there are a few high performing outliers from the regular education group. Nine children (2.25%) had higher scores than all of the others in this group.

Although significant group differences were observed for eight of the measures, high performing regular education outliers were found for only five of them; measures 4, 5, 10, 11, and 12 (see Table 1). On these five measures, a subset of either nine of 400 (2.25%) or six of 400 (1.5%) children obtained scores higher than all the others in their group. All five of these measures required the children to generate responses. A final frequency distribution was computed on

Table 2   Frequency Distributions of the Number of Children in the Regular Education Group on Two Tasks

Picture Recognition Task		Unstructured Information Fruit Task	
Score	Number of Students	Score	Number of Students
16	120	15	2
15	86	13	1
14	77	12	1
13	54	11	1
12	29	9	4
11	9	—— Upper 2.25% of Students[a] ——	
10	11	8	6
9	2	7	14
8	1	6	19
7	4	5	32
5	2	4	81
4	1	3	107
2	1	2	113
1	1	1	19
0	1		
−1	1		
	400		400

[a]The upper 2.25% of regular education students appears above the line.

a total score equal to the sum of scores for measures 4, 5, 10, 11 and 12. This distribution is shown in Table 3.

The upper 2% of the regular education sample (8 of 400) consisted of seven minority children (five B/NH and two W/H) and one nonminority (W/NH) child. Six of these children were male and two were female. All eight regular education children performed at a higher level than 81% (25 of 33) of the sample of kindergarten children identified as gifted by the school system.

If these eight children are candidates for a gifted placement based on their cognitive ability, one might expect them to perform at levels at least above the mean for their school, on Stanford Achievement Tests (SATs). The end of first grade reading comprehension, math computation and math application percentile SAT scores for seven of the eight children for whom such data were available, as well as the median percentile scores for each child's school are shown in Table 4. Two of the seven children did not achieve up to the median percentile for their schools, but five of the seven did earn scores well above the median scores for their school. Three of the five students had two of their three scores in the 90th percentile and a fourth student had one score in the 90th percentile.

Table 3   Frequency Distribution of Regular Education and Gifted Education Students Achieving Each Score and the Race/Ethnicity of the Upper 2% from the Regular Education Sample

Score[a]	Gifted	Regular Education	Race/ Ethnicity
97	0	1	B/NH
75	0	1	B/NH
60	0	1	B/NH
58	1	0	
55	0	2	W/H, B/NH
54	1	0	
50	0	1	W/H
49	2	0	
48	1	0	
47	0	1	W/NH
46	1	1	B/NH
Upper 2% of Students[b]			
45–41	4	10	
40–36	3	27	
35–31	5	57	
30–26	6	65	
25–21	5	102	
20–16	2	76	
< 16	0	55	
	31	400	

[a]Score is the sum of scores for measures 4, 5, 10, 11 and 12.
[b]The upper 2% of regular education students appears above the line.

DISCUSSION

The aim of this study was to see if one could identify minority children with a potential for high academic achievement by assessing cognitive abilities and using a sample of high IQ children already identified as gifted as a criterion reference group. Applying two criteria to select the most valid and potentially useful tasks from the nine task battery, it was shown that one could identify minority children currently in regular education who were able to perform at a level above most of the school-identified gifted sample. Indeed, seven of the eight scores in the top 2% were achieved by minority children. These seven minority children were able to score in the same range on all three verbal tasks (five measures) as a predominantly White/NonHispanic mainstream sample, whose IQ scores were in the gifted range. It would appear that verbal measures of cognitive ability need not be "the gifted low SES student's albatross" (Tyler-Wood & Carri, 1993). The effectiveness of the verbal measures used here in identifying high performing minority children may be due to the fact that students were asked to provide information about items familiar to all children, i.e., airplane, banana, cats, fruit and people. The importance of using measures based on events or meanings common to both majority and minority students has been specifically discussed and evaluated by Clasen, Middleton and Connell (1994).

The SAT scores achieved by five of seven high performing regular education outliers indicates that performance on a set of cognitive measures assessed in kindergarten does relate to high performance on academic achievement tests one year later for at least the majority of the children identified by this battery. These data add additional support to the idea that one may be able to identify gifted ethnic minority children in kindergarten using a brief battery of cognitive tasks.

This study is only a first step; it served to show the validity of the method and content area. However, these initial data are compelling for several reasons. First, the upper 2% of the regular education sample demonstrated cognitive skills, albeit on a restricted set, at a level equal to the highest scorers in the gifted sample. Second, the highest performing regular education children were only eight out of a sample of 400, so their high levels of cognitive performance exceeded those obtained by 392 other regular education children, which might be considered a reflection of giftedness on its own (Gallagher, 1991). Finally, these were kindergarten children. In effect, if this method replicates and a longer and broader-based cognitive battery can be developed and validated, it would mean that ethnic minority children could be identified early and be involved in transitional and enhanced educational programs from the beginning of their school years.

There are, of course, limitations to these data and they relate directly to the criterion used to select the tasks constituting the cognitive battery. Originally, these tasks were selected because they differentiated children with and without learning problems. In effect, they were tasks associated with low performing outliers. Consequently, as can be seen in Table 1, ceiling effects were present for some tasks, e.g., standard oddity (measure 6) and sequencing (measure 8). Even those identification tasks associated with significant group differences reflected small mean differences, e.g., picture recognition (measure 3), dot matrix (measure 7) and rhyming (measure 9). On the picture recognition measure, 30% of the regular education sample achieved the highest possible score, while on the dot matrix and rhyming tasks, 26% and 78% of the sample respectively obtained the highest possible scores. It was only for the generating tasks, where individual differences were not restricted by a maximum score, that high performing outliers were observed. The mean differences even here were not large, averaging only 1.9. These results suggest that we should evaluate primarily open-ended generating tasks that ask for information. For other kinds of tasks, more difficult items are needed. These two practices should result in a greater separation between a gifted sample and most of any regular education sample. As a first look, however, these data are certainly encouraging.

Table 4   Student and School Percentile Scores on First Grade Reading Comprehension, Math Computation and Math Application for Seven of the Eight Regular Education Students With Scores in the Upper 2%

Student Scores[a]			Median Percentile of School		
Reading	Math Comp.	Math App.	Reading	Math Comp.	Math App.
99	84	94	29	42	32
94	94	57	50	67	57
79	89	97	43	74	45
61	77	80	29	42	32
84[b]	99	90	51	79	75
		Median Score in School[c]			
59	44	31	61	60	57
29	33	11	32	58	45

[a]Student and school scores for spring 1995.
[b]This is not a minority student.
[c]Students scoring above the median in their school appear above the line.

NOTE

1. The complete protocol is available from the first author.

REFERENCES

Borland, J. H. (1996). Gifted education and the threat of irrelevance. *Journal for the Education of the Gifted, 19*, 129–147.

Borland, J. H., & Wright, L. (1994). Identifying young, potentially gifted economically disadvantaged students. *Gifted Child Quarterly, 38*, 164–171.

Chinn, P. C., & Hughes, S. (1987). Representation of minority students in special education classes. *RASE, 8*, 41–46.

Clasen, D. R., Middleton, J. A., & Connell, T. J. (1994). Assessing artistic and problem-solving, performance in minority and nonminority students using a nontraditional multidimensional approach. *Gifted Child Quarterly, 38*, 27–32.

Gallagher, J. J. (1991). Editorial: The gifted: A term with surplus meaning. *Journal for the Education of the Gifted, 14*, 353–365.

Harris, J. J., & Ford, D. Y. (1991). Identifying and nurturing the promise of gifted Black American children. *Journal of Negro Education, 60*(1), 3–18.

Klausmeier, K., Mishra, S. P., & Maker, C. J. (1987). Identification of gifted learners: A national survey of assessment practices and training needs of school psychologists. *Gifted Child Quarterly, 31*, 135–137.

Lynch, S. J., & Mills, C. J. (1993). Identifying and preparing disadvantaged and minority youth for high-level academic achievement. *Contemporary Educational Psychology, 18*, 66–76.

Maker, J. C. (1996). Identification of gifted minority students: A national problem, needed changes and a promising solution. *Gifted Child Quarterly, 40,* 41–50.

Masten, W. G. (1985). Identification of gifted minority students: Past research, future directions. *Roeper Review, 8,* 83–85.

Matthews, D. J. (1988). Raven's Matrices in the identification of giftedness. *Roeper Review, 10,* 159–162.

Mills, C. J., & Tissot, S.L. (1995). Identifying academic potential in students from under-represented populations: Is using the Ravens Progressive Matrices a good idea? *Gifted Child Quarterly, 39,* 209–217.

Ortiz, V. Z., & Gonzalez, A. (1989). Validation of a short form of the WISC - R with accelerated and gifted Hispanic students. *Gifted Child Quarterly, 33,* 152–155.

Passow, A. H. (1989). Needed research and development in educating high ability children: An editorial. *Roeper Review, 11,* 223–229.

Passow, A. H., & Frasier, M.M. (1996). Toward improving identification of talent potential among minority and disadvantaged students. *Roeper Review, 18,* 198–202.

Richert, E. S. (1987). Rampant problems and promising practices in the identification of disadvantaged gifted students. *Gifted Child Quarterly, 31,* 149–154.

Rycraft, J. R. (1990). Behind the walls of poverty: Economically disadvantaged gifted and talented children. *Early Child Development and Care, 63,* 139–147.

Scott, M. S., Deuel, L. S., Claussen, A. H., & Sanchez, M. (1993). Identifying young children with mild cognitive deficiencies. *Diagnostique, 19*(1), 335–359.

Scott, M. S., Deuel, L. S., Urbano, R. C., Perou, R., Claussen, A. H., Scott, M., & Sanchez, M. (1996). *Evaluating potential test components for a new cognitive screening test.* Manuscript submitted for publication.

Smith, J., LeRose, B., & Clasen, R. E. (1991). Underrepresentation of minority students in gifted programs: Yes! It matters! *Gifted Child Quarterly, 35,* 81–83.

Tyler-Wood, T. & Carri, L. (1993). Verbal measures of cognitive ability: The gifted low SES student's albatross. *Roeper Review, 16,* 102–105.

4

Dynamic Assessment and Its Use With Underserved Gifted and Talented Populations

Robert J. Kirschenbaum

Clover Park School District, Tacoma, WA

A relatively new, nontraditional approach to assessing cognitive ability is to instruct students on how to perform on certain tasks and then measure their progress in learning to solve similar problems. This approach, called *dynamic assessment*, usually consists of a test-intervene-retest format that focuses attention on the improvement in student performance when an adult provides mediated assistance on how to master the testing task. The dynamic assessment approach can provide a means for assessing disadvantaged, disabled, or limited English proficiency students who have not demonstrated high ability on traditional tests of intelligence and creativity. Dynamic assessment methods should be considered by school districts with large numbers of disadvantaged students which are dissatisfied with the effectiveness of traditional methods for identifying students for specialized enrichment programs.

Editor's Note: From Kirschenbaum, R. J. (1998). Dynamic assessment and its use with underserved gifted and talented populations. *Gifted Child Quarterly, 42*(3), 140-147. © 1998 National Association for Gifted Children. Reprinted with permission.

The Jacob K. Javits Gifted and Talented Students Education Program, created by Congress in 1988, has provided grants for programs employing innovative methods for identifying and serving traditionally underrepresented populations. Yet, most school districts still rely on traditional assessment methods. The result, writes Richert (1985), is that certain groups of students are consistently underrepresented in gifted programs, including:

> (a) underachieving, poor and minority gifted children who most need programs to develop their potential; (b) the creative and/or divergent thinkers whose abilities are not tested by standardized intelligence or achievement tests or grades; and (c) other groups including the learning disabled or handicapped gifted. (p. 70)

A relatively new, nontraditional approach to assessing cognitive ability is to instruct students on how to perform on certain tasks and then measure their progress in learning to solve similar problems. This approach, called dynamic assessment, was originally developed as a means of assessing immigrant students in Israel who were largely uneducated in their home countries and appeared to be mentally deficient according to their performance on standardized intelligence tests.

Putting the Research to Use

Educators in the field of gifted education have little difficulty identifying students who score at the highest levels on standardized tests of ability and achievement. Most of these tests represent static assessment situations in which a student is asked to demonstrate what he or she has learned. However, many highly capable students do not do well enough on standardized tests to be considered eligible for participation in gifted programs, even though they can excel in these programs if given the chance.

Dynamic assessment provides a means to collect data about learning and performance ability. There is an instructional component to dynamic assessment that offers students an opportunity to demonstrate what they can accomplish with specialized assistance. The assessment results offer a glimpse of the capacity of students to excel if given mediated instruction.

Dynamic assessment is not being promoted as a substitute for static assessment, but as a supplemental source of information in a flexible identification procedure. In essence, dynamic assessment can be used to determine and document how well students respond to enrichment activities over an extended period of time. This approach is especially valuable for schools that identify few gifted and talented students from disadvantaged and minority populations.

Dynamic assessment has been described as an alternative method to traditional intelligence tests for measuring intellectual ability in minority and poor children (Bolig & Day, 1993). Based on their review of the relevant literature, Bolig and Day present five reasons why dynamic assessment can be useful in the identification of gifted and talented students:

1. It can detect differences in learning ability among students with identical intelligence test scores.

2. It can provide information that helps determine how and what to teach individual students.

3. It was developed to overcome shortcomings of traditional tests with respect to their use with disadvantaged students.

4. Its focus is on learning ability more than knowledge.

5. It provides information on how students attempt to solve tasks; therefore, it sees students' errors as signs of mistaken beliefs, gaps in knowledge, selection of incorrect strategies, incorrect use of strategies, and cognitive deficiencies.

Given that these reasons constitute a strong argument for an expanded use of dynamic assessment in the identification of gifted, talented, and creative students within underrepresented groups, a more detailed understanding of dynamic assessment and a review of gifted programs using this method is desirable.

DEFINITION OF DYNAMIC ASSESSMENT

Dynamic assessment is a *diagnostic* procedure that takes into account the context of the testing situation and the ability of a student to learn from experience in that context. Lidz (1991) describes dynamic assessment as

> a test-intervene-retest format. The specialist first administers a static pretest to establish a level of performance, then provides interventions to try to produce changes in the examinee, and then retests on the static test in order to assess degree and nature of change. . . . A second definitive characteristic of a dynamic assessment is the focus on learner modifiability. "Modifiability" involves both the amount of change made by the learner in response to the interventions provided, and the learner's increased implementation of relevant metacognitive processes in problem solution. (pp. 4–5)

Haywood, Brown, and Wingenfeld (1990) mention other characteristics of dynamic assessment, including an emphasis on assessing cognitive processes through efforts at teaching students to use these processes, attempts at specifying obstacles to more effective learning and performance, attempts at specifying conditions that will enable the student to improve performance, and an effort to distinguish between performance and potential, ignorance and inability. Although a pretest is not an essential characteristic, it must be included if a baseline measure of a student's unassisted performance on a specific task is desired.

HISTORY OF DYNAMIC ASSESSMENT

Reuven Feuerstein, the primary developer of the dynamic assessment approach, worked with Piaget and shared his interest in how children learn to think. Feuerstein was responsible for assessing immigrant children in Israel, many of whom had lived in countries in which Jews were virtual hostages and were forced to live in ghettos with very limited educational opportunities. Using traditional testing methods, many of these students appeared academically retarded, unable to benefit from a normal learning environment in school. Using the dynamic assessment approach, he was able to determine that these students had serious cognitive deficits that hindered academic learning and performance, but they possessed intellectual faculties that were normal. Feuerstein realized that traditional testing methods were inadequate for assessing true intellectual ability in students who were educationally deficient and had no prior testing experience. He was also faced with the task of assessing students who did not speak the languages used on available standardized tests. Feuerstein and his associates eventually constructed the *Learning Potential Assessment Device* (Feuerstein, Rand, & Hoffman, 1979), which is still the only comprehensive test of learning ability that uses the dynamic assessment method exclusively.

The theoretical foundation for the development of the dynamic assessment approach comes from Vygotsky's conception of potential as "the zone of proximal development" (ZPD; Lidz, 1991). Lidz writes:

> The ZPD concept refers to the idea that a child has some fully matured processes that are evident when the child is assessed by traditional means, as well as emergent developmental processes that can become evident when the child interacts with a more knowledgeable partner. The ZPD is the difference between the child's level of performance when functioning independently and the child's level of performance when functioning in collaboration with a more knowledgeable partner. This can also be viewed as a definition of "potential." (p. 7)

The ZPD is the area within which instruction can benefit students by helping them to reach a higher level of competency and understanding. For highly able students working in their area of strength, this zone is much larger than would be the case for less able students.

Vygotsky (1978) assumed that a primary attribute of the developing human central nervous system is flexibility, since children from different cultures who live in very different environments may acquire vastly different knowledge and skills. From his viewpoint, potential is a product of genetic and biological factors as they interact with environmental, cultural, and social conditions.

In keeping with Vygotsky's perspective on intellectual development, Feuerstein and his associates (Feuerstein, Rand, Hoffman, & Miller, 1980) decided that a deliberate program of intervention which focuses on cognitive processes would facilitate the generation of continuous cognitive growth by rendering students receptive and sensitive to internal and external sources of stimulation that they were unable to recognize previously. Dynamic assessment is the method by which they identify and measure cognitive abilities (and deficiencies) as a prelude to students receiving this intervention. The goal of the assessment and intervention procedures is to help students develop cognitive skills commensurate with their true intellectual ability, not to increase their IQ scores or make them smarter than they would have been if they had received an appropriate education, as some might suggest. Similarly, the goal of dynamic assessment in the area of gifted education is to aid in the identification of youth who have gifts, talents, and creative ability that have not been identified or properly developed.

STATIC VS. DYNAMIC ASSESSMENT METHODS

Static and dynamic assessment methods should be considered complementary means for estimating cognitive potential. Static assessment methods are those that measure student ability by presenting tasks that require a student to access previously acquired knowledge and skills to solve a problem without any assistance. Dynamic assessment actually starts with a static measurement, but then allows the examiner to actively guide the student to the discovery of the solution through the use of "scaffolded" instruction (Wood, Bruner, & Ross, 1976).

In static assessment, the examiner administers a test in a precisely scripted manner, records the number of test items answered correctly, and is not allowed to provide any feedback to the student other than nonspecific encouragement. In dynamic assessment, the examiner provides scaffolded instruction that is either based on a standardized, hierarchic sequence of hints and prompts, or is more individualized, helping the student to complete the presented task, then records the effect of the assistance. The goal of static assessment is a highly reliable, quantitative measure of ability. The goal of dynamic assessment is to obtain a more qualitative and clinical record of the types of errors made and the effect of the intervention.

Static assessment of intelligence provides a profile of the extent to which various abilities have developed and highlights cognitive strengths and weaknesses. Dynamic assessment may provide a profile of abilities, but its main purpose is to detect inefficient problem solving strategies and abilities (e.g., creative thinking ability) that are responsive to instruction. To accomplish this purpose, dynamic assessment incorporates an experimental instructional intervention. The results of the intervention can be used to develop a plan for the remediation of deficient academic skills and ineffective strategies, if necessary, as well as the development of effective problem solving skills and strategies.

USE OF DYNAMIC ASSESSMENT IN THE CLASSROOM

Although dynamic assessment can be conducted in a formal, standardized manner, classroom teachers may use the dynamic assessment method to compare the learning curve of their students on specific tasks presented in their classrooms. The pre- and posttest can be a teacher developed test, chapter test, time needed to complete a task, proficiency in using new work strategies, or a measure of creative output.

Depending on the task that is being presented, different aspects of student performance may be measured. Teachers may examine the number of trials or time students need to complete the task correctly, the quality or correctness of their answers, the appropriateness and effective application of problem solving strategies, time on-task, improvement in persistence and rate of task completion, performance on transfer problems, and aspects of creative output such as fluency and originality. Spontaneous and elicited comments during the assessment process are considered very important indicators of how a student perceives a problem task, what strategies are being used to solve it, and errors in thinking.

DYNAMIC ASSESSMENT OF GIFTED STUDENTS WITH SPECIAL NEEDS

The dynamic assessment approach can provide a means for assessing disadvantaged, disabled, or limited English proficient (LEP) students who have not demonstrated high ability on static tests of intelligence and creativity. Zorman (1997) describes the Eureka model which incorporates dynamic assessment as a means of identifying gifted, talented, and creative students. Only a few other studies were found, however, in which a dynamic assessment approach (not identified as such) was used in conjunction with portfolios or other alternative assessment methods to find students from disadvantaged backgrounds with exceptional potential. In these cases, the identification methods used were not labeled dynamic assessment and differed from the standard approach by not including a static pretest phase.

The Eureka model (Zorman, 1997) is being used in Israel in schools catering to students from lower socio-economic backgrounds and new immigrants. All children are provided experiences in various talent areas and their work is evaluated in a dynamic assessment process for two years, through first and second grade. Portfolios are used to examine student performance over time. Science and artistic potential instruments were designed to tap personality components and specific abilities in these talent domains. Low correlations were found between scores on tests of general intellectual ability and ratings on the science and artistic potential instruments.

A study by Jitendra and Kameenui (1993) demonstrated the utility of dynamic assessment for differentiating students who could master a math task from students who failed to do so. Third grade students were selected who were competent in math but still needed some assistance in doing one-step word problems (i.e., highly able math students were excluded). After pretesting, students were instructed on the use of a strategy for solving word problems. Training probes assessed students' ability to solve problems using a strategy taught during an instructional session. A 75% criterion performance on the probes was used to differentiate between more and less able students. Three transfer items were administered next and a prompting procedure was used to assist students. A near transfer posttest measure was given the following day that included problems similar to those used in training but which included distractors. Dynamic assessment of performance on three multistep, far transfer problems was conducted the next day. Finally, a far transfer posttest was given a day later. Significant differences were found between more and less able students during dynamic assessment, with less able students requiring more prompts.

Jitendra and Kameenui (1993) found that only the more able students showed an increase in performance from pretest to the near transfer posttest; similar amounts of improvement were found on the far transfer posttest. The results suggested that dynamic assessment may have differentially facilitated the performance of the two groups of students on the near transfer posttest. The more able students were better able to detect slight variations in the structure of transfer problems that differed from training problems due to the presence of extraneous information. While highly able students were intentionally excluded from this sample, it is reasonable to hypothesize that dynamic assessment might be useful to differentiate between gifted/talented/creative students and their less able peers. It would be a particularly useful method when trying to identify highly able students who are disadvantaged or disabled and are unable to meet a high test score criterion for entry into a gifted program.

Borland and Wright (1994) describe the use of a dynamic assessment task with young, disadvantaged students as part of a gifted identification procedure. The task design was based on Raven's Progressive Matrices and appears very similar to a task included in the *Learning Potential Assessment Device* (LPAD). Borland and Wright recorded the number of correct responses, the number correct following instruction, the child's strategy, and any other behavior worth noting. Testing sessions were videotaped for viewing during case study review. Borland and Wright suggest that a test of this type should be a good measure of fluid intelligence, which is less knowledge-based than crystallized intelligence.

Disadvantaged Israeli students were identified as "talented" on the basis of high scores on group dynamic assessment tasks and school achievement and selected for a two-year intervention by Kaniel and Reichenberg (1992). Three dynamic assessment tasks were used—figural analogy, verbal analogy, and organizer. The figural analogy task is an LPAD task adapted from items B8-B12 on the *Standard Progressive Matrices* (Raven, Court, & Raven, 1986). For each item, a student sees two figures in which a transformation has taken place from the first to the second figure, as well as a third figure and a blank where a fourth figure belongs. Six choices are given as possible answers. The verbal analogy task was also taken from the LPAD and is in the form A-B:C-?. The third task is called Organizer and requires students to follow a number of premises for sorting objects into an increasing number of boxes. The task examines the ability to draw logical conclusions on the basis of written instructions.

DYNAMIC-LIKE ASSESSMENT METHODS

A dynamic-like assessment approach is described by Kay and Subotnik (1994) as being used in an arts program for inner-city, elementary school students. All third and fourth grade students in two schools were given dance and music lessons once a week for seven weeks and were rated individually on their response to each lesson. Teachers were trained to judge how well students mastered criteria grouped under the headings of skills, motivation, and creativity. This identification procedure was designed to avoid selecting students who demonstrated the highest level of skill because of previous training. Instead, students were sought who showed the most artistic talent as defined by the three types of criteria in response to the instruction given each week.

Borland and Wright (1994) suggest that to identify young, potentially gifted, economically disadvantaged students, teachers need to play a larger role in the identification procedure. To overcome the problem of test bias in assessing disadvantaged students, Borland and Wright prefer to rely on the sensitivity and adaptability of human observation and judgment rather than the objectivity of standardized tests. The advantage dynamic assessment has over more objective, static assessment tasks is that it is flexible enough to allow an examiner to explore ways of encouraging the demonstration of ability by helping a student to succeed on the task.

Coleman (1994) examined a program for disadvantaged children in kindergarten to third grade that used a portfolio assessment model incorporating aspects of dynamic assessment. Sample lessons requiring inquiry and problem solving were taught to students. Teachers were trained to observe target behaviors as signs of exceptional potential and individualize instruction to capitalize on student ability. Teachers commented at the end of the study that they now looked at what they had regarded for years as signs of negative behavior and problems as signs of exceptional potential.

DYNAMIC ASSESSMENT OF STUDENTS ENGAGED IN ENRICHMENT ACTIVITIES AND GIFTED PROGRAMS

There are situations in which students are provided gifted program services even though they might not meet all of the criteria traditionally used to select students for participation. Renzulli and his associates (Renzulli, Reis, & Smith, 1981) used the concept of dynamic assessment in developing the *Revolving Door Identification Model* (RDIM). One of the goals of the RDIM is to identify students who demonstrate an aptitude for working in specific areas and are motivated to investigate a topic of interest, but who were not previously identified as gifted on the basis of test scores alone. One method for doing this is to have enrichment activities presented to an entire class by the regular teacher or an enrichment specialist.

In a district using RDIM, students are given enrichment activities, then they are given tasks to perform. Ideally, teachers are trained to provide scaffolded assistance as students encounter difficulties during the activities, are helped to identify salient features of tasks, and learn appropriate strategies for completing the tasks successfully. As part of the identification component of the RDIM, teachers are responsible for observing whether individual students show an exceptional aptitude and keen interest for working in a particular area. Such students are later given an opportunity to develop their project idea under the supervision of an enrichment specialist. Some students who demonstrate excellence on self-selected projects had been considered of average or low ability by their teachers because of deficient academic skills.

Teachers in districts using RDIM might benefit from training in dynamic assessment that enables them to be more systematic and precise in assessing how well students benefit from involvement in enrichment activities. Schack (1993) examined the effect of a creative thinking program on students at different levels of ability. She concluded that the program had a differential effect on the creative performance of students, with more able students demonstrating superior performance. This demonstrates the potential use of creative thinking activities as "tasks" to be solved in a dynamic assessment situation.

One might consider it possible to have a dynamic assessment situation that occurs over an extended time frame. Primary school-aged Hispanic students in Tucson, AZ, and American Indian students living on the Navajo Reservation in Window Rock, AZ, were selected for participation in gifted programs on the basis of high scores on tests of cognitive ability and other indicators, even though their test scores did not reach the "gifted" level which mandated gifted education according to state regulations (see Kirschenbaum, 1993). In both instances, the intent of the school districts was to provide enrichment activities that would help the students to develop thinking skills and to improve academic skills. In many individual cases, students raised their test scores after one to two years to a level that exceeded the state's gifted level.

Similarly, Kaniel and Reichenberg (1992) also found indications of significant overall improvement, when compared to a randomly assigned control group, in the academic performance of a group of talented students from an impoverished area four years after a two year intervention that focused on thinking skills. The conclusion one might tentatively reach is that the significantly improved posttest performance of the student groups involved in these three interventions demonstrates the value of including students in gifted education activities who demonstrate ability but do not have test scores that exceed a criterion level, possibly because of an impoverished background. This conclusion would substantiate the basic assumption behind dynamic assessment, which is that students with background characteristics that tend to impede academic performance can demonstrate significant improvement on academic tasks once they are provided with appropriate cognitive instruction or mediated learning experiences (Feuerstein et al., 1979).

OBSERVATION OF A DISABLED GIFTED STUDENT'S PERFORMANCE ON THE LPAD

There is ample evidence that there are disabled students who are also gifted, talented, and creative (e.g., Whitmore & Maker, 1985). Special efforts are necessary to identify such students and facilitate the development of their exceptional abilities, since their disability is often a much more salient characteristic to teachers. Baum and Kirschenbaum (1984) conducted a case study of a learning disabled student who was a talented photographer and concluded that gifted, talented, and creative students with academic deficiencies need to be encouraged to perform in their areas of interest and exceptional ability by teachers or they are likely to lose interest in school.

Students who have learning or physical disabilities that impede their performance on academic tasks and tests might be able to demonstrate exceptional learning ability or productive talents on dynamic assessment tasks. At a training workshop given by Feuerstein in 1979 at which the author was present, a 10-year-old female from a disadvantaged background was given the LPAD. She had been an average student up until grade three, when she started to have severe headaches. She eventually had an osteositoma tumor removed from her brain. The operation caused blood clots that resulted in partial paralysis. She could speak and move only in a halting manner. In addition, radiation therapy had damaged her hearing. It was noted in passing that she had started talking before she was 1 year old.

The student's performance was viewed on a television monitor by trainees in another room. During the first test session, she showed at least average ability on several subtests of the LPAD, learning fairly quickly during the assistance phase of each subtest. During the second and final test session, she was administered a subtest that required her to replicate a target pattern in a box by choosing a series of component patterns from a chart. There was only one correct sequence for each target pattern. To the amazement of all those who observed her performance, she proceeded through the whole subtest, slowly calling out the number of each component in correct order to match all the target patterns. When the examiner told her in a tone of shocked disbelief that she had done very well, she responded in a croaking voice that was hard to understand, "I am smart." She also said that she wanted to be a clothing designer. This student did not need more than one or two prompts on the initial items of the subtest to understand what she was supposed to do. Her nearly perfect score with little prompting clearly showed her gift for processing complex figural patterns.

The LPAD is a mostly nonverbal, untimed test that allows pointing at answers. It would, therefore, be very useful for identifying gifted and talented students with language problems, a physical disability, or a reading disability, or who have limited English proficiency. Instructions can also be given non-verbally to hearing impaired students. The disadvantage of the LPAD is that it is expensive, difficult to obtain, takes a long time to administer (if all the subtests are used), and there are few people who are trained in its use. For these reasons, school districts might decide to design and standardize their own dynamic assessment instruments. Most school districts lack the expertise and commitment to conduct this type of research, but that is no reason that it should not be strongly encouraged. After all, evaluation of programs is strongly advocated even though it is rarely done with a high level of technical proficiency.

Efforts should be made to collect and analyze data on locally designed dynamic assessment methods and instruments. Research on dynamic assessment methods should determine their utility for identifying students who would otherwise not be selected by traditional methods, but who end up performing successfully in the program. Research should also be done to investigate the utility of information obtained through dynamic assessment for facilitating the success of these students in gifted programs, which is a question of treatment effectiveness in which making diagnostic information available to teachers is the treatment. It should be reiterated here that both static and dynamic information are necessary for developing a diagnostic profile.

School districts that utilize innovative methods like dynamic assessment can pursue grants to fund research, can attempt to attract the interest of experts in the field, and provide opportunities for members of their own staff (or graduate students) to conduct research in their districts while pursuing a higher degree at a nearby university.

EFFECT OF DYNAMIC ASSESSMENT ON TEACHER PERCEPTIONS

While teachers know they spend a great deal of time evaluating student work, they seem to be less aware of how their implicit assessments of students affect their attitudes, expectations, and behaviors toward individual students. Teachers who have been instructed in the use of dynamic assessment by the author tended to perceive it more as an instructional approach than an assessment method. Still, they recognized that, as a result of training, their perception of students changed from one in which they judged a student as either academically proficient or deficient in a global sense to a perception of students as having deficiencies in various cognitive processes but also as being more capable than they thought on certain types of tasks. This change in teacher perspective has been noted in studies of alternative assessment methods in which teachers have learned to recognize student strengths as well as their own desire to help develop these strengths, rather than focusing mainly on academic deficits and directing most of their efforts to remediation (Shaklee, 1993; Wright & Borland, 1993).

Delclos, Burns, and Kulewicz (1987) found that teachers who viewed students in a dynamic assessment situation rated them as more competent and more knowledgeable than teachers who viewed the same students in a static assessment session. In a follow-up study, Vye, Delclos, and McGoldrick (1988) examined the effects on teacher behavior of viewing a videotape of a dynamic assessment session in which a narration explained three types of instruction used by the teacher shown on the monitor. The instructional processes shown and explained in the narration were familiarizing children with task concepts and processes, explicit instruction on task rules and strategies, and corrective feedback. Teachers were asked to teach a task to a transitional first grader both before and after viewing the videotape. Student performance was measured after each instructional session. A control group of teachers was asked to teach the task but the group was not shown the videotape.

The video presentation teachers changed their instructional methods in some important ways. They showed significant increases in the processes of familiarization and corrective feedback. There were also significant decreases in task description that was an indirect means of directing student attention, in giving directives, both verbal and nonverbal, on how to do the task, and in prompting, which was another way of telling the student what actions were preferable. Overall, the video presentation teachers appeared to be more explicit in providing students information about task principles and general procedures. The children who received instruction from the teachers who viewed the videotape on dynamic assessment made significant gains in performance of the task while the children taught by the control group of teachers made small gains. Vye et al. (1988) also found that student performance was negatively associated to a significant degree with the number of directives given by the teachers in both groups. Although this study and the one by Delclos et al. (1987) used low functioning students, they provide support for the contention that a minimal understanding of dynamic assessment and processes used in this approach can have a positive effect on teachers' instructional methods and their perception of students.

CONCLUSION

Dynamic assessment is an approach to measuring ability that has yet to be fully utilized in the education community. Teachers might improve their ability to identify gifted, talented, and creative students from groups underrepresented in gifted education if they learned how to use dynamic assessment. Very few instances of its use have been found in gifted education, but promising results have been obtained with young, disadvantaged students. Since young students from impoverished backgrounds are likely to show academic deficits that are due more to environmental variables than a lack of inherent ability, the use of dynamic assessment with this population should continue to be explored.

Dynamic assessment methods should also be researched and developed for use with disabled and LEP gifted students. One of the main purposes of dynamic assessment is to determine whether students who exhibit performance deficits have cognitive strengths that are not readily observable. During the teaching phase of dynamic assessment, an emphasis is placed on finding ways to facilitate student success on the presented task. Information can be obtained that details how a student's performance was raised from pretest to posttest, as well as the rate of improvement. A faster than normal learning rate would demonstrate above average ability and raise the possibility that participation in special enrichment activities would be beneficial. Disabled and LEP gifted, talented, and creative students need to be challenged in their area of strength in order for them to get the most out of school.

School districts which have large numbers of disadvantaged students and are dissatisfied with the effectiveness of traditional tests of ability and achievement in identifying students with high potential and are considering alternative assessment methods should take a serious look at dynamic assessment. Efforts by school districts to develop and validate dynamic assessment methods for local use are strongly encouraged.

REFERENCES

Baum, S., & Kirschenbaum, R. J. (1984). Recognizing special talents in learning disabled students. *Teaching Exceptional Children, 16*, 92–98.

Bolig, E. E., & Day, J. D. (1993). Dynamic assessment and giftedness: The promise of assessing training responsiveness. *Roeper Review, 16*, 110–113.

Borland, J. H., & Wright, L. (1994). Identifying young, potentially gifted, economically disadvantaged students. *Gifted Child Quarterly, 38*(4), 164–171.

Coleman, L. J. (1994). Portfolio assessment: A key to identifying hidden talents and empowering teachers of young children. *Gifted Child Quarterly, 38*, 65–69.

Delclos, V. R., Burns, M. S., & Kulewicz, S. (1987). Effects of dynamic assessment on teachers' expectations of handicapped children. *American Educational Research Journal, 24*, 325–336.

Feuerstein, R., Rand, Y., & Hoffman, M. (1979). *The dynamic assessment of retarded individuals: The learning potential assessment device, theory, instruments, and techniques.* Glenview, IL: Scott, Foresman & Co.

Feuerstein, R., Rand, Y., Hoffman, M. B., & Miller, R. (1980). *Instrumental enrichment: An intervention program for cognitive modifiability.* Baltimore, MD: University Park.

Haywood, H. C., Brown, A. L., & Wingenfeld, S. (1990). Dynamic approaches to psychoeducational assessment. *School Psychology Review, 19*, 411–422.

Jitendra, A. K., & Kameenui, E. J. (1993). An exploratory study of dynamic assessment involving two instructional strategies on experts and novices' performance in solving part-whole mathematical word problems. *Diagnostique, 18,* 305–324.

Kaniel, S., & Reichenberg, R. (1992). Instrumental enrichment—Effects of generalization and durability with talented adolescents. *Gifted Education International, 8,* 128–135.

Kay, S. I., & Subotnik, R. F. (1994). Talent beyond words: Unveiling spatial, expressive, kinesthetic, and musical talent in young children. *Gifted Child Quarterly, 38,* 70–74.

Kirschenbaum, R. J. (1993, April). *Wherefore art thou potential?: Developing a diagnostic profile of gifted and talented students.* Paper presented at the sixth annual Conference of the Education of Gifted Underachieving Students, Portland, OR.

Lidz, C. S. (1991). *Practitioner's guide to dynamic assessment.* New York: Guilford.

Raven, J. C., Court, J. H., & Raven, J. (1986). *Manual for Raven's Progressive Matrices and Vocabulary Scales, Section 1 (1986 edition).* London: H. K. Lewis & Co.

Renzulli, J. S., Reis, S. M., & Smith, L. H. (1981). *The revolving door identification model.* Mansfield Center, CT: Creative Learning Press.

Richert, E. S. (1985). Identification of gifted children in the United States: The need for pluralistic assessment. *Roeper Review, 8,* 68–72.

Schack, G. D. (1993). Effects of a creative problem-solving curriculum on students of varying ability levels. *Gifted Child Quarterly, 37,* 16–22.

Shaklee, B. (1993). Preliminary findings of the early assessment for exceptional potential project. *Roeper Review, 16,* 105–109.

Vye, N. J., Delclos, V. R., & McGoldrick, J. A. (1988, April). *Effects of dynamic assessment on teacher instruction and child performance.* Paper presented at the Annual Meeting of the American Educational Research Association, New Orleans, LA.

Vygotsky, L.S. (1978). *Mind in society: The development of higher psychological process* (M. Cole, V. John-Steiner, S. Scribner, & E. Souberman, Trans., Eds.). Cambridge, MA: Harvard University.

Whitmore, J. R., & Maker, C. J. (1985). *Intellectual giftedness in disabled persons.* Rockville, MD: Aspen.

Wood, D. J., Bruner, J. S., & Ross, G. (1976). The role of tutoring in problem solving. *Journal of Child Psychology and Psychiatry, 17,* 89–100.

Wright, L., & Borland, J. H. (1993). Using early childhood developmental portfolios in the identification and education of young, economically disadvantaged, potentially gifted students. *Roeper Review, 15,* 205–210.

Zorman, R. (1997). Eureka: The cross-cultural model for identification of hidden talent through enrichment. *Roeper Review, 20,* 54–61.

5

Defining Belief in Self: Intelligent Young Men in an Urban High School

Thomas P. Hébert

University of Georgia

To address the paucity of research on high-ability youth in urban environment, this article chronicles the experiences of six intelligent young men in an urban high school. Through a qualitative research design that integrated features of case study and ethnographic research, the study examined how urban life experiences influenced academic achievement. The six cases reported in this study are a subset of 12 cases (Hébert, 1993) that contributed to a larger study (Reis, Hébert, Diaz, Maxfield, & Ratley, 1995) of talented students in an urban high school. Major findings for the high-ability achieving males were a strong belief in self that incorporated an "inner will," aspirations heightened sensitivity, and a multicultural awareness and appreciation. Data analysis on the participants identified the following factors that influenced the strong belief in self: relationships with

Editor's Note: From Hébert, T. P. (2000). Defining belief in self: Intelligent young men in an urban high school. *Gifted Child Quarterly*, 44(2), 91-114. © 2000 National Association for Gifted Children. Reprinted with permission.

supportive adults; involvement in extracurricular activities, sports, special programs, and summer school experiences; and family support. Implications of the findings are presented along with suggestions for meeting the educational needs of intelligent young men in urban high schools.

Although the gleaming high-rise complexes and impressive skylines of our nation's cities may inspire awe, the urban centers remain a place where education is often neglected, leaving the glittering signs of progress nothing more than a shameful facade. For the past century, urban educators have dealt with the difficulties of educating children from families who face economic hardships. Throughout the nation's cities, serious problems have plagued the public schools. Educators in urban high schools have struggled with problems of low academic achievement, truancy, drugs, and gang warfare (Ayers, 1991; Carnegie Foundation, 1988; Kozol, 1991; Nelson, Palonsky, & Carlson, 1990). South Central High School, the urban school profiled in this article, faced these same problems; however, the young men described in this study who attended South Central survived in their urban environment and excelled in school. They ignored drug dealers; they turned their backs on gangs; they avoided the crime in their neighborhoods; and they went on to become valedictorians, class presidents, star athletes, and scholars and attended some of the most selective colleges in the country. The courage displayed by these young men seemed remarkable, yet they simply accepted their circumstances and appreciated the opportunities available to them. A guidance counselor at South Central High School spoke with conviction when he poignantly described their situation:

> These kids bring a tremendous amount of baggage to school. We don't know what they are carrying with them every day. They may look perfectly healthy and normal, but their households! They are unbelievable. These kids are driven! They are competitive. They compete anywhere because they want it. They're survivors. They've survived in the inner city, so they know they can survive anywhere.

With the counselor's words in mind, a number of questions evolved. What were the personal characteristics of these young men who had high abilities and demonstrated them? The counselor mentioned that they were "driven." What encouraged this drive? How did these young men view their urban high school experience, and where did these bright, competitive students find support? The problems investigated in this study, therefore, addressed the needs of high-ability males in an urban setting and identified the characteristics that distinguished them from their less-successful peers. To provide a theoretical framework for the study, the following review of pertinent research is presented.

Putting the Research to Use

For the six high-ability urban males in this study, a strong belief in self emerged as the single most important factor influencing their achievement. Educators and parents can assist the development of gifted urban males' belief in self in a variety of ways. Interactions with caring adults can influence how gifted young men perceive themselves and their talents. Urban educators may want to consider implementing a mentorship program in which community leaders guide gifted males in the actualization of their talents. Parents may also facilitate the development of their sons' belief in self by providing strong emotional support for them. Additionally, urban parents who have successfully nurtured their sons' achievement serve as a resource to other parents by forming supportive, informational networks.

Urban parents and educators can nurture the development of a strong belief in self in young men by cultivating their empathy and emotional self-awareness. These qualities will enable young men to perceive their emotions as adaptive tools, helping them interpret their life experiences and feel secure as sensitive males. As an outlet for their sensitivity, gifted males should be encouraged to become involved in community service projects.

Finally, this study has shown that a belief in self can be reinforced in urban males through involvement in a variety of extracurricular activities. Gifted males should be encouraged to participate in both summer enrichment programs sponsored by colleges and universities and community-based programs that provide them opportunities to address the problems of urban communities.

THEORETICAL FRAMEWORK

The most important developmental task of adolescence is the formation of a consistent self-identity (Erikson, 1968, 1985). Newman and Newman (1988) defined identity as the integration of an individual's past identifications, future aspirations, and contemporary talents and abilities, formed within a context of cultural expectations. Identity development was defined by DeHaan and MacDermid (1996) as the ability to explore choices and then select important commitments to individuals and institutions, maintain loyalty to these commitments, and arrive at a stable view of oneself. Grotevant (1987) stressed the idea of identity development as being a normal process in adolescence when young people take on problem-solving behaviors and search for information about themselves or their environment in order to make important life choices. He suggested that although adolescence may be a time of anxiety and stress, identity development exploration is a crucial part of reaching adulthood. Exploration is the degree to which an adolescent has critically examined a certain identity choice, a time during which a young person struggles or actively questions in order to arrive at various aspects of personal identity, such as career choice or religious beliefs. Grotevant also acknowledged that identity development could be more concentrated in one area of life than others and took into account personal abilities and environmental context. Garbarino, Kostelny, and Dubrow (1991) noted that the development of a strong identity was an important factor in adjustment for adolescents living in stressful contexts, such as urban environments.

Embedded Identities

Heath and McLaughlin (1993) examined identity issues in adolescents growing up in different urban areas to improve understanding of the achievement levels among culturally diverse students. They proposed that self-identity is made up of a host of "embedded identities" (p. 7) and that ethnicity appears to be more of a label assigned to culturally diverse urban teenagers by outsiders than an actual indication of their real sense of self. To urban youngsters, ethnic labels mean something only later in their lives; achieving a sense of belonging and knowing that they can do something and be someone in the eyes of others has to come first. Ethnicity is important only if it functions within a host of embedded identities that can get a young person somewhere in the immediate community. For instance, being a member of a winning ball team or the sibling of a prominent gang member is more important in daily street life than one's label of ethnicity.

In examining self-identity in urban youngsters, Heath and McLaughlin (1993) found that urban youth were cognizant of the rich cultural diversity in their neighborhoods as they continuously saw different groups moving in and out. As a result, they had learned to develop positive relationships with teenagers from many different cultural backgrounds. Heath and McLaughlin suggested that educators may think first of strong ethnic identification as something that young people need; however, as revealed in their research, the young people's "sense of salience of their own ethnic membership was likely to be either conditional or latent as their embedded identities, or multi-layered self-conceptions, meant far more to these young people than simple labels of ethnic or racial membership" (p. 7). Plummer's (1995) research supported this notion and indicated that since adolescence was a time of change in every aspect of a young person's life, racial identity was often considered unstable and in the "exploratory stage" (p. 178) during adolescence. Verkuyten (1995) found that ethnic group identification was associated with self-esteem; yet, it was not a decisive criterion in the self-concept of adolescents, and Whaley (1993) maintained that emphasis on the development of personal competencies was likely to be more useful in understanding identity development in culturally diverse youth.

Extracurricular Activities

Heath and McLaughlin (1993) found that involvement in youth organizations allowed culturally diverse urban youngsters to have a sense of the possible identities that went beyond their urban environment. Most important, these groups enabled urban youth to know both that they had options in life and that they could determine their own goals for the future. With nothing constructive to do with after-school time and fearful of life on the streets, motivated urban teenagers sought out organizations they judged to be worthwhile: safe places where they could be with their peers and engage in enjoyable activities centered on cooperative team building and reinforced with consistent adult support. Involvement in these organizations provided opportunities for intelligent young people to build a sense of self-efficacy and success in different events and kinds of activities. A strong sense of worth evolved from being a member of a group or team noted for accomplishment; a sense of belonging came from being needed within the organization—to mentor younger members, design activities, and promote the group to the community. These group experiences enabled urban teenagers to construct a positive sense of self and to raise aspirations for the future. Halpern (1992) indicated that involvement in after-school programs in urban areas offered young people structure and predictability that might be missing in their lives and an opportunity to learn about the distinction in behavior required in settings outside their urban neighborhoods.

McLaughlin (1993) noted that involvement in extracurricular activities involving the production of tangible products or performances reinforced this positive sense of self by building a sense of accomplishment and success within the urban teenagers. The activities gave urban youth evidence that something could be gained by sticking with an effort and provided opportunities for success for some who may not have had positive experiences in school. The performances and productions also demonstrated that choices matter, effort can make a difference, and some adults believe what young people can do with their talents is important. Ball and Heath (1993) indicated that out-of-school experiences helped create a sense of connectedness for urban youngsters through strong discipline, group achievement, and mutual expectations of high quality. Culturally diverse inner-city youngsters found opportunities to bond with each other in a group task and a commitment to excellence. Through the sense of belonging emanating from inclusion in such organizations, the youngsters developed a conviction in their talents and abilities.

The value of extracurricular activities in shaping adolescent self-identity was also highlighted in a longitudinal study that examined the motivational importance of extracurricular activities for 200 talented teenagers. In this study, Csikszentmihalyi, Rathunde, and Whalen (1997) reported that extracurricular activities were the most likely school activities that engaged youngsters fully—the most consistent source of interest and flow (Csikszentmihalyi, 1990) for students. Such activities were important in alerting teenagers to the fact that work was not always aversive and alienating and that exciting and involving activities were not necessarily devoid of challenge. They proposed that extracurricular activities combined feelings of spontaneous involvement with a focus on important goals and perceptions of high skill with correspondingly high challenges.

Involvement in extracurricular activities offered adult relationships that influenced how young people viewed themselves. Caring adult relationships were recognized as critical in assuring success in adolescent life, and young people tended to emulate the behavior they saw in others whom they cared about and admired (Bandura, 1977). Heath and McLaughlin (1993) noted that the most essential contribution that experiences in urban youth groups provided was that of an adult who saw them as young adults, cared for them as individuals, and served as their mentor, critic, and advocate. The presence of these extrafamilial sources of support, including identification models or mentors, was also highlighted by investigators of resilience who discovered that relationships with nonparental adults provided psychosocial support and served as a protective factor in stressful environments (Garmezy, 1985; Jones, Bibbins, & Henderson, 1993; Rhodes, 1994; Torrance, Goff, & Satterfield, 1998; Werner & Smith, 1982).

Heath and McLaughlin's findings are also consistent with the literature on coach-athlete relationships, which describes how young people welcome discipline as a way of ordering their lives and as a clear signal of how significant adults want them to perform. Ruenzel (1994) and Hébert (1995) found that young people spoke positively about their coaches. Good coaches, they reported, were like their fathers, and some students admitted respecting their coaches more than their parents or teachers. Both noted that young athletes displaying a respect for good coaches gave credence to the notion that young men were starved for discipline, for the players expressed gratitude that an adult cared enough to demand excellence of them. Researchers have also reported that athletes perceived their coaches as people who had significant influence on their academic achievement (Hébert; Snyder, 1975).

Interracial Friendships

Friendships play a major role in school adjustment (Clark, 1991) and may influence how a young person shapes an identity. Friendships with teenagers from a variety of cultural and racial backgrounds may also have special significance for adolescents. Opportunities for teenagers to enjoy interracial friendships are likely to occur in urban high schools with culturally diverse student bodies. Research results indicate that opportunities for cross-race interaction influence interracial sociability and friendship (Hallinan & Teixeira, 1987; Hallinan & Williams, 1989; Patchen, 1982; Schofield, 1978). Teenagers who experienced successful interracial friendships had cross-cultural contacts in early childhood and became comfortable with these friendship networks from long periods of exposure to young people from diverse backgrounds (Damico, Bell-Nathaniel, & Green, 1981; Sigelman, Bledsoe, Welch, & Combs, 1996). Youngsters who grew up in multicultural settings had an easier time establishing cross-cultural friendships in high school and college. Adolescents who were exposed to a variety of cultural groups throughout childhood were able to show interest in the cultural backgrounds of others without feeling threatened or endangered by groups different from their own. Such interethnic contact allowed for better social and academic adjustment later in college (Bowler, Rauch, & Schwarzer, 1986; Graham, Baker, & Wapner, 1985). Cross-cultural contact beyond the classroom was also encouraged, for several research studies indicated that interracial friendships were fostered through extracurricular activities in which teenagers interacted in situations designed to encourage cooperative activities (Patchen, Davidson, Hofman, & Brown, 1977; Scott & Damico, 1983, 1984).

Sensitivity

Because adolescence is a time of change when teenagers form friendships and struggle with issues of self-identity, how young men view their masculinity and deal with their sensitivity as men also become significant. Macoby and Jacklin (1974) documented that men and women are more similar than different on many behavioral qualities. In their review of 30 studies on empathy, they concluded that women had no advantage over men in their ability to sense the feelings of other people. Pleck (1976, 1987) found there was a trend away from the traditional masculine roles in which men were expected to be tough and inexpressive, and a shift was occurring toward a more modern role that called for interpersonal skills, the capacity for emotional intimacy, and the willingness to express emotions. Levant (1992) proposed that young men's sensitivity had to be validated and that men were capable of developing some of the same skills that women learned as girls, particularly empathy, emotional self-awareness, and emotional expressivity. Developing these skills would help balance a young man's emotional life as he shaped his self-identity. Researchers have found that younger men are less traditional than older males in their beliefs about masculinity and are more likely to show sensitivity and express their emotions (Gurian, 1996; Ross & Mirowsky, 1984). Ballard-Reisch and Seibert (1993) found that high school males who were able to integrate both positive and feminine characteristics perceived themselves more positively and demonstrated behaviors more conducive to functioning successfully in an academic environment. Robertson and Freeman (1995) proposed that young men should consider emotions from a masculine-congruent perspective—seeing emotions as functional and adaptive tools (Plutchik, 1980) to help men make sense of their life experiences and broaden options for their male behavior. Emotional expression can be seen as a proficiency that assists men in becoming more successful in relationships, families, and in professional settings (Goleman, 1995). By developing their sensitivity and emotional expressiveness, men could increase their personal effectiveness (Goleman, 1995; Gurian, 1996; Miedzian, 1991).

Internal Locus of Control

When investigating the formation of a strong self-identity in high-ability young men and considering personal characteristics such as sensitivity, another important personality characteristic to consider is internal locus of control. Locus of control has been well researched as a construct since it was first introduced by Rotter (1954) in social learning theory. Individuals who believe they are in control of their lives are said to have an internal locus of control and attribute the outcome of their actions to ability and effort, in contrast to those with an external locus of control who attribute their outcomes to factors such as luck, chance, or fate. The research on locus of control in high-ability students (Brody & Benbow, 1986; Douglas & Powers, 1982; Karnes & McGinnis, 1995; Knight, 1995; McLelland, Yewchuk, & Mulcahy, 1991; McLaughlin & Saccuzzo, 1997; Yong, 1994) has consistently supported the notion that highly able students have a more internal locus of control than more typical students and has asserted that an individual's belief in the power to control his or her life is related to high achievement.

The formation of a strong self-identity during male adolescence is a complex process and may be even more complex within highly intelligent young men. The complexity of the process deserves the attention of researchers concerned about the achievement levels of high-ability youngsters. Given the paucity of research on this topic, the study described below is an attempt to add to the literature on the self-identity development of high-ability males in urban environments.

RESEARCH DESIGN AND METHODOLOGY

To understand the urban high school experience of the young men described in the study, the investigator chose a qualitative research design that integrated features of case study and ethnographic research. Merriam (1998) defined a qualitative case study as an "intensive, holistic description and analysis of a single entity, phenomenon or social unit" (p. 27). Ethnography refers to research that involves the description of a culture (Creswell, 1998). The primary goal of the study was to examine the lives of high-ability young men and understand how their urban life experiences influenced their academic achievement. To do this, 120 days of one academic year were spent interviewing high-ability secondary students and observing them at South Central High School, a large high school located in an urban area in the northeastern part of the United States. Case studies are often used when attempting to answer "how" and "why" questions, such as those posed in this study (Yin, 1994). Case studies are designed to investigate "a contemporary phenomenon within its real-life context; when the boundaries between context and phenomenon are not clearly evident; and in which multiple sources of evidence are used" (Yin, 1989, p. 23). As a research tool, case studies enable researchers to understand complex social phenomena while retaining the holistic and meaningful characteristics of everyday events (Yin, 1993). They are particularly useful when the researcher needs to understand some specific group of people, a particular problem, or a unique situation in great depth. When the researcher can identify cases within this group, problem, or situation, case study research can yield valuable information (Patton, 1990). Well-developed case studies can provide a better basis for personally understanding what is going on (Stake, 1981).

The six cases described in this study are a subsample of the author's larger dissertation study of 12 high-ability male achievers and underachievers (Hébert, 1993). The dissertation study contributed to a larger study conducted by a research team funded by the National Research Center on the Gifted and Talented (Reis et al., 1995). The author's dissertation research played an important role in the NRC/GT study in that he began the NRC/GT study, immersing himself in the culture of the urban high school for 120 days and completed the first 12 cases before additional researchers joined the three-year NRC/GT investigation. The author's report of the cases described in this article focus specifically on the experiences of the high-ability achievers in his dissertation study. Acknowledging the author's extensive time spent in the field, the cultural diversity represented in his subsample, and his specific focus on high-ability males in the high school, the intent of this article is to report findings from a representative "slice" of a voluminous qualitative data set. In this study, six high-ability male achievers were the phenomena under investigation, and the primary goal of this article is to focus on their experiences in an urban high school. The names of the people, places, and institutions described in this article were changed to protect the identity of the participants involved.

SELECTION OF THE PARTICIPANTS

The six young men featured in this article had all been identified as gifted in elementary or middle school. They were recommended for involvement in the study by the school's guidance counselors and teachers, and information from an academic portfolio was used to document the label of high ability. For the purpose of this study, as well as the larger NRC/GT study, a high-ability student was defined as one who had shown above-average potential as measured by standardized intelligence or achievement test results of above the 85th percentile using local norms during his school career and had demonstrated superior performance in one or more academic areas. The young men identified for the study as achievers met three of the following four criteria: (1) The student had been enrolled in an academically gifted program; (2) was achieving at a superior level academically as evidenced by high grades; (3) had received a teacher/counselor nomination; (4) had received academic awards and honors. Demographic data about the participants in this study are included in Table 1.

DATA COLLECTION

A combination of participant observation, ethnographic interviews, and document review was used to gather data for this qualitative study. Participant observation is a strategy ethnographers use for listening to people and watching them in their natural settings (Spradley, 1979); therefore, observation data were collected from social, athletic, and academic settings. Along with transcribed interviews with participants, the review of formal and informal documents, such as the students' records, samples of their written work, and programs from athletic events or posters advertising extracurricular activities, provided a clearer picture of the urban high school life experiences being studied.

Six or more in-depth interviews were conducted with each of the high-ability males featured in this article. Individual interviews with their teachers, peers, school counselors, and coaches were also conducted. These semi-structured interviews consisted of open-ended or "grand tour questions" (Spradley & McCurdy, 1972) and specific questions. Grand tour questions were designed to explore a few general topics in order to not only gain information directly from the participants, but also to develop insight on how the young men interpreted aspects of their urban high school experience. Such questions helped define the boundaries of the study and focused the investigation (Fetterman, 1989). In this study of high-ability males in an urban high school, a grand tour question was: "Tell me what it's like to attend this high school." Grand tour questions led to information that allowed the researcher to construct a basic map of the culture and isolate preliminary topics. Such information stimulated a flow of specific, detailed questions, followed by more grand tour questions, which again led to more detailed questions until the researcher had constructed a well-designed conceptual framework (Fetterman, 1989).

Once a significant category was revealed to the researcher through grand tour questions, then specific questions about the category became useful. When grand tour questions shaped and informed the researcher with a general understanding, specific questions probed further into an established category and refined and expanded that understanding (Fetterman, 1989). For example, in this study, the researcher posed the grand tour question about what it was like to attend the urban high school. The participants' responses to the question provided an insider's perspective on the high school's cultural diversity. Probing further, the researcher elicited a description of the students' belief in the importance of cultural diversity as part of their educational experience. A sampling of questions used to interview the high-ability males is provided in Figure 1.

By interviewing participants, a picture emerged of what each participant believed was happening, enabling each young man to tell his own story. The following research questions guided the qualitative case studies: What did the high-ability males expect from their urban high school experience? What support systems (family, school, community) were recognized by these young men? What views did they hold of their urban high school environment? What relationships guided their behaviors, attitudes, and aspirations?

DATA CODING AND ANALYSIS

Field notes, observation notes, and transcribed interviews were coded and analyzed according to a three-stage process proposed by Strauss and Corbin (1990). The first stage of analysis consisted of open coding, whereby all transcribed

Table 1   Students' Demographics for Grade Level, Race/Ethnicity, Test Information, and Grade-Point Average

Student	Grade	Race/Ethnicity	Subject	Test Percentiles	GPA Honors Track
Rafael	12	Hispanic	Math	88	B
			Reading	90	
Vaughn	12	White	Math	96	B
			Reading	96	
Lucio	11	Hispanic	Math	99	B
			Reading	99	
Matteo	11	White	Math	97	B
			Reading	98	
Orlando	11	Hispanic	Math	94	A+
			Reading	85	
Wallace	11	African American	Math	88	B
			Reading	88	

Note: Achievement scores (local norms) on either the Metropolitan Achievement Test (MAT) or Comprehensive Test of Basic Skills (CTBS) taken in high school.

field notes and interviews were read and analyzed line by line to generate initial categories. A second stage of coding then identified consistent themes and relationships in each of the three sources: student interviews, participant observations, and interviews with all other participants. After these general categories were determined, each source was reviewed once more to locate additional evidence in the data. Strauss and Corbin described this process as axial coding since it involves analysis focused individually around the axis of each category. A third stage, selective coding, then compared the general themes across all sources of data, identifying even broader, more consistent themes. The inclusion of several data sources not only increased the validity of the specific findings, but also provided a comprehensive perspective of the data. At several points in the research process, member checks (Lincoln & Guba, 1985) were used with some participants to verify or extend the researcher's understanding. An audit trail of data and data analysis has been preserved and includes tape-recorded interviews, interview transcripts, field notes, notes from observations, and field documents and artifacts (Glesne & Peshkin, 1992).

Following a description of the participants, a discussion of the overall findings is provided using data gathered from document review, observations, and interviews, and implications are discussed.

DESCRIPTION OF THE PARTICIPANTS

Rafael

A teacher in the faculty lounge was once overheard saying, "I can't understand why the young women in this high school haven't discovered Rafael!

Figure 1   Sample grand tour and follow-up interview questions

Elementary School Experience

Grand Tour Questions
Describe your elementary school experience.
Describe your elementary school experience in the gifted and talented program.
Describe especially significant events during your elementary school years.

Follow-up Questions
What did Mrs. Scarfa do that was especially significant in shaping your school experience that particular school year?
How did your teacher's offering you a "scholarship" check in fifth grade affect you at that time?
As a student, what impact did the gifted and talented program experience have on you?

Middle School Experience

Grand Tour Questions
Describe your middle school experience.
Describe your middle school experience in the gifted and talented program.
Describe especially significant events during your middle school years.

Follow-up Questions
What did your English teacher do that was especially significant in shaping your school experience that particular school year?
How did your being selected for Project High Tops influence you during your middle school years?
Why was your being elected student council president so important to your family?
How did your friendships change as a result of your move to the middle school?

High School Experience

Grand Tour Questions
Tell me what it's like being a teenager in this community.
Tell me what it's like being a student in this high school.
Tell me what it's like being a high-ability student in this high school.
Describe your program of study at South Central High School.
Describe especially significant events during your high school years.

Follow-up Questions
Describe your experience with honors and Advanced Placement courses.
What did your AP physics teacher do that was especially significant in shaping your passion for that subject?
How did your involvement in the university-based summer writing camp influence you?
How has the diversity of this high school influenced you?
How has your involvement in the jazz band influenced you?
How have your relationships with Coach Brogan and members of the swim team influenced you?
What are your plans for after high school?
If I return to this community 10 years from today in hopes of conducting a follow-up interview with you, where do you predict you will be and what do you hope your life will be like?

What a wonderfully sensitive young man." Rafael knew he was sensitive and realized this quality allowed him to express himself through his poetry. He explained that when he faced obstacles in life, he wrote poems in Spanish since the language allowed him to express his true feelings more clearly. He referred to feelings of "such desolation and despair" when he surveyed his neighborhood and realized how so many young people were turned off to school and had given in to the culture of the streets. Rafael was a dignified young man with a smooth, dark complexion accentuated by a short, conservative haircut and a well-groomed mustache. He had acquired an athletic physique through neighborhood football, as well as training in Spanish folk dancing. He dressed in black jeans, black leather loafers, and brightly colored, flowered, short-sleeved shirts. He claimed that too many teenagers judged people according to the status-oriented designer clothing they wore. He was a man of simple means, and he saw no need to have an elaborate wardrobe.

Vaughn

Vaughn's appearance changed like the weather. In September, he wore his "new grunge look" clothing, his blonde hair parted in the middle and long on the sides. Later in the year, he wore designer athletic sweatshirts, and his hair was cropped very short with long sideburns. Later, he surprised his friends with a mohawk hairstyle with a stripe of spiked hair down the center of his head dyed peroxide blonde. By mid-winter, his smooth, oval-shaped head was completely shaved. Throughout these changes, Vaughn wore wire rimmed glasses, a mischievous grin, and a retainer over his sparkling white teeth. He was a polite, soft-spoken young man who was known in his senior class as an athlete and scholar. As a well-respected senior on the school's swim team, he admitted that many of his friends took their personal problems to him, for he was known as a good listener and a true friend.

Lucio

Lucio looked like a Latino version of a Hollywood teen idol. A handsome, muscular young man with an athletic build, a creamy complexion, and a mesmerizing smile, Lucio's reputation as a casanova was well established among the students at South Central. Lucio presented himself as an easy-going, care-free member of the swim team, who was known for his charisma and good-natured pranks. Though he was known throughout the school corridors as a hellraiser, the handsome young Cuban American had a quiet, sensitive side that not too many people knew about. This side was reflected in Lucio's art work, which he kept secret, and the poetry, which poignantly described his friend-ships with important young women in his life.

Matteo

Matteo talked incessantly, and many people listened. The young politician with the "gift of gab" took his campaign into every junior homeroom class at South Central High in September and spoke to the members of his class about his plans as junior class president to eradicate student apathy. His emotional plea to the students was convincing, and they elected him. Matteo was a high-energy young man who spoke with emotion, providing his audience with animated facial expressions, sincerity, and a wide, toothy grin. He used analogies throughout his daily conversations and had the vocabulary of an MIT professor. Using a personal metaphor to explain how his mind operated, he compared his thought processes to a computer that provided him with separate files. One file controlled his responsibilities for the junior class presidency, another stored information for his leadership role in Junior Achievement, another file stored the academics, and, finally, one file controlled the heart, where Matteo organized his "romantic projects." An active young man who was constantly on the go, he was known by all faculty members and students.

Orlando

As president of the Bible Study Club, Orlando's day began in prayer as he conducted a morning prayer session in Spanish. He and 12 other students met each morning in the school cafeteria, stood in a circle with their eyes closed, and prayed fervently together. The sincerity he displayed in his religious beliefs and his commitment to his studies brought him the respect of his peers. Orlando was ranked first in his class and had been number one since arriving at South Central as a freshman.

Orlando was a polite, soft-spoken Puerto Rican young man who wore his short black hair combed neatly and dressed in jeans, black Reeboks, and colorful, long-sleeved shirts completely buttoned to the neck. Over his shoulder was the ever-present black leather backpack filled with a heavy load of textbooks. He carried himself throughout the day with a real sense of dignity, and he would greet adults and friends with a warm smile. When Orlando ran for class office, he was unopposed by any of his peers; as one student explained, "Orlando is such a nice guy. Who would want to see him not win?"

Wallace

South Central High sports fans looked to Wallace as a local hero, and the community's sports commentators had only praise for the multitalented Black athlete. Along with playing football and competing in track, Wallace was a strong academic achiever and popular leader who enrolled in honors-level courses, competed in state science fairs, worked as a reporter for the school's newspaper, and served South Central High as student council president. The handsome, ebony-skinned teenager with the rugged physique of an athlete was easily spotted in the corridors of the high school as he stood over six feet and weighed 270 pounds. Wallace's physical stature may have overshadowed his smaller-sized peers, yet his warm smile, soft-spoken manner, and friendly personality made him stand out in the crowd. He dressed in jeans, sneakers, and brightly colored crew-necked jerseys, and he carried a large overstuffed book bag slung over one shoulder with his maroon South Central High varsity letter jacket.

DESCRIPTION OF THE SETTING

Opened in 1974, South Central High School was one of three high schools in a large metropolitan community in the Northeast, and its student population was the most culturally diverse in the city. In this high school, 60% of the students were Latino, approximately 20% were African American, and the remaining 10% were a mixture of White, Asian, and other racial or ethnic groups. The majority of students were from working-class to low-socioeconomic-status families. The multicultural student body was a transient population, with approximately one-third of the students transferring in or out of the high school during any academic year. Located in the south end of the city, South Central High was a metallic brown, four-story structure that housed 1,656 students and a faculty and staff of 200. With an architectural style of the '70s and few windows, a passersby might mistake the high school for an industrial plant.

FINDINGS

The competitive, survivor quality described by the guidance counselor in the introduction appeared to be a reflection of a strong belief in self within these six young men. Several qualities merged to form this belief in self-including sensitivity, inner will, aspirations, and multicultural appreciation. A part of that strong belief in self was a heightened sensitivity. They knew they were sensitive and appreciated that quality within themselves because they knew it allowed them to be better men. With that sensitivity came an appreciation for people from diverse cultures. These young men looked at the multitude of different hues in the faces of their high school peers and saw beauty in that diversity. They knew their association with people of diverse cultural backgrounds provided them with opportunities to understand humanity better; and, with this knowledge of diverse people, they came to understand themselves better, believing in themselves. Also, they had an internal fortitude that helped provide the strong drive for reaching their goals in life. This strong belief in self naturally incorporated aspirations, for these young men had dreams, goals, and visions of a future where they would make the world a better place.

This strong belief in self was reinforced in the six young men in three ways. First, they had had their belief in self nurtured by caring adults who helped make a difference in how they saw themselves and whether they would achieve their goals. Along with adults who cared, they had families who believed in their abilities. Along with their strong families and other supportive adults in their lives, they became involved in a variety of experiences that allowed them to develop their talents and be exposed to another world outside their urban community. The combination of family support, support from significant adults, and experiences in which they began to see themselves as valued individuals enabled their belief in self to become stronger, and they knew they were well prepared to succeed.

Belief in Self

Vaughn was one of only four males in the senior class at South Central who belonged to the National Honor Society. He was proud of this accomplishment, but he explained that his pride in his academic standing had developed as he matured. As a freshman, he was awarded a jacket at an awards assembly for his strong academic record, but he did not wear it the following school year to avoid ridicule from peers who may not have appreciated his academic achievement. He explained that he was comfortable wearing the jacket as a senior. He was more assured of himself, and he knew he maintained the respect of his peers. In all the conversations with Vaughn, he emphasized his independent spirit and how this attitude affected the ways he perceived his academic responsibilities. He explained, "I don't worry about my grade-point average. I worry about learning. I don't care what the teachers think of me, as long as I am learning. Grades aren't important to me. It's what I'm learning that counts." His strong belief in self may have developed at poolside during his four years of swimming for Coach Brogan, a man who served as a mentor and role model to Vaughn. Through his experiences with the team, he learned to deal with competition and learned about himself in the process. He explained, "I'm not worried about the competition. "I'm just going to do the best for the team and for myself."

Rafael described his view of the importance of having a strong self-identity when he discussed the main character in *Catcher in the Rye*, explaining that Holden Caulfield was someone with whom he could not identify. He said,

> Caulfield was out there! He was too wacko for me. But, as teenagers, some of us go through that. You have to come out of being a teenager realizing who you are and what your purpose is. I think I've done that. I've learned that if you concentrate on what you're doing rather than what others are doing, you'll get ahead.

While observing Lucio in an English Literature class, it was apparent that he, too, believed in himself. In a discussion about the novel *Jane Eyre*, Lucio led the group with thoughtful questions for the teacher, as well as insightful comments made to other students throughout the class discussion. When asked about the discussion, he explained the reason for his intense involvement:

> I think I resemble that little girl in the novel. That's why I am enjoying it. She was different. I feel the same way. I never really cared about being the most noted, being class president. I never really cared for that kind of stuff. I just want to be able to be myself. If people don't like the way I talk or the way I think, there are a couple of adjectives I can use to describe them! [laughs] I'm happy with who I am and I have friends.

Lucio discussed an incident that occurred during his adolescence that had a great impact on him and affected the way he perceived himself. Lucio had been accused of being an accessory to the rape of a 12-year-old girl when he was in junior high school. He went to trial with another young man and was found not guilty. The young man who was responsible for the crime was someone with whom Lucio no longer associated, for he learned to choose his friends more carefully. This event proved to be both traumatic and significant in shaping Lucio's life. Lucio had the support of his family at the time of the incident; and, through their understanding and his own reflection, he learned at an early age that his peer group could affect his life goals. He explained, "After that happened, I kept everyone at a distance and started to choose friends a little better. Since then, I am constantly thinking ahead. If I do this, then X, Y, and Z will happen. I learned a lot." This event had a major impact on Lucio. He realized that his earlier years had not been problem-free, but he had an enhanced self-understanding. He commented, "I have lived more in my little 16 years than most people will until they are 30. That's helped me figure out who I am." He noted, 'I've had a lot of the younger swimmers on the team come to me for help at times. Because I've done a lot of things that others have never thought of doing, they consider me 'wiser.' I have the respect of my peers."

Orlando had developed a strong belief in self through his religious beliefs. Orlando had fervent moral convictions. As he walked down a corridor of the high school, he explained that he was nervous about having to give an oral presentation to his Urban Literature class. The topic he had selected was abortion. He was pro-life and was determined to make his peers understand his point of view on this emotionally charged issue. He realized he was presenting a controversial issue to a group of young people who might not appreciate his point of view. Among his inner-city high school peers were several pregnant women and teenage fathers. He described his experience:

> I prayed before going up there, and I said, "Lord, just help me and please make the right words come out." I spoke to the Lord, and I said, "Use me so that with this oral report, someone's mind might be changed, even if it is only one person. I'll feel as though I have accomplished something for You." I went up to the front of the class with my report, and I told them they had to neutralize themselves for a few minutes and listen to what I would be speaking. I spoke about the alternatives to abortion. It went well. Thank God.

Throughout all conversations with Orlando, he emphasized that his belief in self was shaped through his relationship with God. As a teenager at South Central, there were many people who questioned him, but he explained, "It's difficult. It's difficult. But, as long as there is a connection with God, that relationship with the Lord, you'll be fine. A lot of people don't understand that. They think I'm crazy, but I know what I am talking about."

Wallace may have gained some of his strong belief in self from his achievements in athletics at an early age. He reminisced about being recognized for his athletic prowess in junior high school. He described his experiences in baseball:

> When I got to the plate, the whole team would go back in the field. It was an ego boost, but I had to live with it. They were playing me so

deep. It was a high school field we were playing in so they would play me as far back as they wanted to. I'd start to run the bases, and they were right under the ball already. It got frustrating. My coach told me not to kill it all the time. I had to learn to drop it in between players so I could get to see a lot of the bases.

The well-respected athlete who had to keep his ego under control as early as seventh grade was faced with adulation from the South Central High School staff and students. College recruiters closely watched his success in football, baseball, and track, yet he was able to cope with his athletic popularity. School administrators bragged about his scholarly success at a regional science fair, and the student body looked to him as a leader in his role as student council president. He explained, "You take it in stride. The way I deal with it? I think I've learned to just block it out. I block out how the school population perceives me. It's just a matter of going out there and concentrating, knowing what I have to do."

A close friend of Wallace's was Matteo, an officer in the city's chapter of Junior Achievement. He spoke of an experience in Junior Achievement where he was interviewed as a candidate for the state title of "Outstanding Young Entrepreneur of the Year." Matteo described the experience as intimidating, yet he relished the challenge of the competition. Matteo's strong belief in self can be seen in the description of that interview:

The president of Junior Achievement in [the state] interviewed me. The top dog himself, Dr. Hubbard, sat down with me! Actually, he stood up. I walked into his office, which was pretty intimidating. I walked into his office, and he said to me, "Good evening, Matteo, I am Dr. Peter J. Hubbard, president of Junior Achievement." I walked in very forward-like and said, "Good evening, Dr. Hubbard, I am Matteo V. DiSanto, vice-president of finance of Ethnic Vibrations [Junior Achievement company name]. Delighted to meet you!" He started cracking up. That was the ice breaker I needed. I thought, "Yeah! I got that one down!"

Matteo's belief in self incorporated his philosophy that "nothing is impossible," and he approached every challenge he undertook with sheer enthusiasm. He led a research team of three students from his physics class to a statewide science competition after selecting cold fusion as a topic to investigate. He explained,

The idea of cold fusion was mine, and that made me chief researcher, I was turned onto this topic because someone else said I couldn't do it. Across the physics world, everyone said a high school student could not do a project on cold fusion! That's why I became determined to do the project.

Sensitivity

As part of the strong belief in self, the young men in the study displayed a heightened sensitivity. Their belief in self appeared to involve a sentimental, intuitive, and caring quality, and they did not follow the traditional cultural patterns dictated by a macho society. In fact, one participant specified that his cultural background allowed him to be openly sensitive as this quality was highly valued by members of his family. Lucio, a Cuban American, explained that he was raised in a Latino family that was "an old-fashioned household" where people openly expressed their emotions, and men were comfortable showing their affection for each other. Lucio jokingly pointed out that restrictive emotionality was a problem that plagued the culture of Caucasian males. Lucio explained that his closest friends were often females, and during the summer months, he especially enjoyed the company of college-age female friends from his neighborhood who appreciated his maturity and many hours of intense conversation they spent on sensitive topics. A female friend of Lucio's mentioned that as a member of the women's swim team, she watched Lucio's boisterous behavior with his peers on the men's swim team every day around the pool. She explained that she was also happy to know the softer, sensitive side of Lucio who had written her poems to thank her for her friendship. She commented, "Lucio is very deep."

In an initial interview with Rafael, sensitivity was a quality that emerged early, as he reflected back to his early childhood in Puerto Rico and described in great detail scenes from his homeland. He was able to portray vividly his reminiscences in color, describing the landscape, aromas, and significant people from his memories of Ponce, Puerto Rico. He shared his love for writing poetry and explained that he wrote in Spanish because his native language was more precise in allowing him to describe his emotions. He pointed out that he did not write poetry "about flowers and trees," but about "human turmoil." Rafael experienced great sadness over a failed relationship with a young woman during his junior year of high school, and he claimed the poetry helped him "clear his thoughts" and deal with the anguish he felt during the experience.

Rafael's English teacher noted that he was able to use his bilingualism as an asset in his writing, and she encouraged him to submit his poetry for publication, as she was impressed "with the sensitive quality of his work." He wrote a character sketch in another English class that earned him an A+. This piece was about his guidance counselor, Mr. Thomas. He was proud of his work and wanted to let his counselor know he had written it. When he shared it with his counselor, he explained that Mr. Thomas read it in his presence. Rafael commented, "He didn't say anything to me, but I could tell in his eyes that he liked it."

Rafael described the feelings of despair and depression he felt when he returned to his home in the "projects" after having experienced special summer programs on college campuses throughout New England. Though he felt overwhelmed by the poverty seen in the projects and the high number of young people in his neighborhood who were "tuned out to education," he attempted to solve a small piece of the problem. He volunteered as a tutor at an elementary school near the projects, where he worked with bilingual students. Rafael thought he would be able to "relate to these young children who might be having trouble with their reading or learning English."

Vaughn, the senior member of the men's swim team, was appreciated by his peers for his sensitive qualities. A friend of Vaughn's reported that he had a reputation for watching out for the freshman members of the team, for he enjoyed the role of "big brother" to the younger athletes. In his senior résumé where he listed his strengths, he wrote, "Over the years, I've noticed my friends appreciating my understanding, willingness to listen, and my trustworthiness. When it comes to talking to me about a sensitive topic, people feel very comfortable with me. That is the quality I am most proud of."

Multicultural Appreciation

All of the high-ability achievers in the study acknowledged that appreciation for cultural diversity was an integral part of their strong belief in self. All six made frequent reference to the pride they had in the culturally diverse population of their high school and how their appreciation for diversity and their interracial friendships helped them become better adults. Lucio expressed his appreciation for his environment and explained how the multicultural quality of the population affected him personally:

> You have such diversity here. The girl I am going out with is from Guiana. I talk to Puerto Rican people every day. My family is from Cuba. You have Black kids here. You have Polish kids. You have all these different people. Everyone comes together at South Central. It's nice. It's something that you learn outside of your textbooks. You learn 5% in class and 95% in life. The more diversity you have, the more cultures you come in contact with, the more you learn.

Vaughn was a lifeguard at a municipal swimming pool in the city during the summer months. He was proud he used the Spanish he learned in language classes in high school in his dealings with Latino children at the pool. Following his middle school years, rather than enroll Vaughn at South Central, his father considered sending him to a private academy in an affluent suburban community. Vaughn was opposed to that plan at the time. He appreciated the diversity of his high school environment, and he explained how the environment affected him personally when he commented, "I wouldn't be the person I am today had I gone to a private school. I have been exposed to so many more kinds of people and cultures here. Private school is not the real world, and I know that I am a real people person now."

Matteo reflected on his multicultural awareness and appreciation when he shared an experience he had in another community. He described new insights when he said,

> I have a strong multicultural awareness in attending school in the city. I know the Hispanic cultures, the African-American culture, the

Asian-American cultures, and my own Italian culture right here on Jefferson Avenue. I went to a dance a few nights ago with my new friend from Walton High School. There were no Hispanic people. There were no African-American people. There were no Asian people. It was just White people. I was the only person in the gym who could have said this and I did: "I have never been in a room with so many White people who can't dance! "It was a real shock to me. I never realized how I take cultural diversity for granted.

Aspirations

The aspirations of the six achievers were closely tied to their strong belief in self. They all expressed a desire to graduate from college and pursue a professional career, and most of these intelligent, sensitive young males knew what they wanted to do in life. They had dreams and definite goals towards which they were striving, and these dreams, goals, and career aspirations were closely connected with who they were as people. Their personalities were often reflected in their choices for the future.

Rafael, the sensitive young Puerto Rican whose family overcame economic hardships, was proud of his bilingual background and wanted to pursue a degree in elementary education so he could teach young children who faced bilingual problems. He thought he would serve as a strong role model for many other Hispanic children who were feeling disenchanted with the educational system. Wallace knew that athletic scholarships might become a possibility if college recruiters continued to attend South Central's sports events; yet, he was not depending strictly on athletics to determine his life goals. The personable young man, who served as student council president and had the respect of his peers, considered public relations or law as possible career paths. Orlando, the Bible Study Club president, explained he had to deal with ambiguity over his career choice for awhile, but through prayer, he hoped to find an answer to his question. He was torn over whether to pursue a degree in theology or a "college degree with a Christian perspective." Regardless of the decision made, he planned to apply his degree through work in Christian philanthropy. Vaughn, whose interest in science had been strong throughout school, was interested in a future in environmental studies. He talked of working for Greenpeace after completing a degree, and he sincerely explained his reason for this choice was a concern for the environment. He commented, "The environment isn't working right now. Something has to be done."

Lucio had not focused on a definite college major; however, he knew that he had another year to consider the issue, and he believed he would pursue post-secondary education in liberal arts. He explained he was considering oceanography, engineering, or architecture. Matteo had the most definite career aspirations of any of the young men in the study. He spoke of the U.S. Air Force Academy throughout all his interviews. His plans for a college degree through the military appeared to be consuming a large part of his life. Matteo decided he wanted a degree in civil engineering combined with environmental science; and, because of his family's economic hardships, he decided to gain his college education through the military. He described the Air Force Academy as the "ticket" to his dreams; yet, he did not necessarily see himself pursuing a career with the military. He explained his plans in his unique, analogous speaking style:

> The military is the way I will get to my goal. The question is whether I will keep the car. I will have been enjoying the joy ride for all it's worth, but I am not sure if I will be staying with the Air Force. That's what will have gotten me the engineering degree. It's kinda like staying [in the car] after New York and deciding whether or not you want to continue on to Baltimore. [laughs] I may make a career out of it. I might hate it. I don't know. I'll see down the road.

Inner Will

Early in the interviews, the six participants referred to an internal motivation that kept driving them to succeed in their urban environment. Matteo referred to this drive as an "inner will," and this inner will was an important aspect of the strong belief in self observed in these young men. Matteo explained his theory of "inner will" and its importance in his achievement. He said,

> It sounds off the wall, but it's an internal will. For example, if I am curious about something and I want to learn about it, like my science fair topic—cold fusion. I didn't care if the material I needed was radioactive or not. I said to the professor, "Send it to me in a lead bottle UPS. I'll pay the shipping!" Nothing is going to stop me. I am going to do this experiment. If I get this inner drive pointed toward academics, I'll do well. That's basically it. It's like a driving force. If I find some reason to motivate myself to push for something, I'll do it.

Both Lucio and Rafael explained their inner will as the result of family hardships. Rafael's parents had brought their seven children from Puerto Rico to the United States. He explained, "I have watched my father struggle, and I know my parents want me to have a better life." His love of family provided him the motivation he needed to meet his challenges in school. He explained,

> I realized the burden my parents had taken. I knew the roots of where I was coming from. I realized that they had made so many sacrifices for me for so many years. Just to give up now would be such a disappointment, not just to me, but to my mother. . . . I found encouragement from their situation, where they came from, where they were born. They were born in the countryside. They were very poor. I got the motivation from that.

Orlando's inner will, according to him, could be attributed to his strong religious convictions. He explained this succinctly when he said, "I believe in the Lord. I believe that I have to put forth my part, also, but there is no doubt about it. If you help yourself, God will help you. My gifts and talents come from the Lord. My success is through Jesus Christ."

Vaughn indicated a combination of factors that explained what constituted his motivational force. He saw the ingredients of his inner will as a combination of "friends, hard work, and evaluation." He explained his theory:

> Most of my friends have faced problems that I haven't had to deal with—alcoholic parents, difficult home lives. I'm grateful that I haven't faced these problems. That's made me appreciate what I have. Hard work is involved, and I appreciate criticism from adults. I like that. It has helped my development.

Family Support

The six achievers in this study appeared to have supportive families that nurtured them in a variety of ways, and they acknowledged and described the emotional support they received from their families. Matteo's family lived in an apartment house, his grandparents lived below them, and an uncle's family lived above. Matteo's grandfather spent much time at the family's kitchen table reminiscing about the old days in Sicily and passing on advice to his son and grandson. Matteo described the relationship between his father and his uncles as very close: "When one brother moves, they all move." Matteo's father was dealing with an expected layoff from the manufacturer for which he worked, and the family support systems appeared strong as the entire family prepared for the unemployment. This supportive family feeling was apparent in Matteo's discussion of a family conversation regarding his father's situation. He explained that his grandfather had paid off the mortgage on the family home, and his family didn't have to worry.

He said, "My grandparents wouldn't mind if Dad couldn't pay the rent as he does now. The same is true for my aunt and uncle. They will forgo the rent money so we can have a place to live. That's a consoling thing." The hardships faced by Matteo's family brought him closer to his parents, as evidenced in his discussion of the family's lack of financial resources. He said, "I had the money built up for my birthday. I gave it to my parents to put into the family budget because, at the time, it was getting pretty low."

The strong family emotional support was also noted in the experiences of Lucio, whose mother and stepfather had emigrated from Cuba. He explained that he worried about his parents, who were exhausted from working over 60 hours a week to provide for him and his younger brother. He realized that his parents had accomplished so much with limited education. He explained, "I do owe them a lot. It's because of them that I try to get good grades."

Rafael described the important role his family's support played in keeping him focused academically. He said,

I remember when I was younger, my parents used to sit me down, often after dinner, with no interruptions at all. I'd go off to my room or off to watch TV, and my father would call me back to the kitchen and have me sit down and listen to him tell me how it was way back when they were growing up in Puerto Rico. They really instilled the idea that I have to do well in school. They're always telling me that. They didn't have the opportunities for education, and ever since I was a young kid, I've had that drilled into my brain. Even today, they say, "Keep working hard."

Rafael explained that his academic success in high school had impacted his family's decision not to return to Puerto Rico. He explained,

I'll be the only one in my whole family, the extended family, as a matter of fact, who will have gone to college. They're staying here for me. It would be such a disappointment to my mother if I didn't graduate and go on to college.

As Lucio was being interviewed at home, his mother approached him at the kitchen table and jokingly discussed the length of his hair. She lovingly teased him about its condition and offered to cut it stylishly. She explained she could live with his rather long hair, but she admonished, "Wear an earring, and you lose an ear!" Lucio's extended family was also very important to him. He was awed by the struggles they faced in Cuba under the Castro regime and shared details of their hardships. Members of his extended family were visiting from Havana, and as one aunt passed by, she planted a loud kiss on his cheek. He explained, "When they arrived, she had just been in the house for a few minutes, and she started to tell me to cut my hair! That's why I love her so much," he said laughing.

This love of a supportive family was also described by Orlando, whose parents had emigrated from Puerto Rico when his father was in search of employment as a teacher. Teachers' salaries in Puerto Rico were so low that Orlando's father came to the United States for better economic and educational opportunities for their eight children, The family's religious strength provided them with support in a variety of ways. Orlando explained that his parents wanted their children to appreciate their cultural background, and the family had prayed so that he and his older brother, Diego, could travel to Puerto Rico for a summer visit. Diego was the same brother Orlando was delighted to have in his chemistry class. Diego was the valedictorian of his senior class, and rather than compete, the two brothers studied together every night. When Orlando conducted the daily morning prayer meeting in the school's cafeteria, Diego stood to his right in the prayer circle. When Orlando told his family he was torn over his indecisiveness about his plans after high school, his family responded, "Seek the Lord through prayer, and He will help you."

Wallace also described a supportive family who helped him believe in himself. Wallace and his younger brother had a mother, father, and grandmother who regularly monitored their academic and athletic progress. He described his father's support: "When he goes to work, he takes our report cards. He shows them to the guys at work. When I see his friends, they know who I am before I even meet them. Mom and Dad are proud." Wallace received a similar message from his maternal grandmother, who called him and his brother daily and admonished, "Stay in shape, stay cool, and keep hitting the books." He also pointed out that his grandmother took savings from her small salary as a nurse's aide and rewarded his brother and him for impressive grades on their report cards. Their grandmother collected newspaper clippings from the city's paper each time her grandsons were listed in the high school honor rolls or mentioned on the sports page and brought them to her job to show her co-workers.

Supportive Adults Beyond the Family

All six of the young men in the study indicated that the guidance of supportive adults beyond their families was essential to their academic success and reinforced their strong belief in self. They each cited teachers at the elementary or middle school level who had been influential in their school lives and had had an impact on their current success. Matteo commented on an influential first-grade teacher and the powerful impact she had on him. He explained,

Mrs. Scarfa was my first-grade teacher. My parents have told me I loved her. She gave me one theory that I still walk around with, and I think it's my major driving force. When people tell me that things are impossible, there is no such thing as "can't." That word is not in the English dictionary. Mrs. Scarfa told me that you can do anything and everything you want just as long as you have the drive and the power to do it. That's one thing I still carry around. Nothing stops me from doing what I want. There is no "can't."

Rafael described an influential teacher when he said,

My fifth-grade teacher was the best I had throughout my elementary school career. She'd encourage me to work hard. When I was in junior high, I'd go back to visit her. One day, she handed me a check. She called it my "scholarship." She said, "I don't know how your family stands financially, but I know you'll be able to get into a good college." She was always so encouraging, and she never allowed me to put myself down. She said I had great potential.

In addition to supportive elementary and middle school teachers who inspired the young men, teachers or other adults at South Central High School continued to provide support and helped to strengthen their strong belief in self. An interesting finding in the study was that better teachers who were mentioned by the young men were described as people who cared and helped. The six participants appreciated teachers who challenged them intellectually, yet the majority of the teachers discussed were regarded as supportive adults who nurtured their belief in self, their motivation, and their overall well-being as young adults.

Mrs. Lowell, a freshman English teacher, was mentioned by more of the participants than any other faculty member at South Central High School. Throughout their descriptions of the woman and her style of teaching were signs that she was reaching out to them in such a way that they knew she really cared about them. Wallace described her class:

> Mrs. Lowell taught with a lot of enthusiasm. She told us on the first day of class that we were never leaving the room. "This is not a democracy!" she said. "Whatever you need from the nurse, I have right here. You gotta get sick, there is the trash can. You want a drink of water? I have bottled water" She had bottled water! "People come in from the rain some days and your hair is all wet, I have a blow dryer." She really did, and she let people use it. She had people keep their jackets in her teacher's closet. She was a real good teacher. I loved her from the first day. It was a really good class. She was my best teacher. She was at every football game. You know who your true fans are. When you are winning, everybody is there, but when you are losing, only your real fans are there. She was there at every game. I connected with her from the start.

This concern for connecting with teachers who respected them as young adults was also evident when Matteo joined Wallace and another student in physics class to compete in the state science fair with a project on cold fusion. The sophisticated topic caused some anxiety for several science department teachers, yet these students were happy to report they found an advocate in their physics teacher. Matteo explained,

> Mr. Proctor was the only one supporting the idea. With the platinum and other elements we needed, Mr. Willis and Mr. Jenkes didn't want anything to do with it. The metals are so expensive. They knew there was no way we could get the money for that. We talked to Mr. Proctor, and he said he would sign for the metals. We found a company that deals in precious metals that agreed to let Mr. Proctor sign for them. We have to bring the metals back in April. Mr. P. said he'd be responsible.

Rafael had several teachers who spoke highly of his work, yet he found his most supportive relationship with his guidance counselor, Mr. Thomas. Rafael's counselor apparently had helped him through some difficult times, such as a time Rafael described when he was dealing with the ending of a serious relationship he had had with a young woman. He had difficulty dealing with his hurt, and his counselor had been very supportive. He described Mr. Thomas as a regular person. "He attempts to understand you, to comfort you, to provide you with advice, and he listens." He explained how supportive Mr. Thomas had been during his very painful experience when he said,

> When he helped me with my problems, he really saw what I was going through. He listened and provided me with support. Sometimes, he would come to my home and talk. Mr. Thomas was there for me through that whole year.

Mr. Thomas was one of the busiest guidance counselors at South Central High School. Observing him in action every day involved watching a constant line of students who were waiting outside his office door. Two or three students were typically inside his office enjoying animated conversation with him or a private conference behind a closed door. His office walls were covered with snapshots, photographs, and newspaper clippings of students at South Central High School. The popular counselor was a support system for many young people. Throughout the study, the young men explained that they went to Mr. Thomas for advice after having seen their own guidance counselor. They explained they did not want to offend their own counselor, but they trusted Mr. Thomas's counsel. His reputation as a caring, trustworthy counselor who worked hard for his students was well established.

A large number of the high-ability young men who achieved in this high school were supported by Coach Brogan, the men's swim team coach, who was recognized throughout the building by other faculty members and students as a man who shaped his swimmers to become achievers both athletically and academically (Hébert, 1995). Throughout the conversations with Vaughn and Lucio, there were constant references made to a "family" down by the pool. This feeling of a supportive family under the guidance of Coach Brogan, a man whom Vaughn described as a "very ethical man" for whom "everyone has a lot of respect," was described by Lucio when he said,

> He is a father figure to a lot of us. If something goes wrong, he'll talk to us about a lot of things, like the gang stuff that's going on around here. He doesn't want to see us make major mistakes. He takes the time to listen and he tries to understand. If there is an individual personal problem, he'll talk to the swimmers individually. With things in general that are going on in school, we'll all sit together, and he'll talk to all of us.

A father of one of the team members poignantly described the powerful impact Coach Brogan had on his son. He said, "If it weren't for Coach Brogan, my son wouldn't survive here. His relationship with Coach has given him so much self-confidence. This man has really changed my son. He's really saved my son. Coach really cares about the kids here, and they'll do anything for him."

Participation in Special Programs,
Extracurricular Activities, and Summer Enrichment Programs

Along with athletics, the six participants in the study were all involved in a variety of school clubs and activities both after school and in the summer. These special programs and extracurricular activities appeared to have an impact on their belief in self and the development of their intention to achieve academically.

In addition to competing in three varsity sports and serving as student council president, Wallace was a reporter for the "Student Page" in the city's newspaper, a participant in the Upward Bound Program, and served as class president during his freshman year. Wallace was spotted for his potential as a seventh grader and had been nominated for the High Tops Program. This program provided middle school students with a series of field trips and seminars with professional architects and city planners who were involved with the design and construction of several modern high-rise buildings in the city. The students were provided with exciting tangible experiences in math and science through this program, which was designed to raise the aspirations of high-potential inner-city youth.

Rafael benefited from special programs in summer months. He was recommended by his guidance counselor, Mr. Thomas, for two experiences at competitive private-school summer programs where he studied French and English literature. He left those programs with a different attitude about education. He described his experience at one school and explained its impact on his views:

> I met people from all over the world. It was the most exciting thing that has ever happened to me. Through the people I had the opportunity to meet, I realized the world isn't just [community's name]. The world is much bigger than it seems from here. I met people from Switzerland, Japan . . . I had a chance to meet a young man whose father was the president of the Gillette Corporation, another was the son of a Communist leader in Vietnam. I met all sorts of people from all walks of life. When I came back, I told Mr. Thomas that I was interested in going to some private school like that. The standards were so high, the teachers didn't have to stress the importance of education because it was already understood. There was a different atmosphere there; there was an excitement for learning that I don't see here.

Rafael was involved in an enrichment program for students interested in engineering. He was a member of the French Club and was proud of his induction into the National Honor Society. He became involved in the Cadet Club and VISION, both youth groups involved in community service projects. He also taught religious education classes to young children and tutored elementary school children in his neighborhood.

Orlando put his strong religious convictions to work through extensive involvement in Christian philanthropy projects throughout the community. Through the Christian youth groups with which he was associated, he visited convalescent homes and organized students to volunteer at drug rehabilitation centers and soup kitchens. He did volunteer work with the Salvation Army. He worked as a tutor at South Central, and on weekends, he was busy preparing religious worship services with the church's youth group, as well as volunteering with Habitat for Humanity. Orlando's many hours of volunteer work were recognized by the community, and he was one of three teenagers awarded a prestigious corporate-sponsored citizenship award. A full page from the city's newspaper describing the award and Orlando's involvement hung on the door of Mr. Thomas's office.

Vaughn and Lucio, the two members of the men's swim team, were both involved in National Honor Society. Vaughn competed in two other sports. For these two young men, the swim team was the center of their high school experience. Both worked as lifeguards at municipal swimming pools during the summer months. There, they recruited new swim team members for South Central High. The impact the swim team experiences had on their individual belief in self was very pronounced, as Vaughn explained, "Swimming has given me everything. Without it, I'd be totally different. Socially, I'd be a much different person." Lucio commented, "Swimming has given me a control, a goal, something to stick to. It's been a straight line to follow so I don't travel perpendicular!"

Matteo, the lively class politician, was extremely active. He was constantly updating the résumé he had prepared for his guidance counselor's file. He was determined to get to the U.S. Air Force Academy. He was actively involved in Junior Achievement, student council, National Honor Society, the high school band, and a number of enrichment programs held during the academic year and in the summer. In each activity, he took on leadership roles. With a strong interest in engineering and science, he became involved in a statewide pre-engineering program in a university setting and served on a state-wide executive board that oversaw collaboration of high school programs such as Upward Bound. Along with the training in applied math and science in the pre-engineering program, he attended the Young Scholars Program, a collaborative program sponsored by the Project to Increase Mastery of Math and Science (PIMMS), an enrichment summer program for inner-city students throughout the state. Through PIMMS, he enjoyed a five-week summer experience at Wesleyan University, where he enjoyed dormitory life, interaction with "Ph.D. types," and the mentorship of older college students who were majoring in applied sciences. Whether he was campaigning "for the end to the administration's red tape" in preparing for the junior prom, competing in the regional high school band competition and "blowing the other schools out of the stratosphere," or dealing with "a blue-chip audit of the Junior Achievement books," Matteo was a young man with a strong belief in self who was determined to become successful in life.

DISCUSSION

The results of this study provide a better understanding of the personal characteristics of high-ability males who achieve success in urban environments, how they view their urban experiences, and where they find support. A strong belief in self was identified as the most important factor influencing the success of the urban males in this study. These young men had developed a strong belief in self that provided them with the energy, the drive, and the tools they needed to face life's challenges. This strong belief in self was the driving force that allowed them to succeed in school and will allow them to succeed later in life. They were successful because they had determined who they were and believed in themselves. With this strong belief in self, they were able to determine where they wanted to go in life. Several qualities within these young men merged to form this belief in self: sensitivity, multicultural appreciation, aspirations, and an inner will.

An important part of that strong belief in self was a heightened sensitivity, a quality that allowed these young men to appreciate individual differences in people around them, the beauty of language in a poem, or a relationship with a younger handicapped child learning to swim. These young men had developed empathy, emotional self-awareness, and emotional expressivity, qualities that allowed them to balance their emotional lives as they developed their self-identities. They viewed their ability to express themselves emotionally as a quality that would help them become more successful in life. Their emotions were functional, adaptive tools (Plutchik, 1980) that assisted them in making sense of their life experiences and allowed them to feel secure as sensitive males in an urban setting.

Their sensitivity combined with an appreciation for people from diverse cultures. Friendships with teenagers from a variety of cultural and racial backgrounds had special significance for these young men. They believed that their cross-cultural friendships allowed for better social adjustment as young adults. They felt strongly that their association with teenagers from many different backgrounds provided them with more chances to understand humanity better; and, with this knowledge of diversity, they came to understand themselves better.

As part of their strong belief in self, the participants in the study had definite aspirations that were aligned closely with their personal qualities, strengths, and talents. They had dreams and definite goals toward which they were striving, and these dreams, goals, and career aspirations were connected with who they were as people. Their personalities were reflected in their choices for the future. They saw their aspirations as obtainable since they realized they had an internal motivation that kept them driven to succeed. Just as an inner will had allowed them to succeed in their urban school experiences, a motivational force would keep them focused and allow them to reach their goals in life.

The theoretical framework that guided this study was grounded in the sociocultural literature and offered educators a new lens through which to examine the development of a strong belief in self in high-ability youth. The findings of this study support the view that understanding talents and abilities can occur within a context of cultural expectations. In order to understand identity development in high-ability urban youth, the environmental context must be taken into consideration. For the young men in this study, the "multi-layered self-conceptions" (p. 7) described by Heath and McLaughlin (1993) were developed through a multitude of experiences that helped to create a sense of connectedness with their environmental context through strong discipline, group achievement, and mutual expectations of high quality. Engaging these intelligent males in highly valued extracurricular activities and out-of-school experiences gave them a strong source of interest and an opportunity to develop talents, work with caring adults in supportive relationships, and experience cross-cultural contacts that allowed for better social and academic adjustment, as well as the development of a strong belief in self.

With Heath and McLaughlin's (1993) findings in mind, consider Wallace and Matteo as examples. Along with describing himself as an African-American urban teenager, Wallace might say, I'm a successful scholar, science fair winner, athlete, school newspaper reporter, student body president, and Upward Bound student." Matteo might describe himself as a class politician, scholar, Junior Achievement entrepreneur, jazz musician, science fair winner, and engineering enthusiast. These "multi-layered self-conceptions" (p. 7) were shaped by the variety of experiences they were involved in beyond the classroom and South Central High School. Experiences with extracurricular activities and involvement in projects in their community provided the young men with opportunities to connect with supportive adults such as coaches, bilingual education teachers in elementary school tutorial programs, adults supervising Habitat for Humanity building projects, and university student supervisors during summer school programs on college campuses. Through interactions with these adults and their hard work in enjoyable activities beyond school, the young men met success, interacted with others in cross-cultural experiences, and were able to see themselves as successful competitors in their urban environments. Their identities were shaped by these experiences and became an important part of each individual's strong belief in self.

Self-Concept Theory

The findings of this study allow us to generalize to theories regarding self-concept. Self-concept, in very general terms, refers to the image we hold of ourselves. Byrne (1984) defined it as "our attitudes, feelings, and knowledge about our abilities, skills, appearance, and social acceptability" (p. 429). Theorists have agreed on general definitions of self-concept; however, there is considerable disagreement in the literature over the way in which we operationally define the construct (Hogue & Renzulli, 1991).

Three positions have been proposed to explain the self-concept construct. Unidimensional models propose that the only meaningful way of conceptualizing self-concept is in terms of a global construct of self-worth (Coopersmith, 1967). Multidimensional models constitute the second approach to understanding self-concept. These models generally maintain that self-concept is made up of a set of independent dimensions. For example, Harter (1983) identified several aspects of self-concept: school competence, athletic competence, social acceptance, physical appearance, and behavior or conduct. A similar view was offered by Winne and Marx (1981), who proposed four dimensions: academic, social, physical, and emotional. Hierarchical models constitute a third way of understanding self-concept. These models begin with the multidimensional construct as a starting point; however, they maintain that differentiated facets of the self-concept construct are organized in a hierarchical fashion (Marsh, Byrne, & Shavelson, 1988). All three models have empirical support; however, controversies exist, and more research is needed (Hogue & Renzulli, 1991).

In this study, the findings revealed that the six young men had developed a belief in self that could best be described as "multi-layered embedded identities" (Heath & McLaughlin, 1993, p. 7). The participants saw themselves as a combination of the following: scholars, athletes, class politicians, entrepreneurs, social activists, sensitive males, loyal friends, and sons who brought pride to their families. Each facet of their embedded identities can be compared to the facets of self-concept proposed in both multidimensional and hierarchical models of self-concept. It is interesting to note that ethnographers who have examined urban teenagers beyond the classroom have enlightened our understanding of self-concept and the important role it plays in the development of a strong belief in self.

When considering how a self-concept develops, most theorists acknowledge that both internal and external forces affect self-concept (Hogue & Renzulli, 1991). For example, individuals internally assess their competencies and accomplishments against the expectations they hold for themselves, along with the external opinions expressed by parents, significant adults, and peers. These external factors of social support and positive regard have received considerable attention by theorists. These factors involve the processes whereby individuals use the reactions of significant others in the environment to assess their performance and competencies.

One interesting aspect of this social comparison issue, particularly where academic performance is concerned, has to do with the impact of the role of the larger school environment in affecting self-concept. Marsh (1990) has proposed the Big-Fish-Little-Pond Effect to explain that a young person's feelings of self-worth regarding his or her academic performance will depend to some extent on the average level of performance displayed in his or her school or class, an important issue when considering the effects of high-ability students attending urban high schools where a large proportion of the student population is resistant to an ideology of academic achievement. Although South Central High School was a large school with a student body of 1,656, the proportion of students with an academic-achievement orientation was small. Given the level of competition within that environment, the six participants in this study were "big fish in a small pond." For this reason, the factors that reinforced their belief in self were especially important if they were to succeed following graduation from high school. Experiences with extracurricular activities and special programs in university settings, significant adults, and supportive families were critical in instilling within the young men the belief that their talents and abilities combined with focused effort would enable them to succeed beyond their urban setting and prepare them to compete as "small fish in big ponds."

The experiences of the young men in this study have enlightened us. With meaningful, authentic talent development experiences in their urban, cross-cultural environments, young adults are bound to experience more than an increase in self-esteem. The shaping of a belief in self extends beyond self-esteem or self-concept; it involves a young person realizing "I know who I am, and I have the talents and ability to succeed in whatever I choose; therefore, I know where I want to go in life." When working with intelligent urban teenagers, educators should consider the powerful approach of involving young adults in activities that shape their "multi-layered self-conceptions" through success in experiences that allow for talent development. For those who would suggest building self-concept, the young men in this study would respond with "Build more than our self-concepts. Build our belief in self."

John Ogbu's Theory

In reviewing the experiences of the six participants' families in the study, we are reminded of an influential voice in the anthropology of urban education. John Ogbu, a leading proponent of a controversial school of thought, proposed a cultural model to explain achievement within different cultural groups. Ogbu's (1974, 1981, 1987, 1991) findings from comparative research indicated that what distinguished minority groups who were achieving in school from others who were not was the cultural model that guided them. Ogbu (1991) explained that there were two forms of historical forces that shaped the different cultural models of the minority groups. One was the initial terms of incorporation of these minorities into the society in which they lived; the other was the pattern of adaptive responses that the minorities made to treatment by members of the dominant group. According to Ogbu (1991), minority groups have been incorporated into American society either voluntarily or involuntarily. Those who came to the United States voluntarily were "immigrant minorities," who generally believed the move would lead to more economic well-being and better overall opportunities. They viewed education as the golden opportunity for advancement. In contrast, involuntary or "castelike" minorities were people who were brought to America through slavery, conquest, or colonization. They resented the loss of their former freedom; perceived the social, economic, and political barriers against them as part of their undeserved oppression; and viewed the American educational system suspiciously.

Of the minority students in the study, the families of Orlando, Rafael, and Lucio arrived in this country as immigrants, while Wallace's African ancestors came involuntarily. When we reflect on the experiences of these young men in school, the experiences of the immigrant Latino families is consistent with

Ogbu's model; however, what we have learned about Wallace's family does not support Ogbu's notion of involuntary minorities. Although neither of his parents had an opportunity to attend college, Wallace's parents and extended family members valued education and encouraged Wallace and his younger brother to adopt strategies that enhanced academic success. Wallace's parents communicated a clear instrumental message that education was a method of getting ahead. This finding is consistent with research studies on families of economically disadvantaged African-American students that refute Ogbu's model. Numerous researchers (Clark, 1983; Ford, 1993; Lee, 1984; Prom-Jackson, Johnson, & Wallace, 1987; VanTassel-Baska, 1989) have provided evidence that in spite of social hardships and economic barriers that often limit achievement and social advancement, African American parents have high aspirations and maintain high expectations of their children. Wallace's family experience also highlights another distinguishing feature of the African American family. Nobles (1997) indicated that the traditional African American family is a "unique cultural form enjoying its own inherent resources" (p. 88). Comprised of several individual households, the extended family is visible in the lives of its children and provides needed emotional support for its members. Walker, Taylor, McElroy, Phillip, and Wilson (1995) indicated that the African American extended family served as a major "stress absorbing system" (p. 30) and helped develop positive self-esteem within all of its members. Sudarkasa (1997) maintained that African American families are "some of the most flexible, adaptive, and inclusive kinship institutions in America" (p. 39), which provide nurturance for the children and support for adults.

The role of the extended family as a "stress absorbing system" in Wallace's life is interesting to compare to other participants in the study. All six participants acknowledged and described emotional support they received from their families; however, the role of the extended family appeared to be an important feature of some, but not all families. This finding was evidenced cross-culturally. For example, in Matteo's Italian household, grandparents lived within the community and provided emotional support for his family, just as Wallace's grandparents did for him. However, the three young men from Latino households did not benefit from having relatives nearby. Orlando and Rafael had extended families living in Puerto Rico. At the time of the study, Lucio was enjoying a visit from an aunt and uncle living in Cuba, and he referred to his love for his extended family; yet, his nuclear family provided him with daily emotional support. It should be noted that within the experiences of six participants, extended family support was evidenced cross-culturally; however, generalizations to specific cultural groups would be inappropriate. Extended families represent an important and consistent support system in the lives of culturally diverse children, providing emotional support and educational encouragement (Ford, 1996). Such families help to blunt social and economic injustices and hardships, and in the process, they promote self-efficacy, self-reliance, and higher self-esteem within their children (Ford, Harris, Turner, & Sandidge, 1991).

IMPLICATIONS

Implications for Practice

The findings of this study provide specific implications for urban educators working with high-ability students. The sensitivity evidenced in the stories of the six participants highlights the need for educators, parents, and counselors to reconsider what it means to grow up as a young male in contemporary America. With more understanding of the social and emotional needs of intelligent males, our homes and classrooms could become places where bright young men are comfortable expressing themselves as individuals concerned about people. The "emotional intelligence" evidenced in the lives of the six participants in the study, according to Goleman (1995), can be nurtured and strengthened. The young men in this study who were involved in projects such as helping physically challenged youngsters in a high school swimming pool, tutoring bilingual young children who faced difficulty in learning English, or working with Habitat for Humanity remind educators and parents that intelligent young men could be given more outlets for expressing their sensitivity. Such outlets would help to validate them as young men capable of developing their emotional qualities into the adaptive tools for life as described by Levant (1992) and Plutchik (1980). Such self-expression would only help young men better form their self-identity naturally. In addition, opportunities to become involved in urban community projects could be strengthened to provide outlets whereby intelligent young men experience the "required helpfulness" (Garmezy, 1985) that may be crucial to shaping a resilient belief in self. School administrators would serve their students well by connecting their schools to community organizations in need of the talented students serving as volunteers.

Counselors, teachers, and parents in urban schools can feel encouraged by the six participants' experiences with extracurricular activities and the importance of these after-school experiences in shaping their individual self-identities. The extracurricular activities, athletic teams, and special programs in which the six high-ability scholar-athletes were involved throughout their experiences at South Central High School had a powerful impact on shaping their belief in self. Such successful experiences, under the guidance of adults who cared for and supported their psychosocial development as young men, helped to shape what Heath and McLaughlin (1993) referred to as their "embedded identities" (p. 7). The experiences of the six young men beyond their schoolday highlight the need for urban school systems to continue to provide strong after-school, extracurricular experiences and athletic programs to nurture the talents of high-ability males. Summer enrichment programs associated with private colleges and state universities and community-based programs whereby bright teenagers are given opportunities to address the problems of their urban communities through a proactive, hands-on approach should be emphasized and strengthened. Such experiences continue to expose young people to multi-ethnic groups, elevate aspirations, provide opportunities for talent development, and help direct young men to share their talents in pursuit of fulfilled lives.

The six participants' experiences with teachers and coaches who cared about them as young individuals remind urban school administrators to consider personality traits that are appropriate for success in working with urban youngsters. The voices of the six young men have informed us that young people appreciate content experts in high school classrooms, but they also gravitate to professionals who let them know that their self-identities are valued. Personnel directors in urban schools may want to pay close attention to the personality traits characteristic of the successful urban educators noted by the participants in this study. In addition, the significance of the relationships between several of the participants and men such as the coach, the guidance counselor, and the physics teacher, indicates the powerful impact same-gender mentors may have on intelligent males. Torrance, Goff, and Satterfield (1998) proposed multicultural mentoring strategies appropriate for nurturing the talents of young people from economically disadvantaged environments. An ongoing relationship with a caring adult or mentor has tremendous potential for changing an intelligent young man's life. Urban school systems may want to consider implementing such mentor programs in which successful urban community leaders assist public school educators in fostering the talents of high-ability males.

The work of successful urban educators, similar to those described in this study, needs to be showcased in urban school districts. Administrators in urban high schools may want to provide special recognition for counselors like Mr. Thomas, teachers like Mrs. Lowell, and coaches like Coach Brogan. These successful individuals should serve as mentors to beginning counselors, coaches, and teachers in urban schools. The expertise and experience of the adults who make a difference in the lives of urban youth need to be shared with prospective educators in university degree programs. Internships arranged with the most successful urban educators may help to nurture another generation of successful urban teachers, counselors, and coaches.

In addition, the findings of this study indicate that the evaluative feedback of teachers holds great potential for influencing the attributional thinking of high-ability young men. Teachers who consistently reinforce the message that ability combined with hard work will result in success have a powerful impact on students. The participants in this study explained the role that teachers played in shaping their internal locus of control when they described how earlier teachers delivered the message that these young men had the ability to achieve success, and, with hard work and effort, they could reach their goals in life. If teachers actively shape their students' thinking, it is important that they be trained to use evaluative feedback messages conducive to encouraging attributional thinking in students. University teacher-training programs designed to prepare urban educators may want to consider training prospective educators in strategies for delivering such feedback effectively to children.

Implications for Parents

The findings of this study also provide food for thought for parents of teenagers throughout the United States. The awareness of cultural diversity, which had been part of the urban neighborhood and classroom experience of all six of the participants, evolved into a real appreciation for their multi-cultural student body. This appreciation for people from a variety of cultural backgrounds had an impact on how they viewed themselves as bright young men who were better able to compete in a diverse society.

Researchers and theorists maintain that multicultural appreciation should be fostered in schools through a social reconstructionist approach (Ford, Grantham, & Harris, 1996; Ladson-Billings, 1994). Such an approach to education embodies a comprehensive view of culture that provides for the awareness of group similarities and differences. Experiences with diversity help students see how race, gender, and socioeconomic status interact and provide opportunities for young people to develop ways of thinking and analyzing that allow them to become more proactive in making changes in society. Parents concerned about their youngsters' ability to cope in a multicultural society will be encouraged to hear from the participants in this study. The young men at South Central High School shared with us the importance of experiences with cultural diversity in developing their strong self-identities. Their appreciation for diversity supports the literature on interethnic contacts allowing for better academic and social adjustment (Bowler, Rauch, & Schwarzer, 1986; Graham, Baker, & Wapner, 1985) and provides American families with an important message. Families in some communities in this country often consider this issue when deciding which elementary, middle, or high school their children will attend. These young people then face college selection decisions and may be influenced by the diversity of a university campus. Parents of teenagers may want to listen closely to what the six young men in this study have offered and consider their experiences when making important decisions in choosing a school experience that will prepare their children for success in a multicultural society.

The family stories of the six young men should encourage parents in urban environments to continue providing their sons with strong emotional support throughout their school experiences. Urban parents who are successful in nurturing their sons to become achievers in high school would make excellent discussion leaders in homes throughout urban neighborhoods. High school guidance counselors could easily assist successful parents in organizing and facilitating evening discussion groups in private homes. The parents in this study were not affluent, yet they provided their sons with constant emotional support that helped them believe in themselves and their ability to make a better life for their own families. Many urban families would appreciate hearing from such successful parents. Hackney (1981) reported that parents of gifted students felt a sense of relief when they learned that parents of other high-ability youngsters had similar experiences and the same feelings about parenting. Creel and Karnes (1988) reported that a majority of parents of high-ability students would benefit from networking with parents of other high-ability youngsters.

Implications for Future Research

This study highlights a need to continue examining the belief in self within high-ability students in a variety of contexts. Future research studies should investigate the phenomenon in high schools that have different configurations of cultural diversity, perhaps a setting where two cultures (i.e., Black and White) co-exist side by side, or in high schools where only one cultural group is present. Such studies would help to broaden our understanding of the role experiences with diversity play in young people developing a strong belief in self. This study should be replicated in rural and suburban settings and in different regions of the country.

Furthermore, since this study was conducted with only high school students, there is a need to replicate the study to include high-ability males in middle schools and perhaps elementary schools to help determine when a strong belief in self begins to form within high-ability youngsters. This study has gender-specific implications for future research. It should be noted that the same study was conducted simultaneously at South Central High School with high-ability females and has been reported in the literature (Reis et al., 1995). Finally, it is important to follow high-ability students over time through longitudinal research and across contexts in order to fully describe the role that a strong belief in self has on the life experiences and achievements of high-ability youth.

In conclusion, the prophetic words of the guidance counselor and the voices of the six young men from South Central High School provide compelling messages for urban educators and parents. When examining the challenges faced by young people in their struggle to achieve a better life, we learn that some who realize their goals face greater obstacles than others. However, many are successful because they have established a strong belief in self, and with this strong belief in self, they are able to tackle life's challenges, determine what they want to achieve in life, and reach their goals successfully.

REFERENCES

Ayers, W. (1991). Perestroika in Chicago's schools. *Educational Leadership, 48*(8), 69–71.

Ball, A., & Heath, S. B. (1993). Dances of identity: Finding an ethnic self in the arts. In S. B. Heath & M. W. McLaughlin (Eds.), *Identity and inner-city youth: Beyond ethnicity and gender* (pp. 69–93). New York: Teachers College Press.

Ballard-Reisch, D. S., & Seibert, D. R. (1993). Academic self-concept, gender orientation, and communication apprehension in adolescents. In C. Berryman-Fink, D. S. Ballard-Reisch, & L. H. Newman (Eds.), *Communication and sex-role socialization* (pp. 283–310). New York: Garland.

Bandura, A. (1977). *Social learning theory.* Englewood Cliffs, NJ: Prentice Hall.

Bowler, R., Rauch, S., & Schwarzer, R. (1986). Self-esteem and interracial attitudes in Black high school students: A comparison with five other ethnic groups. *Urban Education, 21*(1), 3–19.

Brody, L. E., & Benbow, C. P. (1986). Social and emotional adjustment of adolescents extremely talented in verbal or mathematical reasoning. *Journal of Youth and Adolescence, 15*(1), 1–18.

Byrne, B. M. (1984). The general/academic self-concept nomological network: A review of construct validation research. *Review of Educational Research, 54,* 427–456.

Carnegie Foundation for the Advancement of Teaching. (1988). *An imperiled generation.* Princeton, NJ: Author.

Clark, M. L. (1991). Social identity, peer relations, and academic competence of African American adolescents. *Education and Urban Society, 24*(1), 41–52.

Clark, R. (1983). *Family life and school achievement: Why poor Black children succeed and fail.* Chicago: University of Chicago Press.

Coopersmith, S. (1967). *The antecedents of self-esteem.* San Francisco: Freeman.

Creel, C. S., & Karnes, F. A. (1988). Parental expectancies and young gifted children. *Roeper Review, 11,* 48–50.

Creswell, J. W. (1998). *Qualitative inquiry and research design: Choosing among five traditions.* Thousand Oaks, CA: Sage.

Csikszentmihalyi, M. (1990). *Flow: The psychology of optimal experience.* New York: Harper and Row.

Csikszentmihalyi, M., Rathunde, K., & Whalen, S. (1997). *Talented teenagers: The roots of success and failure.* New York: Cambridge University Press.

Damico, S. B., Bell-Nathaniel, A., & Green, C. (1981). Effects of school organizational structure on interracial friendships in middle schools. *Journal of Educational Research, 74,* 388–393.

DeHaan, L., & MacDermid, S. (1996). *Identity and poverty: Defining a sense of self among urban adolescents.* New York: Garland.

Douglas, P., & Powers, S. (1982). Relationship between achievement locus of control and expectancy of success of academically talented high school students. *Psychological Reports, 51,* 1259–1262.

Erikson, E. H. (1968). *Identity: Youth and crisis.* New York: Norton.

Erikson, E. H. (1985). *The life cycle completed.* New York: Norton.

Fetterman, D. M. (1989). *Ethnography: Step by step.* New York: Sage.

Ford, D. Y. (1993). Black students' achievement orientation as a function of perceived family achievement orientation and demographic variables. *Journal of Negro Education, 62*(1), 47–66.

Ford, D. Y. (1996). *Reversing underachievement among gifted Black students.* New York: Teachers College Press.

Ford, D. Y., Grantham, T. C., & Harris, J. J. (1996). Multicultural gifted education: A wakeup call to the profession. *Roeper Review, 19,* 72–78.

Ford, D. Y., Harris, J. J., Turner, W. L., & Sandidge, R. F. (1991). The extended African-American family: A pragmatic strategy to blunt the blades of injustice. *The Urban League Review Policy Research Journal, 14*(2), 1–13.

Garbarino, J., Kostelny, K., & DuBrow, N. (1991). *No place to be a child: Growing up in a war zone.* Lexington, MA: Lexington Books.

Garmezy, N. (1985). Stress resistant children: The search for protective factors. In J. E. Stevenson (Ed.), *Recent research in developmental psychopathology* (pp. 213–233). Oxford: Pergamon.

Glesne, C., & Peshkin, A. (1992.) *Becoming qualitative researchers.* White Plains, NY: Longman.

Goleman, D. (1995). *Emotional intelligence.* New York: Bantam Books.

Graham, C., Baker, R., & Wapner, S. (1985). Prior interracial experience and Black student transition into predominantly White colleges. *Journal of Personality and Social Psychology, 47,* 1146–1154.

Grotevant, H. D. (1987). Toward a process model of identity formation. *Journal of Adolescent Research, 2,* 203–222.

Gurian, M. (1996). *The wonder of boys.* New York: G. P. Putnam's Sons.

Hackney, H. (1981). The gifted child, the family and the school. *Gifted Child Quarterly, 25,* 51–54.

Hallinan, M. T., & Teixeira, R. B. (1987). Opportunities and constraints: Black-White differences in the formation of interracial friendships. *Child Development, 58,* 1358–1371.

Hallinan, M. T., & Williams, R. A. (1989). Interracial friendship choices in secondary schools. *American Sociological Review, 54,* 67–78.

Halpern, R. (1992). The role of after-school programs in the lives of inner-city children: A study of the "urban youth network." *Child Welfare, 71,* 215–230.

Harter, S. (1983). Developmental perspectives on the self-system. In E. M. Hetherington (Ed.), *Handbook of child psychology: Vol. 4. Socialization, personality, and social development* (pp. 275–386). New York: John Wiley.

Heath, S. B., & McLaughlin, M. W. (1993). *Identity and inner-city youth: Beyond ethnicity and gender.* New York: Teachers College Press.

Hébert, T. P. (1993). *An ethnographic description of the high school experiences of high ability males in an urban environment.* Unpublished doctoral dissertation. The University of Connecticut, Storrs, CT.

Hébert, T. P. (1995). Coach Brogan: South Central High School's answer to academic achievement. *The Journal of Secondary Gifted Education, 7,* 310–323.

Hogue, R. D., & Renzulli, J. S. (1991). Self-concept and the gifted child (Research Monograph No. 9104). Storrs, CT: The University of Connecticut, National Research Center on the Gifted and Talented.

Jones, D. J., Bibbins, V. E., & Henderson, R. D. (1993). Reaffirming young African American males: Mentoring and community involvement by fraternities and other groups. *The Urban League Review, 16*(2), 9–19.

Karnes, F. A., & McGinnis, J. C. (1995). Self-actualization and locus of control of gifted children in fourth through eighth grades. *Psychological Reports, 76,* 1039–1042.

Knight, B. A. (1995). The influence of locus of control on gifted and talented students. *Gifted Education International, 11,* 31–33.

Kozol, J. (1991). *Savage inequalities: Children in America's schools.* New York: Crown.

Ladson-Billings, G. (1994). *The dreamkeepers: Successful teachers of African American children.* San Francisco, CA: Jossey-Bass.

Lee, C. (1984). An investigation of psychosocial variables related to academic success for rural Black adolescents. *Journal of Negro Education, 53,* 424–433.

Levant, R. L. (1992). Toward the reconstruction of masculinity. *Journal of Family Psychology, 5,* 379–402.

Lincoln, Y., & Guba, E. (1985). *Naturalistic inquiry.* Beverly Hills, CA: Sage.

Macoby, E. E., & Jacklin, C. N. (1974). *The psychology of sex differences.* Stanford, CA: Stanford University Press.

Marsh, H. W. (1990). Influences of internal and external frames of reference on the formation of math and English self-concepts. *Journal of Educational Psychology, 82,* 107–116.

Marsh, H. W., Byrne, B. M., & Shavelson, R. (1988). A multifaceted academic self-concept: Its hierarchical structure and its relation to academic achievement. *Journal of Educational Psychology, 80*, 366–380.

McLaughlin, M. W. (1993). Embedded identities: Enabling balance in urban contexts. In S. B. Heath & M. W. McLaughlin (Eds.), *Identity and inner-city youth: Beyond ethnicity and gender* (pp. 36–68). New York: Teachers College Press.

McLaughlin, S. W., & Saccuzzo, D. P. (1997). Ethnic and gender differences in children referred for gifted programs: The effects of vulnerability factors. *Journal for the Education of the Gifted, 20*, 268–283.

McLelland, R., Yewchuk, C., & Mulcahy, R. (1991). Locus of control in underachieving and achieving gifted students. *Journal for the Education of the Gifted, 14*, 380–392.

Merriam, S. B. (1998). *Qualitative research and case study applications in education.* San Francisco, CA: Jossey-Bass.

Miedzian, M. (1991). *Boys will be boys: Breaking the link between masculinity and violence.* New York: Doubleday.

Nelson, J. L., Palonsky, S. B., & Carlson, K. (1990). *Critical issues in education.* New York: McGraw-Hill.

Newman, P. R., & Newman, B. M. (1988). Differences between childhood and adulthood: The identity watershed. *Adolescence, 23*, 551–557.

Nobles, W. W. (1997). African American family life: An instrument of culture. In H. P. McAdoo (Ed.), *Black families* (3rd ed., pp. 83–93). Thousand Oaks, CA: Sage.

Ogbu, J. U. (1974). *The next generation: An ethnography of education in an urban neighborhood.* New York: Academic Press.

Ogbu, J. U. (1981). School ethnography: A multilevel approach. *Anthropology and Education Quarterly, 12*, 3–29.

Ogbu, J. U. (1987). Variability in minority school performance: A problem in search of an explanation. *Anthropology and Education Quarterly, 18*, 312–334.

Ogbu, J. U. (1991). Immigrant and involuntary minorities in comparative perspective. In M. A. Gibson & J. U. Ogbu (Eds.), *Minority status and schooling: A comparative study of immigrant and involuntary minorities* (pp. 3–33). New York: Garland.

Patchen, M. (1982). *Black-White contact in schools.* West Lafayette, IN: Purdue University Press.

Patchen, M., Davidson, J. D., Hofmann, G., & Brown, W. (1977). Determinants of students' interracial behavior and opinion change. *Sociology of Education, 50*, 55–75.

Patton, M. Q. (1990). *Qualitative evaluation and research methods* (2nd ed.). London: Sage.

Pleck, J. H. (1976). The male sex role: Definitions, problems and sources of change. *Journal of Social Issues, 32*, 155–164.

Pleck, J. H. (1987). The theory of male sex-role identity: Its rise and fall, 1936 to the present. In H. Brod (Ed.), *The making of masculinities* (pp. 21–38). Boston: Allen & Unwin.

Plummer, D. L. (1995). Patterns of racial identity development of African American adolescent males and females. *Journal of Black Psychology, 21*, 168–180.

Plutchik, R. (1980). *Emotion: A psychoevolutionary synthesis.* New York: Harper & Row.

Prom-Jackson, S., Johnson, S. T., & Wallace, M. B. (1987). Home environment, talented minority youth, and school achievement. *Journal of Negro Education, 56*, 111–121.

Reis, S. M., Hébert, T. P., Diaz, E. I., Maxfield, L. R., & Ratley, M. E. (1995). *Case studies of talented students who achieve and underachieve in an urban high school.* Storrs, CT: University of Connecticut, The National Research Center on the Gifted and Talented.

Rhodes, J. E. (1994). Older and wiser: Mentoring relationships in childhood and adolescence. *The Journal of Primary Prevention, 14*, 187–196.

Robertson, J. M., & Freeman, R. (1995). Men and emotions: Developing masculine-congruent views of affective expressiveness. *Journal of College Student Development, 36*, 606–607.

Ross, C. E., & Mirowsky, J. (1984). Men who cry. *Social Psychology Quarterly, 47*, 138–146.

Rotter, J. B. (1954). *Social learning and clinical psychology.* New York: Prentice-Hall.

Ruenzel, D. (1994). Playing by the rules. *Teacher Magazine, 6*(3), 32–37.

Schofield, J. (1978). School desegregation and intergroup relations. In D. Bai-Tai & L. Saxe (Eds.), *The social psychology of education: Theory and research* (pp. 329–363). New York: John Wiley.

Scott, E. S., & Damico, S. B. (1983). The effect of extracurricular activities on interracial contact for university and high school students. *Integrated Education, 21*(1), 140–142.

Scott, E. S., & Damico, S. B. (1984). The role of extracurricular activities in the promotion of cross-race contact by White students from high school to college. *Urban Review, 16*, 165–176.

Sigelman, L., Bledsoe, T., Welch, S., & Combs, M. W. (1996). Making contact? Black-White social interaction in an urban setting. *American Journal of Sociology, 101*, 1306–1332.

Snyder, E. E. (1975). Athletic team involvement, educational plans, and the coach-player relationship. *Adolescence, 10*, 191–200.

Spradley, J. P. (1979). *The ethnographic interview.* San Francisco, CA: Holt, Rinehart and Winston.

Spradley, J. P., & McCurdy, D. W. (1972). *The cultural experience: Ethnography in a complex society.* Palto Alto, CA: Science Research Associates.

Stake, R. (1981). *The art of progressive focusing.* Paper presented at the annual meeting of the American Educational Research Association, Los Angeles, CA. (ERIC Document Reproduction Service No. ED 204–358)

Strauss, A. L., & Corbin, J. (1990). *Basics of qualitative research: Grounded theory procedures and techniques.* Newbury Park, CA: Sage.

Sudarkasa, N. (1997). African American families and family values. In H. P. McAdoo (Ed.), *Black families* (3rd ed., pp. 9–40). Thousand Oaks, CA: Sage.

Torrance, E. P., Goff, K., & Satterfield, N. B. (1998). *Multicultural mentoring of the gifted and talented.* Waco, TX: Prufrock Press.

VanTassel-Baska, J. (1989). The role of the family in the success of disadvantaged gifted learners. *Journal for the Education of the Gifted, 13*, 22–36.

Verkuyten, M. (1995). Self-esteem, self-concept stability, and aspects of ethnic identity among minority and majority youth in the Netherlands. *Journal of Youth and Adolescence, 24*, 155–175.

Walker, K., Taylor, E., McElroy, A., Phillip, D., & Wilson, M. N. (1995). Familial and ecological correlates of self-esteem in African American children. In M. N. Wilson (Ed.), *African American family life: Its structural and ecological aspects* (pp. 23–33). San Francisco: Jossey-Bass.

Werner, E. E., & Smith, R. S. (1982). *Vulnerable but invincible: A study of resilient children.* New York: McGraw-Hill.

Whaley, A. L. (1993). Self-esteem, cultural identity and psychosocial adjustment in African American children. *Journal of Black Psychology, 19*, 406–422.

Winne, P. H., & Marx, R. W. (1981, April). *Convergent and discriminant validity in self-concept measurement.* Paper presented at the annual conference of the American Educational Research Association, Los Angeles, CA.

Yin, R. K. (1989). *Case study research: Design and methods.* London: Sage.

Yin, R. K. (1993). *Applications of case study research.* London: Sage.

Yin, R. K. (1994). *Case study research: Design and methods* (2nd ed.). Thousand Oaks, CA: Sage.

Yong, F. L. (1994). Self-concepts, locus of control, and machiavellianism of ethnically diverse middle school students who are gifted. *Roeper Review, 16,* 192–194.

6

Jermaine: A Critical Case Study of a Gifted Black Child Living in Rural Poverty

Thomas P. Hébert

The University of Georgia

Teresa M. Beardsley

Gifted students exist in the culture of rural poverty; however, these children often are not identified, and schools fail to provide appropriate educational programs, preventing young people from realizing their potential. In this account of a gifted Black child living in an impoverished rural environment, a university researcher and a classroom teacher collaborated in order to describe a young man's creativity, his resilience, his struggle to find a place for himself in his community, and the significant

Editor's Note: From Hébert, T. P., & Beardsley, T. M. (2001). Jermaine: A critical case study of a gifted black child living in rural poverty. *Gifted Child Quarterly, 45*(2), 85-103. © 2001 National Association for Gifted Children. Reprinted with permission.

factors that influenced the early formation of a strong self-identity. The findings of the study offer educators helpful suggestions for identifying and addressing the educational needs of gifted Black children living in rural poverty.

A s I travelled the silent rural highways of Alabama, I reflected on the special significance of kudzu. Having grown up near the rocky coast of Maine, I always imagine kudzu as a powerful tidal wave that overtakes the Southern countryside. Every spring in the South, the kudzu vine washes over the entire countryside, covering telephone poles, buildings, and all vegetation in its path. It blocks the sunlight from the tall pine trees and shrubs it covers, silently draining the life out of them. Though it appeared beautiful as it draped over the vegetation along the red clay roads I traveled that day, I was reminded of the choking qualities of this vegetation, and I thought about how this might reflect the rural isolation and poverty in the life of the gifted child I would come to know in my research. I approached this community as an ethnographic researcher to join a public school teacher named Teresa Beardsley and begin a three-year case study of her student, Jermaine, a gifted Black child living in rural poverty. During my travels, I pondered the question, "As kudzu chokes life out of vegetation, does the isolation of an impoverished, rural environment have a similar effect on the creativity of a gifted child?"

As I spent more time in the rural Alabama county, I continued to admire the beauty of the South; yet, I grew to understand how an impoverished environment negatively affected children. Together, the data Teresa provided me on Jermaine's creativity and the data I collected as a researcher interacting with him allowed me to explore the role environment plays in developing the gifts and talents of children.

BACKGROUND

America's public schools are increasingly under attack. Beginning with *A Nation at Risk* (National Commission on Excellence in Education, 1983), numerous studies have identified serious problems in the education of our young people. These criticisms are not new to rural educators; Nachtigal (1992) noted, "Even before the turn of the century, educational leaders were concerned about the rural school problem" (p. 66). An unspoken perception exists in rural communities that people should settle for less in rural schools (Nachtigal, 1992). Herzog and Pittman (1995) reported that students in rural settings suffered from negative stereotypes because of their rural background and internalized antirural prejudices, and they "exhibited an inferiority complex about their origins" (p. 114). They found that students educated in rural communities attended poorly funded schools and experienced both a lack of quality facilities and limited educational programs, while their teachers struggled with limited access to cultural and information resources and university teacher training programs that did not adequately prepare them with specialized training for working in rural schools (Herzog & Pittman, 1995; Spicker, Southern, & Davis, 1987).

Putting the Research to Use

Gifted Black children exist in rural, impoverished communities and need support to reach their full potential. As evidenced in this case study of a young child named Jermaine, adults who provided emotional support and an understanding of his intelligence and creativity were critical to his success. Jermaine's story highlights the significance of extended African American families in nurturing the talents of their children. The extra-familial support Jermaine received was also crucial to him, which emphasizes the importance of a mentor for a child living in rural poverty. In addition, this study suggests that a child's creativity can be nurtured with existing resources available in a rural community. Valuing the bucolic qualities of a rural life may also enhance a child's creativity. Jermaine's case highlights the need for connecting gifted youngsters in rural schools with the world beyond their communities via technology. This examination of Jermaine's experiences also calls for significant changes in educational policies to overcome racial discrimination in school districts across this country.

In addition, rural schools also face an exodus of intelligent young adults due to limited professional employment opportunities (Seal & Harmon, 1995; Spicker, 1992a; Stern, 1992). Young adults whose families have deep generational roots in rural communities often decide not to remain or return not only because of a lack of opportunities, but also because of inadequate health care and underfunded schools (Spicker, 1992b).

Although cognizant of serious problems facing rural schools, fewer researchers undertake studies in rural settings in this country than in urban or suburban settings. In addition, there is limited research on special populations of students in rural settings. Unfortunately, one population of students missing from much of the research literature on rural schools is gifted students. Consistent with other special populations in rural America, gifted students in rural communities face serious challenges. Spicker, Southern, and Davis (1987) highlighted major obstacles in providing for the special educational needs of rural gifted youngsters. They indicated that, within rural school districts, acceptance of the status quo and resistance to change made it difficult to initiate new programs for gifted students. Along with limited financial resources for programs perceived as benefitting a few students, rural schools were unable to provide adequate specialized teachers, counselors, school psychologists, and curriculum specialists to assist in providing appropriate services for high-ability youngsters. Finally, Spicker, Southern, and Davis indicated the rural belief in self-sufficiency and local control decreased the likelihood that school officials might seek outside assistance from educational experts to address the needs of gifted students.

Poverty adds another layer of complexity to problems facing schools. According to a study conducted by the United States Department of Education (1993), children living in poverty faced the following obstacles: less access to formal learning opportunities, more serious physical and mental health problems, and more environmental barriers that affect their education. Dudenhefer (1994) highlighted the lack of research on rural, impoverished children, indicating "when researchers—or at least the principal sponsors of poverty research— think poverty, they think city, not town or country" (p. 4). Poverty is as much a serious problem in rural America as in urban America. Books (1997) indicated that, although more than nine million people in rural areas of the United States lived in impoverished conditions, rural poverty is overshadowed by the media's fixation on issues of urban poverty, including drugs and violence.

Understanding the effects of poverty remains especially important when examining the life experiences of Black children since they face a higher rate of poverty than children of any other racial or ethnic group in the United States (Sum & Fogg, 1991) and often live in conditions that may impede their school achievement (McLoyd, 1990). Ford (1996) noted that the poverty rates for Black families and children in this country have been high, both historically and currently. According to the 1990 federal census, over 55% of the rural poor, and nearly 97% of the rural Black poor, lived in the South (Dudenhefer, 1994). African American children in the South have borne a disproportionate share of the burden of poverty in America for decades. Though Black children in rural, impoverished environments face adverse conditions, Frasier (1987) cautioned us not to oversimplify the problem when she indicated that "there are too many examples of gifted adults who come from less advantaged backgrounds to make a tenable argument that culture, class, or environment are permanent obstacles to achievement" (p. 174). In examining diverse ethnic groups, both Frasier (1991) and Kitano (1991) identified within-group heterogeneity as prevalent as in the majority culture; therefore, socioeconomic status should not serve as a predictor of aptitude or academic achievement. Ford noted that "poverty is a circumstance, not a measure of inherent worth" (p. 72). Using the metaphor of "undiscovered diamonds," Baldwin (1987) encouraged educators to continue searching for the gifts and talents of Black children and urged policy makers to pursue increased research on gifted Black children in rural environments. Renzulli (1973) reminded policy makers over 25 years ago that gifted minority children in impoverished environments were being lost as he pointed out:

> There can be little doubt that our nation's largest untapped source of human intelligence and creativity is found among the vast numbers of individuals in the lower socioeconomic levels . . . an invaluable natural resource is being wasted daily by a system of education that has shut its eyes and turned its back on [these children]. (p. 437)

Efforts to bring about change for these young people must be monumental when we consider "the great number of youngsters whose day-to-day school experience is nothing short of an educational and psychological disaster" (Renzulli, 1973, p. 439). Little research exists on gifted students in rural environments, and even less research has examined gifted Black students who live in impoverished, rural communities. This study attempts to add to the limited information on this population by examining the life experiences of a gifted Black child living in rural poverty. To do so, the following research questions guided the study: What relationships guide the behaviors, attitudes, and aspirations of a gifted Black child in an impoverished, rural environment? What factors influence the creativity of a gifted Black child in an impoverished, rural setting?

THEORETICAL FRAMEWORK

Critical theory served as the framework for the study. The emergence of critical theory began in the 1920s with a group of German scholars collectively known as the Frankfurt School. These scholars focused on merging theory, practice, and inquiry with an historically grounded understanding of contemporary social, political, and cultural issues. Since then, critical theorists have been influenced by the work of Habermas (1970, 1971, 1974, 1989), who believed human beings are unnecessarily oppressed by implicit cultural ideologies. Therefore, the goal of critical theory research is to make these unconscious belief systems explicit, thereby freeing individuals by providing alternatives through self-reflection and social action. Critical theorists work for social justice by constantly challenging and questioning societal values and practices (Crotty, 1998). Critical theorists undertake research with a concern for issues related to power and oppression. Critical inquiry "keeps the spotlight on power relationships within society as to expose the forces of hegemony and injustice" (Crotty, p. 157). Themes addressed through critical inquiry include examining social institutions and highlighting historical problems of oppression and social struggles (Morrow & Brown, 1994). Although the ultimate goal of a totally free and just society may not be attainable, critical theorists believe that their research can at least improve contemporary societal conditions (Crotty). Merriam and

Simpson (1995) noted that critical research "brings to focus the possibilities of how culture can sustain irrationality, unfulfilling lifestyles, and social injustice, revealing the degree to which certain ways of life within a culture are strategically organized to preserve the interests of some members of society at the expense of others" (p. 132).

In the present study, I used a critical theory framework to structure my examination of the environmental factors influencing the education of a gifted child. Incorporating a critical interpretive lens in the design of the study enabled me to explain how the ideology of an impoverished, rural community impacted his life. A critical inquiry approach was best suited for this study, for it is only through developing an understanding of the community's ideology that educators and policy makers will be able to determine appropriate methods of enabling gifted children in rural, impoverished communities to realize their potential.

METHODOLOGY

The primary goal of the study was to examine the life of a gifted Black child living in rural poverty and to understand how his rural environment influenced his academic achievement. To accomplish this goal, I chose a qualitative research design that integrated features of case study and critical ethnographic research. *Ethnography* refers to research that involves the description of a culture (LeCompte & Preissle, 1993). Merriam (1998) defined a qualitative case study as an "intensive, holistic description and analysis of a single entity, phenomenon, or social unit" (p. 27). Case studies provide researchers with an understanding of complex social phenomena while preserving the holistic and meaningful characteristics of everyday events (Yin, 1994). Case studies are a valuable tool for understanding human behavior in depth (Stake, 1995). Patton (1990) differentiated *critical cases* as "those that can make a point quite dramatically or are, for some reason, particularly important in the scheme of things" (p. 174). Patton noted that a clue to the existence of a critical case is the statement to the effect that "if it happens there, it will happen anywhere," or vice versa, "if it doesn't happen there, it won't happen anywhere" (p. 174). In this critical case study, Jermaine, a gifted Black child living in poverty, is the phenomenon under investigation, and the primary goal of the article is to focus on his experiences in his rural environment. The study was conducted in Pine Grove, Alabama, a community of approximately 200 people situated in Milledge County.

Data Collection

In this study, the data-collection process incorporated the following four distinct phases described below: (1) review of a portfolio and entry into the community, (2) three weeks of participant observation, (3) one-year correspondence with the child and his teacher, and (4) a final visit to the community and an in-depth interview with the child. (Note. With the exception of Teresa and her husband, James, the names of the people and places within Alabama were changed to protect the identity of the participants involved.)

Phase One: Entry Into the Community With the Help of a Gatekeeper. Jermaine was introduced to me during his third-grade school year. Teresa Beardsley was my student enrolled in a graduate gifted education degree program. As I came to know Teresa, I learned of Jermaine and her work with him. She explained that, since having Jermaine as a student, she continued to provide after-school enrichment experiences for him and two other students. Teresa shared many intriguing stories of this highly creative Black child and helped me to gain entry into the rural community in which she lived.

Teresa and her husband, James, had been living in Pine Grove, Alabama, since 1972, when they arrived in the community with Volunteers in Service to America (VISTA) following the civil rights movement. Although the civil rights movement had brought about significant changes in other areas of the South, when Teresa and James arrived in Milledge County, they found a segregated society remained, with "Whites Only" signs hanging in the windows of local establishments, Following their work as VISTA volunteers, they were hired as teachers by the county school board and have remained there as dedicated rural educators. Since 1972, Teresa, James, and their two children have been the only Caucasian citizens in the rural, Black community of Pine Grove.

Teresa had maintained a portfolio of Jermaine's work in her first-grade classroom and continued to save examples of his creative writing and the art he produced during their continued after-school enrichment sessions. She shared those products with me and gave me the opportunity to examine the highly creative responses of this gifted young child. Personal documents such as Jermaine's portfolio of work provided rich, stable sources of information (Lincoln & Guba, 1985). My examination of this material was intended to assist me in developing a comprehensive understanding of the gifted young child under study.

Teresa helped me in gaining access to Jermaine and entry into the Pine Grove community. Having lived in Pine Grove for more than 20 years, she served as a key "informant" (Glesne & Peshkin, 1992, p. 34) in the study, an insider in the community who knew the individuals and the politics of the community and who could assist me in "traversing the often sensitive territory" (Glesne & Peshkin, p. 34) of the research setting. Following my review of Jermaine's portfolio, I arranged to visit Pine Grove and spent time travelling throughout Milledge County with Teresa. I toured the community of Pine Grove and several surrounding communities. I visited Pine Grove's schools and spent time in conversation with local citizens of this rural town. During my visits with the community members, several shared their perceptions of Pine Grove's children with me and expressed how their children had enjoyed having Teresa as their teacher.

Phase Two: Participant Observation. A local paper mill had provided philanthropic funding for a summer tutorial reading and science program for the children of Pine Grove for two years. The company recruited Teresa and James to coordinate the program each summer. During the three-week experience known as "Rocket Readers," local high school students worked as tutors with elementary school children by providing them with remedial drill activities to improve vocabulary and reading comprehension. In addition, James provided the youngsters with a curriculum unit on crustaceans to train them in scientific methodology. With parents and grandparents carpooling the children, approximately 50 youngsters arrived at a modest country church every morning for a four-hour academic program and some time for softball during a physical education period. Teresa and James explained that their rationale for providing the program each summer was to help children with reading and give them time to be together during the summer when they tended to become removed from each other, living many miles apart in isolated areas.

Teresa explained that, during the previous year, Jermaine had attended the Rocket Readers program, and the experience had not been productive. Though they realized the tutorial sessions were inappropriate for him, Teresa and James encouraged Jermaine to attend the program simply for social interaction, thinking that Jermaine might benefit from seeing other children. Within a short time, Jermaine was bored and had become a discipline problem for his high school tutor. The following summer, Teresa and I agreed that the Rocket Readers summer experience would be an ideal time for me to continue working with Jermaine in creative writing. Throughout the three-week summer experience, I travelled from my university community to Pine Grove and spent the mornings working with Jermaine on the front steps of the country church. I had an ideal opportunity to observe him with his peer group during the softball games, interview him regarding his life experiences, and provide him with time to pursue his writing craft.

Phase Three: Correspondence With Jermaine and Interviews With Informants. While working with Jermaine during the Rocket Readers program, I learned that the reading materials used with the children had been provided by outside educational consultants hired by the local paper mill to provide the reading curriculum. I noted that the paperback books used throughout the summer were worn copies of low-level children's literature. They featured simple vocabulary and rather mundane stories that were completely removed from the life experiences of African American children living in a rural, isolated community. I also realized that none of the books featured African American characters.

At the end of the three-week summer experience, graduation day would be held, and the children would be receiving a Rocket Readers t-shirt for having participated. Since Jermaine would not be receiving a t-shirt, I was prepared to provide him with his "graduation" present: a children's novel featuring African American youngsters. I explained to Jermaine that I wanted to continue working with him during the school year by corresponding with him. During his fourth-grade school year, I mailed children's novels each month and looked forward to hearing more about Jermaine's response to them. I selected Newbury Award-winning novels, novels that featured African American children as main characters, and other reading material that I thought might appeal to Jermaine's creativity. Throughout that period, I regularly scheduled telephone conversations with Teresa regarding Jermaine's progress in school.

Phase Four: A Final Visit to Pine Grove and an Interview With Jermaine. The final phase of data collection consisted of a visit to Pine Grove during Jermaine's fifth-grade school year. I spent a day with Teresa and Jermaine, catching up on news of the community, and concluded the data collection with an in-depth interview with Jermaine.

Fieldwork Techniques. I used a variety of techniques for ethnographic data collection to elicit the insider's perceptions of reality. Fetterman (1989) emphasized the importance of field notes in ethnographic research, describing them as "the brick and mortar of an ethnographic structure" (p. 107). According to Fetterman (1989), field notes take on a variety of forms including observations, speculations, cues, and lists,. The field notes were transcribed at the conclusion of each day I visited Pine Grove. They formed an early stage of analysis during data collection and contained raw data necessary for more elaborate analyses in the study. The field notes were used as outlines of the interviews themselves, with the purpose of shaping subsequent interviews. In this study, tape recording did not substitute for direct field notes. Due to cross-cultural differences in dialect, I chose to record handwritten notes rather than tape record interviews. I determined that this less obtrusive strategy was a more culturally sensitive approach while working with Jermaine and the residents of Pine Grove.

I also used a variety of unobtrusive measures that supplemented observation and interview data and analysis. Fetterman (1989) defined outcroppings "as a portion of the bedrock that is visible on the surface, in other words, something that sticks out" (p. 68). For example, outcroppings in ethnographic research in an impoverished, rural community might include abandoned automobiles in the yards of Pine Grove residents, the citizens of the community seated in front of the country store, or the condition of the furniture in the vestibule of a small country church. As a researcher, I had to place these visible cues in a larger context, assess the information carefully, and not ignore it or take it for granted.

In this study, one example of an outcropping that became salient was the appearance of the television satellite dishes in the yards of the Pine Grove residents. The important role that satellite television programs played in the lives of children living in rural isolation gave me a better understanding of how important being connected to the world beyond Pine Grove through the satellite dish was to Jermaine and the development of his creativity.

In addition to examining outcroppings, photography was included in the data-collection process and was useful in documenting my observations.

Photography enables an ethnographer to create a photographic record of specific behaviors. Collier and Collier (1986) noted that "the camera with its impartial vision has been, since its inception, a clarifier and a modifier of ecological and human understanding" (p. 8). Photography is a useful research tool, for the camera enables researchers to "see without fatigue [since] the last exposure is just as detailed as the first" (Collier & Collier, p. 9). Fetterman (1989) also indicated that photographs can serve as mnemonic devices for researchers. While researchers are involved with data analysis and writing of findings, photographs can jog their memory, allowing access to detail that they may otherwise have been unable to recall. Photographing prior to beginning a research study enables researchers to capture the culture being examined before developing a schema that may later cloud their interpretive lens after data collection has been completed.

Researcher's Journal. To further enhance data collection, I maintained a researcher's journal that included a record of my "experiences, ideas, fears, mistakes, confusions, breakthroughs, and problems" (Spradley, 1980, p. 71) that arose during fieldwork in Pine Grove. Fetterman (1989) noted that personal reflections such as these may also be included as data in the form of field notes. These diary-like reflections were not only cathartic; they also provided me with a record of my feelings, attitudes, and subjectivities during data collection. Later, during data analysis and writing, this record provided me with a context for understanding the observational field notes I had taken at the same stage of the data collection process. The record of my personal reflections allowed me to take into account how my personal reactions to my experiences in Pine Grove may have influenced my data collection.

DATA ANALYSIS

In case study research, data analysis consists of making a detailed description of the case and its context. In analyzing my data of Jermaine in the Pine Grove community, I followed the four procedures advocated by Stake (1995). I began "categorical aggregation" (p. 74) by searching for a collection of instances from the data, looking for issue-relevant meanings to emerge. I then examined single instances in my data and drew meaning from them without looking for multiple instances. Stake referred to this "direct interpretation" (p. 74) as a process of pulling the data apart and then putting them back together in more meaningful ways. I then worked to "establish patterns" (p. 78) and looked for any correspondence between two or more patterns or categories. Following this, I attempted to present my findings descriptively to facilitate my readers' forming "naturalistic generalizations" (p. 85), which are conclusions readers develop through vicarious experiences so well constructed that they feel as if the experience was their own. Therefore, in my data analysis process, the themes that emerged began with the analysis of my initial observations, were constantly refined throughout the data collection and analysis process, and continuously shaped the formation of categories (LeCompte & Preissle, 1993). To conclude my analyses, I developed generalizations about Jermaine's story in terms of patterns and how they compare and contrast with published literature on gifted students in rural communities.

To enhance the validity of the findings, I conducted intensive direct observations and interviews until data saturation occurred when new information collected was redundant and did not offer any additional insights to elucidate further understanding (Bogdan & Biklen, 1998). I also provided a detailed description of how I conducted the investigation, the measures I took to ensure the accuracy of the observations, and the evidence on which the findings were grounded. In addition, I arranged to have fellow university researchers play the role of "devil's advocate" in reviewing my data analysis and the interpretation of my findings.

The Context of the Study: Pine Grove, Alabama

Graue and Walsh (1998) defined context as "a culturally and historically situated place and time" (p. 9). The context of this study played an important role in understanding the way of life in Pine Grove and Jermaine's experiences. The study was conducted in Milledge County, Alabama. Historically significant events had taken place less than 30 miles away in Selma, Alabama. On March 7, 1965, over 600 civil rights marchers were stopped at the Edmund Pettus Bridge in Selma, where state and local lawmen attacked them with billy clubs and tear gas and drove them back. Two days later, Martin Luther King led another symbolic march to the bridge. Later that month, over 3,000 marchers walked from Selma to the state capital in Montgomery. Shortly after, President Johnson signed the Voting Rights Act of 1965. The memories of those events remained clear in the minds of residents of Pine Grove. Several community members had been with Dr. King and expressed how they hoped that children in Alabama appreciated "the gas they had to breathe" during those horrendous times in America's history.

The prevalent lifestyle in Milledge County for generations was rooted in a cotton plantation and sharecropper economy. This prosperous economy began to deteriorate with the invasion of the boll weevil following World War I. The cotton economy was further devastated by land erosion, the Great Depression, and the emergence of modern farming techniques. Timber growing and wood-pulp industries eventually replaced the fledgling cotton economy. During this time, a conversion from sharecropper to wage hand farming also took place. Landless Black tenants were slowly eliminated as machines replaced the work of physical laborers and more cotton fields were cleared for timber growing.

According to the federal government's census, the estimated population of Milledge County in 1998 was 13,468. Noted as the poorest county in the state of Alabama, the per capita personal income reported was $10,759, with 45.20% of the county's population falling below the poverty level (Alabama Department of Archives and History, 1998). A journalist for *The Montgomery Advertiser* described the county as "one of the poorest parts of the country" (Benn, 1988, p. 1C) and indicated that the majority of people living in Milledge County were forced to rely on public assistance to survive. The McDonald Billings Company, a manufacturer of corrugated cardboard, is the only industry in Milledge County, employing only several Pine Grove residents. Residents of this rural community commute 30–40 miles beyond the county lines to work in catfish-processing plants. Others are employed in the fast food restaurants in Selma.

Jermaine's Family and School

Jermaine is an ebony-skinned child with large brown eyes, a warm smile, and finely sculpted features. A small, slender child, he is animated and vivacious. Jermaine lives with his mother, his older brother and sister, and an aunt. According to his teachers, Jermaine and his 16-year-old sister, Tamara, are frequently left responsible for his elderly aunt, who is physically handicapped and mentally retarded. Residents in the community often noted Jermaine's mother's absence from the home. She is part of a group of Pine Grove residents who sit in front of an abandoned country store for long periods during the day and evening hours. Jermaine's older brother, Tyrell, also spends time in front of the store. Tyrell is a high school junior and receives services from the program for educable mentally retarded (EMR) students.

Jermaine attends the elementary school in Pine Grove, a prekindergarten through sixth grade facility serving 255 children. All students are African American, and 98% are eligible for a federally subsidized free-lunch program. The children are bussed from six small communities, all within 25–30 miles of Pine Grove and separated by rural highways. The school facility, a red-brick building constructed in the late 1940s, is in great disrepair, with rain leaking through the roof, dilapidated furniture, and equipment in need of repair. It consists of three classrooms and a modest lunchroom, with nine overcrowded mobile trailers housing classrooms behind the school. There is no media center, gymnasium, art room, or music facility. Special education classes and physical education classes share a classroom referred to as the "auditorium." The grounds surrounding the school consist of red clay, and no awnings cover the walkways between the main building and the portable classrooms. When it rains, the school is saturated with mud. A letter I received from Teresa one winter provided evidence of the difficulties faced by teachers in the school. She sounded discouraged when she wrote: "School is difficult this time of year . . . rain and mud seem constant, and my children slip and slide coming and going. Then there are SAT objectives. That's all we hear about, and apparently all we are expected to teach."

Administrators in Milledge County watch teachers closely. Schools throughout Milledge County have annually been on a list of school districts threatened to be taken over by the state department of education if achievement test scores do not increase substantially. Schools are designated "on alert," "under caution," or "clear" depending on the testing performance of students.

Evidence that these conditions have existed historically in Milledge County was found in an investigative report published in 1967 by The National Education Association (NEA) Commission on Professional Rights and Responsibilities entitled *[Milledge] County: A Study of Social, Economic and Educational Bankruptcy*. The problems facing Milledge County schools also affect special education programs. Although the state legislature in Alabama mandated identification and programming for gifted students in 1972, Milledge County has not complied with the law since its inception.

Standardized testing in Pine Grove consists of the Stanford Achievement Tests conducted each spring. Throughout the three-year investigation, Jermaine's achievement scores ranged from the 86th to the 99th national percentiles in language arts and reading, with vocabulary and language expression ranked as his most prominent strengths. Jermaine's scores in math were in the average range. His Otis Lennon School Ability Test scores ranged from 118 to 120. According to Teresa and several of Jermaine's former teachers, when his test scores are compared with the above-average students in his class scoring in the 40th to 50th percentiles, Jermaine's performance is considered remarkable. In addition, it is important to consider how the items on verbal IQ tests favor the acculturation experiences of urban children. For example, Jermaine has never experienced a modern shopping mall. As Spicker (1992a) noted, a child living in an isolated rural area who had never seen a shopping mall would be hard pressed to describe one. However, he may know more about snakes, fishing for catfish, or summer sunsets than most urban and suburban children his age. Unfortunately, questions involving shopping mails are more likely to appear on aptitude tests than questions that would be a better measure of a rural child's knowledge base.

Jermaine's Home

Pine Grove is a community in which pockets of homes are clustered at intervals along narrow, rural red clay roads. Jermaine's home is up a hill on a dirt road. The house is a cabin with a cinder block foundation. It is heated with a wood stove and cooled by opening windows and doors. In second grade, Jermaine included an entry in his creative writing folder that described an account of his typical morning routine before school and provided evidence of the impoverished conditions in which he lives:

>5:30   Jermaine wakes up the family
>   Gets bathing pan, soap and rag
>   Goes out to bathroom to get water
>   Puts water on heater and bathes
>   Finds some clothes, finds booksack and shoes
>
>7:00   Jermaine goes to bus stop
>   Gets to school and waits for breakfast to get ready
>   Eats and talks until Mr. Jones tells us to go to class

Nestled in the woods, Jermaine's home is surrounded on three sides by trailers. According to the residents of Pine Grove, trailers are considered superior to houses since they come with central heat and air conditioning, furnishings, and appliances. In Jermaine's front yard sit a nonfunctioning automobile and a satellite dish. All of the surrounding residences have television service through a satellite.

FINDINGS

A Struggle to Find a Place in the Community

According to Teresa and other residents, the small, rural community of Pine Grove determines a ranking for its members. Like many small towns, families in Pine Grove have roles according to their perceived place in the community. Jermaine's family falls into the lowest rank; they are considered outcasts and are largely ignored. They are often spoken of in derogatory terms and used as examples of how not to be. A distant cousin of the family explained, "I grew up knowing who to be like, and it sure wasn't them." The reason provided for this by most residents of the community interviewed was the "crazy" factor. Jermaine's handicapped aunt and older brother were mentioned. The whole family was marked as being inclined to odd or "crazy" behavior. The main generalizations that anyone could provide for this attitude was the presence of multiple family members with mental or physical handicaps. Another reason provided was the cemetery near the family property because "no one in their right mind" would live near a cemetery. Apparently, the stigma of the family has not been overcome as Jermaine was recognized by the adult community as a "no-count bad child." The negative status of the family in the community was expressed in several phrases, but the general view was that Jermaine and his family were outside the normal population of the community.

The heart of this small, rural town is the church. In Pine Grove, the church serves as a vehicle for interaction, kinship, for the kind of time spent together that leads to understanding and tolerance. Few families can maintain significant status in the community without church affiliation. Jermaine's family does not attend church. No family relative or member of the community has ever taken Jermaine to church. The functions of the church and the support systems the church can offer have not served Jermaine.

Jermaine dismissed church attendance, indicating it was an intrusion on his television time. His older sister attributed a lack of church clothing and a lack of transportation as reasons for the family absence from Sunday services. Since church is more than a place of worship, services may last until the late afternoon; as Jermaine and his sister explained, "It takes too long." The result is that the community center focus is absent from the pattern of life in Jermaine's family.

Jermaine's lack of church experience became evident during his after-school enrichment sessions with several other students in Teresa's classroom. The holiday season was approaching, and Jermaine asked to hear the Christmas story. Teresa explained:

> We read several versions of the Christmas story. Jermaine didn't know the story. Questions were flowing from him, which isn't unusual. Jermaine wanted to know the details. He concentrated on the three kings and on their travel and their place of origin. He had rather quickly noticed the incongruity of the traditional telling of the Christmas story. Over the next several days he drafted a picture book. He wanted to be clear about things that he felt those around him already knew.

The Role of Family in Jermaine's Life

Although the majority of students in the Pine Grove school are poor, Jermaine knows that he has less than others. Teachers in Pine Grove reported that, when Jermaine first arrived at the elementary school, his clothes were ill fitting, and, on cold winter days he sometimes arrived at school in only a t-shirt and jeans. One teacher explained, "Jermaine knows that he is poor. Other kids have sneakers that cost $89. Some have sneakers that cost $189, but Jermaine's mom buys his sneakers at Bargaintown. 'Bargaintown Nikes' are spotted right away. Jermaine gets teased a lot."

Although Jermaine's situation may seem dismal, he is not discouraged. He is lively, humorous, and self-confident. The family disparaged by others remains very important to him. Jermaine attributes his keen sense of humor to his mother. He respects his mother, but does not make demands of her. He is accustomed to the arrangement that she lives a life separate from his and is absent often. Jermaine's extended family is also important to him. Two of his mother's brothers, Walter and McKinley, are his favorites. They live in Detroit and come to Pine Grove regularly. Two vignettes from Jermaine's autobiography provide evidence of this fondness for his uncles:

> Last Christmas, when I was little, Uncle Walter was there. He came for a visit. He told my mom he had opened my presents to see what was in them, but I had really done it. My Uncle Walter saved my butt just like he used to save my Uncle Carl's butt when they were kids . . . Another time at Christmas when I was a little boy, Uncle Walter and Uncle McKinley were back home at my house. It was Christmas morning, and when I got up, I walked in to see my presents. But I only saw my uncles. They were on the floor playing with cars. Those were my presents! So I ran over to them and we played all morning.

Jermaine's family functions almost as an outlet for his verbal abilities. He is a story teller, and, like most story tellers, he does not limit himself to strictly facts. Not all his stories are true, but Jermaine's friends find them entertaining. Teresa reported that his peers were delighted with a story he wrote about his sister, Tamara. The following is a vignette from the story:

Early one morning, my mother wanted a glass of water. She told Tamara to go to the pump to get her some. Tamara was still asleep. She didn't get up, so my mother yelled at her. Tamara said she wanted to sleep. My mother went to get the shotgun and told her she better get up. Tamara was asleep, so my mother shot the gun. She shot a hole in the roof. Tamara jumped so fast she was pumping water before she saw that she didn't have a water glass in her hand!

Jermaine's Creativity

Teresa explained that the creative behaviors displayed by Jermaine during his early school experiences were not always appreciated by adults in his elementary school. Apparently, his family's reputation in the community extended into Jermaine's experience in school when he first arrived. The assistant principal referred to him as "that bad little boy I have to keep my eye on," while another teacher who had observed Jermaine during bus duty commented, "That boy is just too bad to handle." Teresa reported that, in kindergarten, Jermaine was discovered hanging upside down in his chair while the teacher was presenting a lesson. When the teacher posed a question, Jermaine answered correctly and elaborated. The teacher announced to the class, "If you can do that and still give me the answers, then you can act like Jermaine." Fortunately, Jermaine's kindergarten experience was positive; however, Teresa became involved in many conversations with several of Jermaine's teachers who were not as appreciative of his high energy. Teresa noted that teachers appreciated his advanced vocabulary, but found that she had to serve as an advocate for the creative young child whose classroom antics bewildered his teachers.

The portfolio of creative writing maintained by Teresa provided many fine examples of Jermaine's creativity. Jermaine s love of language and creative expression was evident in his work. As a first grader, he chose to write an autobiography during the after-school enrichment sessions. The following paragraph is the introductory paragraph of his autobiography:

I was tumbling through my mother's stomach—BOOM . . . BOOM . . . BOOM. I came out crying. Everybody comes out crying. Someone was holding me, and I wanted my momma. I was named Jermaine after my granddaddy. He didn't have a nickname or a middle name, so I don't either. He was my momma's daddy.

Also included in the portfolio is a book authored by Jermaine entitled *Jermaine's World*. The book provides readers with a glimpse of Jermaine's view of himself. In his story, he is a hero using his calculating mind to solve problems. The following vignette provides evidence of Jermaine's view of his problem-solving creativity:

I was leaving Jermaine's world, I needed to go see my sister. It was soon to be her wedding. I wanted to stop her from marrying a jerk. I was riding my dragon through the hills. My dragon and I bumped into a gate. I wanted to show off my powers, so I burned the gate down with my powerful triton. We walked to where the gate had been. Suddenly, thousands of dragons arrived. They were breathing fire and smoke. I looked around. I knew we had to get out of there. I saddled up my dragon, grabbed my triton, and tried to escape. One of the dragons fired at my bottom. One fried my hair until I was bald. Another tried to claw me. I spoke out in my kingly voice, "What is this NONSENSE?!" A dragon said, "Who ARE you talking to?" "Who ARE YOU talking to? I am the most powerful king you will ever meet." "OH! HO! Fried king for supper tonight!" All the dragons were happy to hear that. "Fried! No, not fried," I said. "I would taste better boiled. And if you are going to boil me, you'll need water." The dragons turned and began to walk toward a pond several miles away. Dragons do not like to have water too close. It might put out their fire. It took them many hours to get to the pond. They walked so slowly because they were afraid. I turned south and went back to my world. I decided to never return. My dragon agreed with me. He was glad that none of the other dragons had noticed that he was toothless.

Another fine example of Jermaine's creativity follows. His first-grade story entitled "How the Sun Got Hot" included colorful, vivid illustrations that were expressive, detailed, and depicted the emotions of his characters. The complete text of this story is provided below:

Once upon a time, there lived a humongous sun and a smaller moon. They were very cold indeed. They lived in the dark, shivery sky. They kept warm by holding onto each other. One time, millions of years after time began, moon let go of sun, he was tired of holding onto his humongous friend. The sun fell from the sky. It fell to earth and landed in the hottest volcano there was. Moon tried to reach his friend, but he couldn't reach into the hot volcano. Moon cried. Thunder and rain came to earth. The enormous sun sank to the deepest part of the volcano. It turned so red from heat, it exploded from the volcano. The sun was on fire as it shot back into the sky. When the moon saw the sun coming home, he ran to his friend. Moon said, "SUN! What happened to you?" Sun said, "I fell into a warm place and now I won't ever be cold again." The moon had to move far away from the ball of fire that was his friend. And Moon missed holding his friend, Sun. Sometimes he still cries. When you hear thunder and feel rain, you will know that moon is crying for his lost friend.

In my work with Jermaine during the summer reading program, I spent mornings with him discussing ideas for additional creative stories he wanted to publish. I agreed to serve as his secretary, taking dictation as he tilted his head back, closed his eyes, and told his imaginative stories. In my work with him during those morning creative writing sessions, I learned how he obtained his creative ideas and infused them into his writing. At one point in a story in which he described a "virgin black candle," he stopped in midsentence and said to me, "Do you want to know where I got that idea?" When I encouraged him to explain, he pointed out that he had seen a "virgin black candle" in one of his favorite television shows on a satellite television station. Later that morning, he opened his eyes again and said, "That triton I just used. I got that idea from *Hocus Pocus*. It's one of my favorite shows." It was then I began to understand the significant role that the satellite dishes throughout Pine Grove played in the lives of children living in such rural isolation. Satellite television was for many the only connection to a world beyond their rural community, and for Jermaine, satellite television apparently served as a constant source of inspiration for his manuscripts.

I later realized that Jermaine was inspired in a variety of ways. Following my work with him that summer, I mailed him children's novels that I thought would appeal to him, corresponded with him, and continued to interview Teresa concerning his progress in fifth grade. I learned that his creative writing apparently was being inspired by the books I was mailing him. I had sent a copy of Todd Strasser's *Help! I'm Trapped in My Gym Teacher's Body*, an outlandish story about a young boy who undergoes a magical transformation and resides in the muscular physique of his physical education teacher while the gym teacher simultaneously becomes trapped in the youngster's body. Shortly after Jermaine received the book, Teresa reported that his fifth-grade teacher came to her classroom one afternoon after school and exclaimed, "I don't know where he gets all these ideas, but today, he wrote a story about a metamorphosis! Where could he be getting these words?" Apparently the rather whimsical story I had mailed him had served not only as the inspiration for a story, but also a vocabulary booster.

During our writing sessions on the front steps of the country church, we discussed the beauty of Pine Grove's countryside. We once became involved in a rather sophisticated discussion about the solitude and whether or not the quiet of country living would help a young child become more creative. He explained that the quiet of the countryside helped to inspire his ideas, and through daydreaming he was able to foster his creative thinking process. Along with being inspired by the chirping of crickets and daydreaming about what a day in the life of a cricket would be like, Jermaine pointed out that his daydreams also took place at night as he pondered a sunset or watched the dazzling little glow of light from fireflies. He also indicated that daydreaming was an important part of every school day and may have served as a strategy for surviving the boredom he often experienced in school. He explained:

> Most of my day I spend daydreaming. In class, I daydream all the time. I think about my future plans for all the movie scripts I'm going to write when I become a movie producer. I just can't get over daydreaming. I

read a book that explained it was normal for a kid my age to daydream a lot. At night, when I'm not daydreaming, I like to go out and stare out at the dark and think. I call it my "thinking in the dark time." It's my nighttime inspiration. I like to think about some of the movies I've watched and think of ideas for movies I want to write someday.

Jermaine also noted that family members were often the inspiration for his manuscripts. He pointed out how his sister had been an important character in his dragon story. When I questioned Jermaine about his storytelling ability, he also pointed out the influence his family had on his creative abilities:

I think I get my storytelling from my granddaddy. He used to tell really good campfire stories. He always told funny stories about old people. Whenever we had family reunions and my uncles came down from Detroit and Boston, we would sit around a campfire for hours and listen to my granddaddy's stories.

Another source of inspiration for his story writing is Jermaine's fascination with animals. He is extremely knowledgeable about many animals that live in his rural environment. Numerous stories he dictated to me on the front steps of the church were stories about salamanders, catfish, and animals found in south Alabama. The first story he crafted with me was entitled *The Odd Couple: Charley and Grant*, a clever tale about two baby iguanas who survive a severe winter blizzard together. He explained that, although he spent hours watching satellite TV shows, he emphasized his favorite programs were "*National Geographic* shows on wildlife animals, and not *The Jerry Springer Show!*"

Teresa described one scenario in her first-grade classroom that highlighted Jermaine's early expertise on animals. She explained:

The children were invited, if they chose, to handle a small garden snake. Very few volunteered. Jermaine took the snake, the third child to even touch it, and began to talk about snakes. When he got to the part about vestigial legs, Shanika [a child in the class] was stunned. She stood up and told the rest of her classmates, "Jermaine knows everything!" Shanika was impressed.

In a conversation with Jermaine about the books I had mailed him, I asked which book had been his favorite. He did not hesitate as he announced that *Phillip Hall Likes Me, I Reckon Maybe* by Bette Greene had really captivated him. Bette Greene's award-winning novel is about a gifted young Black female in rural Arkansas. The author provided her readers with a better understanding of the lives of Black children in the rural South along with typical elementary school boy-girl rivalries and some of the dilemmas posed by giftedness. Beth, the main character in the book, is an assertive young girl whose impetuosity sometimes gets her into trouble; and, like Jermaine, she is an animal lover.

Jermaine explained that he enjoyed the adventures of the main character, particularly the competition between Beth and her cow against Philip Hall in the county fair. Following the discussion of that novel, I asked Jermaine what type of books he would want me to continue mailing him, and he replied, "I really like those stories, but please send me some nonfiction books about animals!"

Extrafamilial Support

Along with emotional support from members of his extended family, Jermaine found support from people beyond his family. A school relationship with a classmate played an important role in Jermaine's life during his early years in school. Jermaine and Cedric became friends in kindergarten and were assigned to the same classroom from then on. Cedric was a popular boy who enjoyed Jermaine's sense of humor. Teresa explained the importance of their relationship and the effect it had on Jermaine's life:

> Cedric is the grandson of our school's cook. Cedric has connections. When he and Jermaine became friends, Jermaine began to have connections. Cedric's grandmother has always been empathetic to any child who enters the school cafeteria. When a child needs to be encouraged or "bragged on" or needs extra food on the tray, Sister Sophia is the one who provides. She became more familiar with Jermaine through his friendship with her grandson. She learned of specific accomplishments, and she praised him for a book he wrote or a good grade he earned. Cedric's mother, a teacher's aide, also became acquainted with Jermaine through her son. She described him as a "lost child" who was "just too sad for a little boy." She fixed his clothes when they needed a pin to hold them up or combed his hair when he needed it. She supported Jermaine. Eventually Jermaine asked Cedric if he could ride bus #3 and come home with him. Cedric asked and found that both his mother and grandmother were willing to have Jermaine as a guest. Jermaine began spending several weekends with the family. Sister Sophia mentioned that Jermaine was invited to spend Thanksgiving, so "he could get a good meal like everybody ought to have." The visits continued, and Jermaine began to receive a different view of himself.

Along with the support found in Sister Sophia's family, Jermaine also found support within Teresa's family. Teresa, James, and their children have been an important source of extrafamilial support for Jermaine since he was a student in Teresa's first-grade classroom. Jermaine visits Teresa's home occasionally and will join her son for an afternoon of computer games on the family's computer and bowls of ice cream. He enjoys sharing his creative writing with Teresa's daughter. This family has appreciated and celebrated Jermaine's creativity since he was young and have called attention to his gifts and talents. Teresa has served as a strong advocate for Jermaine throughout his elementary school career, struggling hard during his primary grade years to get other teachers to understand his behavior and appreciate his special abilities. Jermaine feels strongly about his special relationship with "Miss Teresa," as he explained, "I don't know what I'd do without Miss Teresa. She's always there to help me. She helps me get my work right. Whenever I have a problem, I know that I can go to her, and she'll help me solve it."

Teresa and her husband have remained in Milledge County since their days volunteering for VISTA. Frustrated with the lack of progress in their school district for over 25 years, they continue to maintain a realistic view of the situation, constantly hopeful that the conditions in Pine Grove will improve. Teresa continues to provide enrichment experiences to talented children after her teaching day has ended. She continues to work with her colleagues to help them understand the needs of children like Jermaine, providing in-service training during staff development days. James is known beyond the county as a scavenger for used science and computer equipment for the Pine Grove school. Two humble individuals, these dedicated teachers remain passionate about their work with children in their rural, impoverished community. This passion was evidenced in an interview with James as he explained:

> Occasionally you see a child like Jermaine, and he gives you so much hope. You know that you play an important role in shaping that youngster's experience and exposing him to a world beyond Pine Grove. You know that if you help him to achieve in school and provide him with the tools he needs to get accepted into a college, he'll leave here. So few ever return since there's nothing here for them. Knowing that the community may never benefit from their talents and abilities is a difficult thing to have to accept, but that doesn't stop you from doing all you can to help them achieve a better life. You chip away at a big problem one child at a time, and you just hope and pray that you're making a difference.

During Jermaine's fifth-grade school year, another significant source of extrafamilial support evolved when Mr. Cooper, a gentleman from Detroit, Michigan, returned home to Pine Grove to retire. Upon arrival, he decided he needed something to occupy his time, so he formed athletic teams for the children in the community to compete against teams from surrounding towns. Along with the athletic program, he organized a Boy Scout troop. Jermaine became involved with a number of sports and scouting. Coach Cooper has played an important role for Jermaine. He recognized Jermaine's intelligence and selected him as the quarterback for the new football team. Jermaine explained the coach's rationale for selecting him for such a prestigious position: "Coach Cooper saw that I really knew my plays, and I knew how to call them. That's what it takes to be a quarterback. Coach said he chose me to play quarterback because I'm smart and fast. Because I'm the quarterback, I'm getting new respect. A lot of kids who didn't used to like me now wave to me in school and say, 'What's up?'"

The Emergence of Jermaine's Self-Identity

In the three-year period during which I collected data on Jermaine, evidence of an emerging self-identity was noted. The young child known for hanging upside down in his chair behaved differently by fifth grade. Jermaine's belief in self had appeared in his creative writing; however, his fifth-grade school year seemed significant for him in a number of ways. Along with an emerging reputation as the community's elementary school quarterback, Jermaine's school year was positively influenced by the books he received in the mail. The children's novels did more than serve as inspiration for his creative writing. According to Teresa, when Jermaine finished the books, he shared them with Jerome, Lamont, and Niesa, his three new best friends who were grouped with him in the highest fifth-grade reading group. They were seen proudly carrying the books out to daily recess. Jermaine's small personal library was valued by his new peer group, and apparently he was becoming more highly regarded.

Along with enjoying new books together, Jermaine's friends collaborated with him in partnerships for the fifth-grade science fair, winning first place together in the countywide competition. He and his three best friends were also successful in earning another award for a Black History Month project in their school. Jermaine and his three friends designed a timeline of the life of Harriet Tubman to accompany an historical biography about the famous historical figure. Continuous success as a team helped Jermaine maintain healthy relationships with other children who appreciated his intelligence and creativity.

Another important factor that made a difference for Jermaine during fifth grade was the school district's decision to implement a school uniform. According to Teresa, early in Jermaine's school career, he was viewed as the child in ill-fitting clothes with a constant habit of holding his pants up with one hand while the other hand was free for whatever task he was attempting. During his fifth-grade year, the uniform became a socioeconomic equalizer that allowed Jermaine to arrive at school looking like everyone else. Teresa described the impact on him:

> The talk of Pine Grove is the implementation of a school uniform. The uniform consists of khaki pants and a hunter green polo shirt and "tie-up Sunday dress shoes." They are being sold by stores in Selma, and everyone ends up with the same quality. Jermaine's uncles have paid for his. They are a real equalizer here, and they've really helped in creating a sense of community. This has really helped Jermaine this year. Fifth graders are so much more aware of brand-name clothing.

Jermaine has begun to find a place for himself in the community and has found a small group of students who appreciate his creativity and with whom he can compete academically. With the exception of a B in math, Jermaine achieved straight As in fifth grade. The appreciation of his creativity and the community respect for his new role as quarterback has helped redefine

Jermaine's self-identity. As a 10-year-old, he is constructing a strong sense of self, with a new confidence that is apparent in a number of ways.

Jermaine noted that problems typically associated with more urban communities were beginning to creep into his rural community. According to him, gangs were beginning to form in the county's middle and senior high schools, and he appeared worried. This concern was evidenced when he commented, "There's a lot goin' on in the country nowadays. There are gangbangers and kids are doin' smoke. There are kids in the middle school with blades. Even here in Pine Grove, young brothers need to get off the streets and get jobs."

Jermaine assured me he wanted nothing to do with gang culture. He sees himself as a 10-year-old who is perfectly comfortable being a fifth grader. He sees no need to rush the process of becoming more worldly or sophisticated before his time. He described an experience at a birthday party that highlighted his desire to remain naive for a while longer.

> I went to a birthday party a few weeks ago. So many of the kids were talking about having boyfriends and girlfriends. They were playing games, kissing games. Tongue-suckin' kissin'. I talk to a girl like a friend. I just want to play games, and not that tongue-suckin' stuff! My mom says that stuff will affect your life.

Rather than become a teenager before his time, Jermaine appears happy being 10. He sees himself as a good person with special talents and is feeling positive about his abilities that are now valued by his peers. Jermaine's emerging self-identity and the positive view he has of himself was also evidenced in a story he crafted as part of a fifth-grade essay contest sponsored by the county teachers' association. The guidelines for students in the third- through sixth-grade category were to write a creative essay about themselves tackling problems of crime and misguided youth in Milledge County. In his essay, Jermaine decided to address a community problem by transforming himself into a super-hero. The introduction to his essay entitled *The Adventures of Turbo Man* read as follows:

> I live two lives. The first one is when I am Courtney Davis, a well-respected lawyer. My other life is as Turbo Man. That is my name when I help people who are in trouble. I wear a red suit of hard steel. I can bend metal with my bare hands and see through walls with my super-sonic eyes. I have turbo disks on my arms that can knock out evil characters, and I drive a Turbomobile.

In this manuscript, Turbo Man's adventure concludes with Jermaine's character capturing a kidnapper and returning his community to safety.

In my work with Jermaine, I questioned him as to what he saw as his greatest strengths, and he quickly responded with "my creativity and my ability to write stories" and "my talent as a football quarterback." When asked to think about filling a time capsule for posterity with 10 items that would best represent him, he included his primary-grade creative writing books entitled *Jermaine's World* and *How the Sun Got Hot*, further evidence of his pride in his ability as a creative writer.

Teresa reflected on a favorite memory of Jermaine during an after-school enrichment session in her classroom. She described how he opened a conversation by saying, "You know what the real meaning of life is? It is to care about each other." Teresa explained that, after this profound statement, he decided to read by himself. His only follow-up comment was that "he did not hear it on TV." What is apparent is that Jermaine wants to be cared about and wants others to care for each other.

Along with an empathy for others, Jermaine has a solid sense of ethics. He described an incident at school in which a jar of pennies being collected by students for a fund-raising project was stolen. He found this upsetting and could not understand how young people could steal from one another. He shook his head and expressed his concern for his community. The young man who was troubled by the school crime dreams of becoming a lawyer one day, but explained that his legal career may serve as his second profession, as he intended to first spend several years working as a Hollywood film producer.

DISCUSSION AND IMPLICATIONS

The Role of the Extended Family

If kudzu symbolizes the effects of rural poverty and isolation in the life of creative youngsters, then what could serve as a weed killer in fighting off the effects of this life-choking vine? In this study, filling the role of "weed killer" in helping to combat the kudzu were members of Jermaine's extended family who supported him. His relationships with his uncles were significant to him. Mentioned throughout the three-year study, Uncle Walter and Uncle McKinley gave him emotional support and were there for him via long-distance financial support, as evidenced in their purchase of Jermaine's school uniform in fifth grade. Also noted was his pride at having inherited his story-telling talents from his grandfather. Jermaine's relationship with his uncles highlights a distinguishing feature of the African American family. Nobles (1997) indicated that the traditional African American family is a "unique cultural form enjoying its own inherent resources" (p. 88). Comprising several individual households, the extended family is visible in the lives of its children and provides needed emotional support for its members. Walker and colleagues (Walker, Taylor, McElroy, Phillip, & Wilson, 1995) indicated that the Black extended family served as a "stress absorbing system" (p. 30) and helped develop positive self-esteem within all of its members. Sudarkasa (1997) maintained that Black families were "some of the most flexible, adaptive, and inclusive institutions in America" (p. 39) that provided nurturance for the children and support for adults.

Extrafamilial Support

The findings in this critical case study of Jermaine highlight the importance of strong emotional support and understanding from adults who understand and value creativity in young children. Teresa's appreciation for Jermaine's creative abilities at an early age and her advocacy for him as a student made a significant difference. Teresa struggled for years to develop an understanding within the faculty that giftedness was a multifaceted construct and a child's ability to think creatively was something to be celebrated. The child whom teachers initially perceived as a problem child eventually was appreciated by more teachers in Pine Grove, as well as by his peers. Teresa and her family also provided Jermaine with friendship, hospitality, and a receptive audience for sharing his creative ideas.

In addition to the support Jermaine received from Teresa, other adults beyond his family provided support in a number of ways. Sister Sophia, the school's lunchroom chef, and her daughter, who provided time for Jermaine to spend with his friend Cedric, were also significant sources of emotional support early in his elementary school experience. The child perceived by the community as a "bad little boy" was understood by this family, and they provided nurturance they regarded as basic. Coach Cooper also appeared to serve as a significant "weed killer" in fighting off the kudzu in Jermaine's experiences. By selecting Jermaine as the football team's quarterback, he did much to elevate Jermaine's status in the community. Coach Cooper's recognition of Jermaine's ability to think quickly appeared to have helped Jermaine develop a positive view of himself. With a stronger sense of self, Jermaine's creativity could continue to flourish. This finding supports what urban researchers Heath and McLaughlin (1993) and Hébert and Reis (1999) found in studies of urban youth, in which supportive relationships with significant adults helped to nurture resilience and shaped a belief in self within culturally diverse teenagers.

Nurturing Creativity

Two additional "weed killers" that were important in Jermaine's experience were the satellite television stations beamed into Jermaine's home and the collection of children's literature he received through the mail, enjoyed, and shared with his friends. These connections with a world beyond his isolated, rural community provided Jermaine with exposure to new ideas and new ways of thinking and served as an important source of new information about one of his childhood passions, wild-life animals. The information Jermaine was able to absorb through television viewing and reading from his new collection of books eventually was infused into his creative writing, helped to strengthen his vocabulary, and allowed his creativity to flourish.

Although Jermaine's exposure to satellite television may have supported his creativity, we must also critically consider the negative impact television may have on children in communities such as Pine Grove. Realizing that nearly

99% of all American households have at least one television set (Abelman, 1992), Jermaine's experience with satellite television in his impoverished, rural community should not surprise us. Abelman described television as "the great cultural denominator, the one environmental factor that all children have in common" (p. 18), and noted that parents should consider it "a potentially positive and negative force in children's lives" (p. 18). Through his critical inquiry of the television industry, Williams (1974) noted that, while television may be educational, it may also undermine intellect and critical thought, creating generations of passive individuals. Jermaine was exceptional in that his creativity was nurtured, rather than stifled, by his television viewing. However, we are reminded of the important conclusions drawn by Gray (1995) regarding the portrayal of Blacks on television programs:

> Black representations in commercial network television are situated within the existing materials and institutional hierarchies of privilege and power . . . television representations of blackness work largely to legitimate and secure the terms of the dominant cultural and social order by circulating within and remaining structured by them. (p. 10)

Since this medium was Jermaine's primary source for learning about the world outside his community, his impressions of life beyond Pine Grove may have been very distorted. When Jermaine watches television, does he ever see anyone like himself portrayed? No. More likely, he sees middle-class Black characters in situation comedies or urban Black youths portrayed unfavorably in dramas, both of which reinforce social stratification and social disharmony, as well as legitimate the status quo of White dominance (Spigner, 1991; Tait & Perry, 1994). For this reason, African American children in isolated, rural communities bombarded with racially stereotyped messages delivered through culturally insensitive television programs may eventually question their self-worth and their ability to achieve success in life.

The need that children in Pine Grove had for intellectual stimulation through satellite television and enriched educational materials calls attention to a serious problem facing schools in isolated areas. This finding supports what Descy (1992) proposed in linking rural schools to universities and other school districts via interactive technology. Interactive television would allow students in isolated, impoverished areas to take advantage of unique educational opportunities. In order to compete in an increasingly technological society, students from communities such as Pine Grove will need the same knowledge and skills as young people in suburban and urban communities. Since it is not always possible to take students to where educational opportunities may be available, such opportunities must be taken to students and teachers. If an interactive technology system is to be established in an impoverished area such as Pine Grove, a collaborative effort may have to evolve between the industrial community and the public schools. Given the impoverished conditions evidenced in Pine Grove and the philanthropic efforts of the local paper mill in Milledge

County, the McDonald Billings Corporation might serve as a source of financial support for such efforts.

Although interactive technology may assist educators in addressing the needs of students in isolated, rural areas, we need to realize that rural isolation may benefit some children in some ways. Surprisingly enough, the quiet solitude of the rural environment in which Jermaine lived appeared to help nurture Jermaine's creativity. This quiet solitude essentially was another "weed killer." Although isolated, Jermaine found that his quiet surroundings gave him high-quality thinking time and inspiration for his creative writing. This finding suggests that educators need to examine rural life and realize that, for those who are born and raised in a rural culture, the cultural qualities of their experiences are to be appreciated and respected. Kearney (1991a) noted the importance of this appreciation for rural life in the experiences of gifted children living in isolated, rural communities. She suggested that

> to support the optimal development of these children without asking them to deny or denigrate the culture which has produced them requires an appreciation of the cultural foundations of rural life, and a willingness to use the strengths of the culture itself to support the child's development. (p. 16)

Jermaine's appreciation for rural solitude and his evening thinking time are important in highlighting a significant issue to consider when educating gifted students in rural, isolated areas. Gifted students growing up in such areas may actually enjoy some advantages. Jermaine's love of animals and his use of nighttime quiet for creative thinking may have helped him to build an important knowledge base as he developed his creativity. What we have seen with Jermaine's experience is consistent with what Kearney (1991b) suggested when she noted that rural gifted children may "share the benefits of nature as a science laboratory, quiet places in which to reflect, and an independence and autonomy not always available to their city cousins—elements which can support the inner dynamics of a creative and intellectual life" (p. 16).

Creative Positives

Regardless of the kudzu-like rural impoverished conditions in which Jermaine lived, his creativity continued to flourish. In reviewing Jermaine's experience, it becomes apparent that a number of his personal characteristics as a creatively gifted youngster were similar to those mentioned in the literature. The findings of this study regarding Jermaine's creative abilities support Torrance's (1969) research in which he identified 18 creative positives, characteristics that occurred to a high degree and with high frequency among economically disadvantaged African American children. In the case study of Jermaine, evidence of the following eight creative positives identified by Torrance exist: an ability to express feelings and emotions, articulateness in role-playing and storytelling, enjoyment and ability in visual art, expressive speech, responsiveness to the kinesthetic, a sense of humor, richness of imagery in informal language, and originality of ideas in problem solving.

Following five years of research with African American children, Torrance (1977) called attention to a number of critical issues. He noted that attention should be given to those kinds of giftedness that are valued by the particular culture to which a person belongs. He suggested that creative positives should be used in designing learning experiences. In addition, Torrance emphasized that learning activities should be planned and executed so as to help culturally different children cope with and grow out of any feelings of alienation by developing pride in their strengths and providing opportunities for sharing their creative strengths with others.

Emerging Self-Identity

The findings of the study regarding Jermaine's emerging self-identity allow us to generalize to theories regarding self-concept. Self-concept refers in general terms to the image we hold of ourselves. Byrne (1984) defined it as "our attitudes, feelings, and knowledge about our abilities, skills, appearance, and social acceptability" (p. 429). The literature on self-concept provides a number of multidimensional models as an approach to understanding self-concept. In these models, self-concept is depicted as a set of independent dimensions. Harter (1983) identified several aspects of self-concept: school competence, athletic competence, social acceptance, physical appearance, and behavior or conduct. Winne and Marx (1981) proposed a model of self-concept with four dimensions: academic, social, physical, and emotional. In this study, the findings revealed that Jermaine had an emerging belief in self that could best be described as a "multi-layered embedded identity" (Heath & McLaughlin, 1993, p. 7). Jermaine saw himself as a combination of the following: scholar, creative thinker, athlete, and ethical young man. The various facets of his embedded identity are consistent with the facets of the self-concept proposed in the above multi-dimensional models. When considering how an emerging self-identity develops, most theorists acknowledge that both internal and external forces affect self-concept (Hogue & Renzulli, 1991). For example, individuals evaluate their performance against the expectations they hold for themselves, as well as the opinions expressed externally by parents, significant adults, and peers.

External influences on self-concept formation may include social comparisons whereby individuals use the reactions of significant others in their environment to assess their competence. One salient aspect of this social comparison issue has to do with the impact that the larger environment has on affecting self-concept. Marsh (1990) has proposed the big-fish-little-pond effect to explain that a young person's perception of his or her self-worth regarding his or her performance in school is partially dependent upon the average level of performance displayed in his or her school or class. This is an important issue when considering the effects of gifted students attending rural, impoverished schools where students may not see the value of education. Given the level of competition Jermaine found in Pine Grove, he was a "big fish in a small pond." Should Jermaine leave Pine Grove, the factors that nurtured his creativity and reinforced his emerging self-identity, the "weed killers combating the kudzu," will be especially important if he is to remain successful following his high school graduation in Milledge County. A supportive family, significant adults who provide extrafamilial support, and perhaps his involvement in athletics and extracurricular activities may enable him to succeed in his rural setting and prepare him to compete as "a small fish in a big pond."

Resilience

Jermaine's life story serves as an example of a child overcoming chronic adversity through resilience. According to Rutter (1987), *resilience* is the term used to describe "the positive role of individual differences in people's response to stress and adversity" (p. 316). The literature on resilient individuals indicates that resilient children are those who, despite severe hardships and the presence of at-risk factors, develop characteristics and coping skills that enable them to succeed in life (McMillan & Reed, 1994). They appear to develop stable, healthy personalities and are able to recover from or adapt to life's adversities (Werner, 1984).

Jermaine's situation was consistent with the high-risk children Werner and Smith (1982) followed in a longitudinal study. These researchers concluded that children who thrived under adverse conditions had at least one person, such as a neighbor or teacher, who provided them with consistent emotional support. Resilient youth mentioned educators who took a personal interest in them as critical to their success. McMillan and Reed (1994) and Rhodes (1994) also reported that resilient students sought out professionals who had respect for them as people, listened to them, took them seriously, and provided them with encouragement. Masten and Garmezy (1990) found children who faced chronic adversity fared better when they had a positive relationship with a competent adult, were good problem solvers, were engaging to other people, and had areas of competence and perceived efficacy valued by self and society.

The significance of the relationships between Jermaine and Teresa, Sister Sophia, and Coach Cooper indicates the powerful impact mentors may have on gifted young children living in rural, impoverished environments. Torrance, Goff, and Satterfield (1998) proposed multicultural mentoring strategies appropriate for nurturing the talents of young people from economically disadvantaged environments. An ongoing relationship with a caring adult or mentor has tremendous potential for changing a child's life. Rural school systems may want to consider implementing such mentor programs in which students from surrounding college or university campuses travel to isolated areas and assist public school educators in fostering the talents of children in these environments. For example, a community such as Pine Grove would benefit greatly from a linkage between African American Greek honor societies at nearby colleges or universities. College students in such organizations often are required to become involved in outreach projects, and such an effort could easily be facilitated through a school administrator.

One interesting question emerging from this study is whether there is a connection between the resilience evidenced in Jermaine's experience and his creativity. Are creative children who face chronic adversity in their environments more likely to develop resilience because of their creativity? The literature addressing this issue is limited. In a six-year research study with the United States Air Force, Torrance (1957) examined the psychology of survival within combat aircrews and identified the following seven skills that were necessary in overcoming adverse conditions: inventiveness, creativity, imagination, originality, flexibility, decision-making ability, and courage. Researchers interested in discovering whether a connection exists between resilience and creativity may want to consider pursuing additional research in order to assist children living in impoverished conditions.

Racial Discrimination

The life experiences of Jermaine highlight many significant issues in addressing the needs of gifted students in rural settings. In discovering Jermaine and investigating the community in which he lived, I have called attention to a significant issue in this country. The impoverished conditions uncovered in Pine Grove, Alabama, resemble what Renzulli (1973) described as an "educational and psychological disaster" (p. 439). Although Jermaine has managed to survive in this community, we cannot overlook the fact that other children are "wasted daily by a system of education that has shut its eyes and turned its back on [them]" (Renzulli, p. 437). We must ask ourselves these questions: How many other children like Jermaine have gone unnoticed in similar communities? How many lives have been wasted? For how many more generations must this problem exist in our country?

What is happening in impoverished communities like Pine Grove, Alabama, is nothing short of educational genocide. No predominantly White school district in Alabama is faced with such impoverished conditions. We must remind ourselves of the events that took place in Selma, Alabama, in 1965 and ask ourselves several serious questions. When will Martin Luther King's message be understood? Why are we turning our backs on African American children in public schools? Why have we allowed social conditions such as those found in Pine Grove to exist? Haynes and Comer (1990) have eloquently provided us with their thoughts on these issues, and it is now time for us to respond:

> Black children are heirs to the effects of the bigotry and racial prejudice that have guided national policy prior to the 1960s and that have resurfaced during the 1980s. To protect Black children and ensure [that] their rights as American citizens have been protected, an effective national

policy that addresses racial prejudice in all forms must be developed. In particular, policies that divide local school systems racially, so that there are schools for Blacks that are substandard and schools for Whites that are superior, must be changed. (p. 105)

Implications for Future Research

This critical case study highlights a need to continue examining the life experiences of gifted Black children living in rural, impoverished communities in various parts of this country. The study needs to be replicated with gifted African American youngsters in different geographical regions. In addition, critical case studies should also examine the experiences of gifted young females in rural settings. Studies of other culturally diverse populations living in rural isolation would also add to our understanding. Researchers should also consider investigating the phenomenon through a longitudinal approach. This critical case study of Jermaine represents the beginning of such a longitudinal effort in order to broaden our understanding of the role that environment plays in nurturing giftedness and creativity.

SUMMARY

Jermaine's story should serve as a cogent reminder to educators across this country that children who show potential for exceptional performance are present in every segment of society. Jermaine has spoken for children living in rural poverty by sharing his life story and his aspirations for the future with us. Whether the future remains bright for Jermaine and other gifted Black children will greatly depend on educational policy makers and the efforts of educators working to assure a better tomorrow for Jermaine and others like him.

REFERENCES

Abelman, R. (1992). *Some children under some conditions: TV and the high potential kid* (Research Monograph No. 9206). Storrs, CT: National Research Center on the Gifted and Talented, University of Connecticut.

Alabama Department of Archives and History. Retrieved March 8, 2001 from the World Wide Web: http://www.asc.edu/archives/populate/[milledge].html

Baldwin, A. Y. (1987). Undiscovered diamonds: The minority gifted child. *Journal for the Education of the Gifted, 10,* 271–285.

Benn, A. (1988, November 11). Quilting bee cooperative diminishing. *The Montgomery Advertiser,* pp. 1C–2C.

Bogdan, R. C., & Biklen, S. K. (1998). *Qualitative research in education: An introduction to theory and methods* (3rd ed.). Boston: Allyn and Bacon.

Books, S. (1997). The other poor: Rural poverty and education. *Educational Foundations, 11,* 73–85.

Byrne, B. M. (1984). The general/academic self-concept nomological network: A review of construct validation research. *Review of Educational Research, 54*, 427–456.

Collier, J., & Collier, M. (1986). *Visual anthropology: Photography as a research method.* Albuquerque, NM: University of New Mexico Press.

Crotty, M. (1998). *The foundations of social research.* Thousand Oaks, CA: Sage.

Descy, D. E. (1992). On the air in rural Minnesota. *Educational Horizons, 70*, 84–87.

Dudenhefer, P. (1994). Poverty in the United States. *Rural Sociologist, 14*, 4–25.

Edelman, M. W. (1985). The sea is so wide and my boat is so small: Problems facing Black children today. In H. P. McAdoo & J. L. McAdoo (Eds.), *Black children: Social, educational, and parental environments* (pp. 72–84). Newbury Park, CA: Sage.

Fetterman, D. M. (1989). *Ethnography: Step by step.* Newbury Park, CA: Sage.

Ford, D. Y. (1996). *Reversing underachievement among gifted Black students: Promising practices and programs.* New York: Teacher's College Press.

Frasier, M. M. (1987). The identification of gifted Black students: Developing new perspectives. *Journal for the Education of the Gifted, 10*, 155–180.

Frasier, M. M. (1991). Disadvantaged and culturally diverse gifted students. *Journal for the Education of the Gifted, 14*, 235–245.

Glesne, C., & Peshkin, A. (1992). *Becoming qualitative researchers: An introduction.* White Plains, NY: Longman.

Graue, M. E., & Walsh, D. J. (1998). *Studying children in context: Theories, methods, and ethics.* Thousand Oaks, CA: Sage.

Gray, H. (1995). *Watching race: Television and the struggle for "Blackness."* Minneapolis, MN: University of Minnesota Press.

Habermas, J. (1970). *Toward a rational society.* Boston: Beacon Press.

Habermas, J. (1971). *Knowledge and human interests.* Boston: Beacon Press.

Habermas, J. (1974). *Theory and practice.* Boston: Beacon Press.

Habermas, J. (1989). *On the logic of the social sciences.* Cambridge, MA: MIT Press.

Harter, S. (1983). Developmental perspectives on the self-system. In P. H. Mussen (Series Ed.) & E. M. Hetherington (Vol. Ed.), *Handbook of child psychology: Vol. 4. Socialization, personality, and social development.* (4th ed.; pp. 275–385). New York: John Wiley & Sons.

Haynes, N. M., & Comer, J. P. (1990). Helping Black children succeed: The significance of some social factors. In K. Lomotey (Ed.), *Going to school: The African American experience* (pp. 103–112). Albany, NY: State University of New York Press.

Heath, S. B., & McLaughlin, M. W. (1993). *Identity and innercity youth: Beyond ethnicity and gender.* New York: Teachers College Press.

Hébert, T. P., & Reis, S. M. (1999). Culturally diverse high-achieving students in an urban high school. *Urban Education, 34*, 428–457.

Herzog, M. J., & Pittman, R. (1995). Home, family, and community: Ingredients in the rural education equation. *Phi Delta Kappan, 77*, 113–118.

Hogue, R. D., & Renzulli, J. S. (1991). *Self-concept and the gifted child* (Research Monograph No. 9104). Storrs, CT: National Research Center on the Gifted and Talented, The University of Connecticut.

Kearney, K. (1991a, July). Highly gifted children in isolated rural areas (Part I). *Understanding Our Gifted, 3*(6), 16.

Kearney, K. (1991b, September). Highly gifted children in isolated rural areas (Part II). *Understanding Our Gifted, 4*(1), 16.

Kitano, M. (1991). A multicultural educational perspective on serving the culturally diverse gifted. *Journal for the Education of the Gifted, 15*, 4–19.

LeCompte, M. D., & Preissle, J. (1993). *Ethnography and qualitative design in educational research*. New York: Academic Press.

Lincoln, Y., & Guba, E. (1985). *Naturalistic inquiry*. Beverly Hills, CA: Sage.

Marsh, H. W. (1990). Influences of internal and external frames of reference on the formation of math and English self-concepts. *Journal of Educational Psychology, 82*, 107–116.

Masten A. S., & Garmezy, N. (1990). Resilience and development: Contributions from the study of children who overcome adversity. *Development and Psychopathology, 2*, 425–444.

McLoyd, V. C. (1990). The impact of economic hardship on Black families and children: Psychological distress, parenting, and socioemotional development. *Child Development, 61*, 311–346.

McMillan, J. H., & Reed, D. F. (1994, January/February). At risk students and resiliency: Factors contributing to academic success. *The Clearing House, 67*, 137–140.

Merriam, S. B. (1998). *Qualitative research and case study applications in education*. San Francisco: Jossey-Bass.

Merriam, S. B., & Simpson, E. L. (1995). *A guide to research for educators and trainers of adults*. Malabar, FL: Krieger.

Morrow, R. A., & Brown, D. D. (1994). *Critical theory and methodology*. Thousand Oaks, CA: Sage.

Nachtigal, P. N. (1992). Rural schooling: Obsolete or harbinger of the future? *Educational Horizons, 70*, 66–70.

National Commission on Excellence in Education. (1983). *A nation at risk: The imperative of educational reform*. Washington, DC: U.S. Government Printing Office.

National Education Association Commission on Professional Rights and Responsibilities. (1967). *[Milledge] County: A Study of Social, Economic, and Educational Bankruptcy*. Washington, DC: Author.

Nobles, W. W. (1997). African American family life: An instrument of culture. In H. P. McAdoo (Ed.), *Black families*, (3rd ed.; pp. 83–93). Thousand Oaks, CA: Sage.

Patton, M. Q. (1990). *Qualitative evaluation and research methods*. Newbury Park, CA: Sage.

Renzulli, J. S. (1973). *Talent potential in minority group students. Exceptional Children, 39*, 437–444.

Rhodes, J. E. (1994). Older and wiser: Mentoring relationships in childhood and adolescence. *The Journal of Primary Prevention, 14*, 187–196.

Rutter, M. (1987). Psychosocial resilience and protective mechanisms. *American Journal of Orthopsychiatry, 57*, 316–331.

Seal, K. R., & Harmon, H. L. (1995). Realities of rural school reform. *Phi Delta Kappan, 77*(2), 119–120, 122–124.

Spicker, H. (1992a). Innovation in rural and small-town schools. *Educational Horizons, 70*(2), 50.

Spicker, H. (1992b). Identifying and enriching rural gifted children. *Educational Horizons, 70*(2), 60–65.

Spicker, H., Southern, T., & Davis, B. (1987). The rural gifted child. *Gifted Child Quarterly, 31*, 155–157.

Spigner, C. (1991). Black impressions of people-of-color: A functionalist approach to film imagery. *Western Journal of Black Studies, 15*, 69–78.

Spradley, J. P. (1980). *Participant observation*. New York: Holt, Rinehart, & Winston.

Stake, R. E. (1995). *The art of case study research*. Thousand Oaks, CA: Sage.

Stern, J. D. (1992). How demographic trends for the eighties affect rural and small-town schools. *Educational Horizons, 70*(2), 71–77.

Sudarkasa, N. (1997). African American families and family values. In H. P. McAdoo (Ed.), *Black families*, (3rd ed.; pp. 9–40). Thousand Oaks, CA: Sage.

Sum, A. N., & Fogg, W. N. (1991). The adolescent poor and the transition to early adulthood. In P. Edelman & J. Ladner (Eds.), *Adolescence and poverty: Challenge for the 90's* (pp. 37–110). Washington, DC: Center for National Policy Press.

Tait, A. A., & Perry, R. L. (1994). African Americans in television: An Afrocentrist analysis. *Western Journal of Black Studies, 18*, 195–200.

Torrance, E. P. (1957). *Surviving emergencies and extreme conditions: A summary of six years of research.* Unpublished manuscript prepared at the Personnel Research Center at Lackland Air Force Base, Lackland, TX.

Torrance, E. P. (1969). Creative positives of disadvantaged children and youth. *Gifted Child Quarterly, 13,* 71–81.

Torrance, E. P. (1977). *Discovery and nurturance of giftedness in the culturally different.* Reston, VA: Council for Exceptional Children.

Torrance, E. P., Goff, K., & Satterfield, N. (1998). *Multicultural mentoring of the gifted and talented.* Waco, TX: Prufrock Press.

U.S. Department of Education. (1993). *National excellence: A case for developing America's talent.* Washington, DC: Office of Educational Research and Improvement.

Walker, K., Taylor, E., McElroy, A., Phillip, D., & Wilson, M. N. (1995). Familial and ecological correlates of self-esteem in African American children. In M. N. Wilson (Ed.), *African American family life: Its structural and ecological aspects* (pp. 23–33). San Francisco: Josey-Bass.

Werner, E. E. (1984). Resilient children. *Young Children, 40*(1), 68–72.

Werner, E. E., & Smith, R. S. (1982). *Vulnerable but invincible: A study of resilient children.* New York: McGraw-Hill.

Williams, R. (1974). *Television: Technology and cultural form.* London: Fontana.

Winne, P. H., & Marx, R. W. (1981, April). *Convergent and discriminant validity in self-concept measurement.* Paper presented at the annual conference of the American Educational Research Association, Los Angeles, CA.

Yin, R. K. (1994). *Case study research: Designs and methods* (2nd ed.). Thousand Oaks, CA: Sage.

7

The Nature and Extent of Programs for the Disadvantaged Gifted in the United States and Territories

James M. Patton

Douglas Prillaman

The College of William & Mary

Joyce VanTassel-Baska

This article reports results of a study designed to assess the nature and extent of programs for disadvantaged gifted learners in the 50 states and the United States' territories. The primary purposes of the study were:

Editor's Note: From Patton, J. M., Prillaman, D., & VanTassel-Baska, J. (1990). The nature and extent of programs for the disadvantaged gifted in the United States and territories. *Gifted Child Quarterly*, 34(3), 94-96. © 1990 National Association for Gifted Children. Reprinted with permission.

1) to determine the philosophical and definitional considerations utilized by states in addressing issues related to the disadvantaged gifted, 2) to ascertain the major approaches to identification and program interventions utilized with these populations, and 3) to determine the level and extent of state funding patterns, policies, procedures, and program standards. The findings indicated that although states have been consistently positive in their philosophical orientation toward culturally diverse and low socioeconomic gifted students, they have lagged behind in incorporating these concerns for equity and pluralism into the definitional and funding structures of their gifted programs.

INTRODUCTION

Gifted and talented students from culturally diverse and low socioeconomic environments represent untapped potential. State departments of education and local school divisions have found identifying and providing qualitatively different programs for gifted learners challenging, but identifying, developing, and funding programs for gifted minority and low socioeconomic students pose even greater challenges.

The research literature indicates that philosophical and definitional considerations related to these neglected populations of gifted abound and are often contradictory. The interaction of cultural factors and low socioeconomic status has made it difficult to isolate or treat separately the relative effects of either of these two variables (Baldwin, 1987). A study designed to determine the philosophical and definitional considerations used by states to guide the development of gifted programs for culturally diverse and low income gifted learners is needed.

Several researchers (Hilliard, 1976; Torrance, 1971; Baldwin, 1987) have pointed out the need for nontraditional assessment tools to identify giftedness in culturally diverse and low-income student populations. The need to provide differentiated programs for these gifted populations once they have been defined has also been noted in the literature (Maker, 1989; Richert, 1987; Kaplan, 1986; Baldwin, 1987). There has been, however, a paucity of research which has reported on the major approaches to identification, program intervention, and state and local funding patterns utilized with these populations in the 50 states and the United States' territories. Results of responses of the states to these major concerns are reported in this study.

PURPOSES OF THE STUDY

The purposes of this national study were: 1) to determine the philosophical and definitional considerations utilized by states in addressing issues related to the disadvantaged gifted, 2) to ascertain the major approaches to identification and program interventions utilized with these populations, and 3) to determine the level and extent of state funding patterns, policies, procedures, and program standards.

Putting the Research to Use

How do we bridge the gap between what we know in theory about educating at-risk gifted learners and what we do with these students in practice? The results of this study tell us that assessment, identification, and intervention practices used by most states for at risk gifted learners lag behind what is known about the best practices for these students. The study results reveal a limited application of our knowledge base to state programs in this area. In fact, despite broad conceptions of giftedness and pleas for the use of nontraditional assessment measures and personalized intervention, this study shows that conventional practices are still the norm even where these populations are receiving service.

The use of more alternative identification measures, affirmative selection processes, and differentiated curriculum and instruction emerges as an effective means of insuring that more racial, cultural, and low socioseconomic status learners are identified and served in gifted programs. The recommendations offered in this study should prove helpful to policy makers, administrators, teachers, and all those interested in enhancing the education and lives of at-risk gifted learners.

METHOD

A mail questionnaire was designed to assess the nature and extent of programs for disadvantaged gifted students in the 50 states, the District of Columbia, and the United States' territories of Guam. Puerto Rico, and the Virgin Islands. After field testing, the final version of the questionnaire contained 20 questions. A majority of the questions consisted of Likert-type scale items; several questions were categorical choice and forced choice.

SAMPLE

The study sample consisted of state directors of gifted programs or their designees in all 50 states, the District of Columbia, Guam, Puerto Rico, and the Virgin Islands. The questionnaires were returned by 49 of the states and all of the United States' territories surveyed for a total of 52 states or state entities. Three states indicated that they did not have any programs which focused on disadvantaged gifted learners and, accordingly, did not complete any survey items. For convenience, states, or state entities, refers to all respondents, including the District of Columbia and United States' territories.

RESULTS

States were asked to indicate the philosophical and attitudinal considerations used to define gifted programs for disadvantaged students. The results show that slightly more than 30% of the states reported the use of low socioeconomic status (SES) "a lot" or "to a great extent" in identifying students for gifted programs, and 34.6% of the responding states used this variable "a little" or a "not at all."

When asked to what extent they included the variable of race or ethnicity in the process of identifying students for gifted programs, 28.8% (15) of the states indicated that this factor was used "to a great extent" or "a lot"; 34.6% (18) of the states responded that race was used "not at all" or "a little"; 26.9% (14) of the states indicated moderate use of this variable. The questionnaire probed several areas related to identification and intervention issues for disadvantaged gifted learners. It specifically asked states to respond to questions related to types of measures used to identify these learners, as well as the names of actual instruments employed. The questionnaire also asked how these learners' needs were served in gifted programs. In some instances states responded by citing specific program types used for this purpose.

In general, directors of state programs perceived that their states embraced a moderate stance toward the use of a broadened conception of giftedness in terms of identification issues, with a mean response rate of 3.3 on a 5.0 scale. The mean response rate of 3.5 was slightly higher on the question related to the conceptual issues of using nonbiased assessment instruments and approaches to identifying the disadvantaged gifted. When the question shifted to the extent of nontraditional testing actually used in the states, the mean response rate dropped to 2.7. In fact, the study found that 90.4% of the states used norm referenced tests "to some extent" in identifying the disadvantaged gifted population. Less than half of the states (40.4%) indicated moderate or great use of a nontraditional approach. The mean response of the states to the use of observational techniques to identify the gifted was 3.5; 38% of the states did not use this technique at all.

The intervention section of the state questionnaire sought to explore ways in which disadvantaged gifted students were being served in programs. A majority (78.8%) did not differentiate programs or services "at all," or only "a little" for this population. Ten states did not provide data for this section of the report.

Survey respondents were asked about funding patterns related to programs for disadvantaged gifted students. Only one respondent cited "set asides" and "identification" standards as the approaches utilized. "Documentation in the state plan" represented an approach that was utilized by 11.9% of the states surveyed. Similarly, evidence of "goals for disadvantaged participation" was cited by 19% of the states as a criterion to determine funding. The largest number of responding states (11) indicated that "other approaches" were utilized to encourage funding for disadvantaged gifted students. Very little usable information describing these "other approaches" was offered.

Finally, 43 respondents (82.6%) reported that no specific or defined percentage of state funds was allocated for disadvantaged gifted students. When asked if other state funding sources were set aside for this population, 96% of the state directors gave a "no" response. Three questions regarding the development, monitoring, and dissemination of program standards and guidelines were posed. None of the states indicated that separate state program standards existed for the disadvantaged gifted. The largest percentage of respondents, 42.3% (22 states), indicated that their standards were the same for all gifted students. Thirty-six states reported that no guidelines or handbooks had been developed. However, 19 states revealed that these materials either existed or were in the process of being developed.

DISCUSSION

The findings indicate that although states have been philosophically consistent in considering culturally diverse and low socioeconomic gifted students, they have lagged behind in incorporating their expressed concerns for equity and pluralism into the definitional and funding structures of their gifted programs. Given the present and projected increase of students from diverse cultural, racial, and social class backgrounds in public schools, the implications of the lack of congruence between states' philosophies regarding policies and these demographic factors are a matter of concern.

Study results reveal a strong use of traditional approaches to the identification and assessment of disadvantaged gifted learners. No other techniques were so extensively utilized by states in the identification process as norm referenced tests and teacher nominations. Yet the limited numbers of disadvantaged students in present gifted programs lead us to believe that greater use of other measures and approaches is needed to identify and assess this population better.

A majority of states do not differentiate programs or services for the disadvantaged gifted. If we accept the premise that disadvantaged gifted students have some characteristics and needs different from those of other gifted students, then we must also accept the premise that differential programming for these students will be required in order to meet differential needs. Additional avenues and opportunities for accessing advanced skills such as mentorships, counseling, and special tutorials seem warranted.

Results of this study indicate that states have not developed action plans for identification and intervention with disadvantaged gifted learners. These students should be included in gifted programs at a level commensurate with their representation in the school age population. Nontraditional instruments and more affirmative selection processes should be attempted so that more children from racial and cultural minority groups are identified for gifted programs.

RECOMMENDATIONS

The recommendations from this study are based upon a careful consideration of the data, including the noticeable lack of data in several key areas of the questionnaire. The major recommendations are:

1. STATES NEED TO TRANSLATE THEIR EXPRESSED PHILOSOPHICAL CONCERNS FOR CULTURALLY DIVERSE AND LOW SOCIO-ECONOMIC STATUS LEARNERS INTO THEIR STATE DEFINITIONS OF GIFTEDNESS. Furthermore, states should eliminate the use of the term "disadvantaged" to describe culturally diverse and/or low income populations because of its negative connotations. "Cultural diversity" and "low socioeconomic status" acknowledge the condition without placing a value judgment on it.

2. STATES NEED TO DEVELOP PROGRAM PROTOTYPES FOR USE WITH ATYPICAL GIFTED LEARNERS. Schools should provide additional levels of programming for at-risk learners, e.g., tutoring, mentoring, and counseling. This value-added concept of programming might occur in the context of the regular gifted program through an IEP model, individual contract, or more personalized delivery of services. Special groupings of such learners based on the particular risk factor might have merit in some contexts.

3. STATES NEED TO COLLECT SYSTEMATIC DATA ON AT-RISK STUDENTS IN GIFTED PROGRAMS. As this study has revealed, few states are capable of providing incidence data regarding at-risk gifted populations. Moreover, even those capable of this level of reporting are not systematically collecting evaluation data on classroom/program effectiveness with this kind of learner. Some funding and energy should be targeted at data collection efforts on this population. Because the evaluation problem is endemic in the gifted education field, accomplishing this needed program measure may be difficult. Yet the success of future work with at-risk gifted learners depends heavily upon having access to good data about program practices.

REFERENCES

Baldwin, A. (1987). I'm black but look at me. I am also gifted. *Gifted Child Quarterly, 31,* 180–85.

Hilliard, A. G. (1976). Alternative to IQ testing: An approach to the identification of the gifted "minority" children (Report No. 75 175). San Francisco, CA: San Francisco State University. (ERIC Document Reproduction Service No. ED 147 009).

Kaplan, S. (1986). Qualitatively differentiated curricula. In C. J. Maker (Ed.). *Critical issues in gifted education Defensible programs for the gifted* (pp. 121–134). Rockville, MD: Aspen Publications.

Maker, J. (Ed). (1989). *Critical issues in gifted education: Defensible programs for the gifted* (Vol II). Rockville, MD: Aspen Publications.

Richert, S. E. (1987). Rampant problems and promising practices in the identification of disadvantaged gifted students. *Gifted Child Quarterly, 31,* 149–154.

Torrance, E. P. (1971). Are the Torrance tests of creative thinking biased against or in favor of disadvantaged groups? *Gifted Child Quarterly, 15,* 75–80.

8

The Seven Plus Story: Developing Hidden Talent Among Students in Socioeconomically Disadvantaged Environments

Alexinia Y. Baldwin

University of Connecticut

The Javits 7+ Gifted and Talented Program awarded to Community School District 18 of Brooklyn, New York, was designed to provide an opportunity for socio-economically disadvantaged children to receive intensive school-based activities which would prepare them for programs for the

Editor's Note: From Baldwin, A. Y. (1994). The seven plus story: Developing hidden talent among students in socioeconomically disadvantaged environments. *Gifted Child Quarterly*, *38*(2), 80-84. © 1994 National Association for Gifted Children. Reprinted with permission.

gifted. The philosophical approach of this grant was derived from Gardner's concept of multiple intelligence. The program was designed to involve teachers, parents, district staff, and students in program design and implementation. This article outlines the components of the grant, its operation, and its evaluation as viewed by the author.

Joyce Rubin and Joel Rubenfeld have led Community School District 18 administrators, teachers, parents, and students on an exciting journey of innovation and inspiration. The following quote, taken from a video of the program, captures the essence of their efforts.

> When will we also teach them who they are? . . . We should say to them you are unique, you are a marvel. In this whole world there is no one like you and there will never be again.

> —Pablo Casals

Community School District 18 of Brooklyn, New York, received funding through the Jacob Javits Gifted and Talented Students Education Act to design a program which would find and nurture giftedness within its school population.

DATA COLLECTION

My on-site introduction to the program included a visit with directors, parents, teachers, students, and principals. As I interacted with each group, a sense of joy and anticipation of the continuation of this effort was evident.

In order to obtain appropriately descriptive data within the time frame allotted, interviews, questionnaires, observations, and program documents were used as resources. I was provided with the grant proposal, the teacher training strategies, a description of the identification process, parent communications, the evaluation document of Metis and Associates (1992), and a program video. An analysis of the relationship of objectives to the procedures used in operationalizing the program was done. A series of questions for parents, children, teachers, and administrative staff was designed to be used during the interview process. I was given permission to tape these answers and any extemporaneous discussions regarding the program. I observed class activities and spent time working with some of the students.

PROJECT COMPONENTS

Demographics

District 18 is considered a "blue collar" community with a wide range of ethnic groups, including Haitians, Dominican Republicans, Puerto Ricans, and

African Americans. The district serves 18,000 students who bring to the classroom varying cultures and mores. The Javits 7+ Program serves 399 students from Kindergarten to Grade 3 and two special education classes for developmentally delayed students. The grant supported three sites; however, the concept of the program was so well-received in the district that two principals decided to support the same program in their schools by various fund raisers and rerouting of available funds. Seventy-five students, including an additional special education class, were sponsored by their principals and became part of the total number of students benefiting from the concept of this grant. The ethnic breakdown of the students participating in the Javits 7+ program is as follows:

1. Black ($n = 337$) Includes African Americans and students from French- and English-speaking Caribbean islands

2. Hispanic ($n = 32$) Includes students from Spanish-speaking islands/ countries

3. White ($n = 25$) Includes all students classified as Caucasian

4. Asian ($n = 5$) Includes students of all Asian groups, that is, Korean, Japanese, Chinese.

The teaching staff includes 17 teachers and 5 paraprofessionals who have day-to-day contact with the students. The program planning, workshops, and other aspects of the program involved the Division of Instruction and Development and other offices of the district.

Conceptualization of Program

The administrative team of the Javits 7+ program has defined giftedness as " . . . evidence of high performance capability in areas such as intellectual, creative, artistic, or leadership capacity, or in specific academic fields." The title, 7+, refers to Gardner's (1983) concept of multiple intelligences, the theoretical rationale for the identification strategy and instructional design used in this program.

Gardner defines intelligence as the ability to solve a problem or to fashion a product in a way that is considered useful in one or more cultural settings. He further suggests that an individual could be identified as talented in at least seven intelligences, including linguistic, logical-mathematical, spatial, bodily-kinesthetic, musical, interpersonal, and intrapersonal intelligences.

The project designers knew that they would be exploring new territory for their district. The objectives of the program had to be clear, and the cooperation of district-wide administrators, teachers, and parents had to be evident.

Objectives

The project objectives addressed each aspect of the proposed program and participants.

1. Target teachers and administrators will demonstrate increased capacity to assess the cognitive strengths and interests of students.

2. Project teachers will demonstrate increased capacity to individualize instruction based on the cognitive strengths and interests of students.

3. Target teachers will develop, field test, and distribute assessment tools which will evaluate the broad spectrum of intelligences.

4. Target teachers will develop, field test, and distribute activity kits which will provide materials to nurture all of the child's intelligences.

5. Project staff will produce a videotape that will be used to disseminate the teacher training model.

6. Participating students will exhibit improved competencies in the areas of fluency, flexibility, originality, elaboration, risk taking, and higher level thinking.

7. Project teachers will produce a project newsletter which will be disseminated throughout the district, the city, and the state.

8. Participating parents will develop skill in nurturing the cognitive and affective performance of their children.

After I reviewed these objectives, I asked the director what she felt the impact of the program was in the district as a whole. She responded enthusiastically that she had just received a call from one of the principals who had provided her own funds for the program indicating that she would be taking the program to the fourth grade in her school. Additionally, she had received a call from a teacher in one of the other gifted programs in the district requesting that she be transferred to this program because she was convinced that the approach used by Javits 7+ teachers was the philosophical approach with which she agreed.

PROGRAM OUTCOMES AND BENEFITS

Teachers/Assessment

The assessment process required that teachers become familiar with Gardner's seven plus talents. Consultants were brought in to work with the teachers and the school district personnel who would be involved with the program. Participants immersed themselves in typical performance-based activities for each of the intelligences.

The assessment strategy included the intelligences outlined in Gardner's *Frames of Mind* (1983). For purposes of assessment, interpersonal and intrapersonal intelligences were combined. An assessment model was developed for use in identifying the students for the program. Each of the assessment areas included two phases: experience and performance. When I inquired further about the assessment process, the director explained it this way:

> Before the assessment is made, there is an experience period. From September to December the teacher gives specific lessons to the entire class because children come from different backgrounds and we want all of the children to have an opportunity to respond to the best of his or her ability. Children work on pattern blocks, telling stories, responding to music, and becoming more flexible thinkers. The students are exposed to all aspects of the proposed assessment strategy. When the time for assessment arrives, the student is familiar with the various aspects of the assessment; [for example], he or she is familiar with a story board hence lack of knowledge about this aspect would not hamper the child's opportunity to show off his or her basic abilities. Teachers are asked to make broad generalizations, to use materials in a unique way, and [to] engage children in becoming more fluent thinkers. During the assessment, new material is given: [for example], when the story board is used, the students are given new material so they can incorporate what they know with new situations.

The rationale for each aspect of the assessment model was given to teachers for their use in assessing students as follows:

Linguistic: designed to identify strength in oral expression through coherent, sequential, and effective presentation of ideas:

Logical mathematical: designed to identify strength in reasoning through recognition of patterns and order;

Spatial: designed to identify strength in representing and manipulating spatial configurations through visual presentation of ideas;

Musical: designed to identify strength in musical ability through recognition and production of elements such as rhythm, pitch, and theme;

Bodily-kinesthetic: designed to identify strength in the ability to use all or part of one's body through the performance of tasks or in fashioning products; and

Interpersonal/Intrapersonal: designed to identify strength in the ability to understand other individuals through interactions and/or to draw upon one's own range of abilities as a means of guiding one's own behavior.

Before the assessment begins in December, teachers are given refresher workshops. Each teacher receives a packet, and a set of simulation activities are presented so that the teachers will be aware of possibilities of exceptional abilities. The activities are open-ended, and there is no way to give students the answers. Much depends on the training and insight of the teachers.

Following Gardner's recommendations, scenarios were developed and teachers were given the kinds of abilities they should be looking for as they observed students who were engaged in the scenarios. A video outlining the process of this model was developed and shared with the district and others who wanted to know more about the process.

The students were given an opportunity to become involved in a scenario which would provide them with some experience; observations were then made of their performances. An example of this process for the linguistic intelligence assessment follows:

1. Experience phase: Teacher introduces the storyboard village to the class and students tell their own stories. This activity can be done until students are familiar with the process.

2. Performance phase: Teacher displays in random fashion the storyboard kit with items next to the kit. Students then proceed to tell a story and the teacher listens and looks for the following things: variety of vocabulary: variety in sentence structure; use of voice effectively; use of dialogue to communicate ideas; coherence and sequential nature of story: and unusual or imaginative presentation of ideas. A score is given based on the following scale: 1 = *not evident*; 2 = *somewhat evident*; 3 = *evident*; 4 = *highly evident*; 5 = *extremely evident*. This score is then recorded on a matrix of all the abilities. Each of the intelligences has a score which could show strength or weakness in the particular area.

According to the summative evaluation of the first year by Metis Associates (1992), teachers noted that they found the model more useful than standard measures of assessment. When I asked questions regarding their experiences with assessment, teachers enthusiastically endorsed the use of this type of assessment technique. As one teacher expressed it, "these children are exhibiting a combination of attributes that cannot be judged by standard tests; however, they are the essence of what has been defined as giftedness-creative problem-solving ability, flexibility of thinking, and ability to judge and create ideas." These teachers felt that this assessment technique had given them insight into both the abilities of these students and the basic approaches they should consider taking in their instructional strategies.

Instructional Changes

After students were selected and placed in classes, the teachers stressed the importance of relating the assessment to the instruction. They indicated that the strengths of each child could be used to help him or her develop in other areas. They felt that they could be creative in designing the appropriate program for the students with whom they were working. This did not imply that they were not responsible for having students acquire the skills and content needed for successful completion of their programs but rather that the depth and breadth of their planning provided students with a differentiated program. This was evident in a student's response to questions about his activities in class. He talked about animals that were now extinct and made use of data collected on these extinct animals, that is, dinosaurs, to determine evolution, processes of archeology, mathematical equations to determine time, and so forth. Additionally, the development of the ability to understand the artist's perception of his or her environment was evident in the children's knowledge of great artists. The methods of design and the framing of perspective involved the students in mathematical/logical reasoning. This is how teachers used strengths to enhance weaker areas. Resource teachers in dance, music, art, and science were teachers-in-residence to work with teachers and students.

Teachers continued to refine the assessment tools with an understanding of Gardner's intelligences and the formative evaluation of year one of the grant. In the process of refining their assessment instrument, parents informed teachers that the report card traditionally used did not effectively assess what these students were doing. A special report card was designed for the purpose of assessing the growth of students in the program.

Activity Kits

Target teachers also worked to develop activity kits for use in the classroom. As noted in the Metis evaluation (1992), one teacher said: "We did pick themes that we used throughout the year. We meet twice a week and have selected themes and are writing different tasks." Another indicated, "basically, we are trying to write the curriculum in a way that captures all of the various intelligences."

The activity kit package that I reviewed was titled "Teaching for Discovery." The themes of this sample packet were identity, change, culture, and communication. The horizontal axis of the matrix indicated the intelligence and the vertical axis indicated the content. The content areas included social studies, communication arts, mathematics, and science. Reading vertically and horizontally, teachers were given ideas for a topic and a content area. A teacher matching spatial intelligence with social studies from the theme *identity*, would be given the suggestion that students could design a sculpture called "The Real Me." Each theme was accompanied by the generalization, the unit topic, the content objectives, thinking-skills objectives, and activities and directions for teachers and students.

Evaluation of Student Progress

The administrators were interested in a formative evaluation strategy. Although their design did not include a control group, they were able to collect enough data to help them in future planning. In order to document the change in students after their first experiences in the Javits program, a Likert-type scale was designed to measure the following specified behavioral characteristics:

Table 1   Pre and Post T-test Analyses for Composite Scores for Behavioral Characteristics of Identified Intelligence and In General Intelligence

Behavioral Characteristic	In the Identified Intelligence			In General		
	Pre	Post	Diff.	Pre	Post	Diff.
Fluency	5.69	7.80	2.11*	5.51	7.12	1.61*
Flexibility	5.25	7.33	2.08*	5.13	6.64	1.51*
Originality	5.48	7.60	2.12*	5.26	7.00	1.74*
Elaboration	5.04	7.39	2.35*	4.84	6.89	2.05*
Commitment	6.19	8.59	2.40*	5.72	7.61	1.89*
Performance	2.77	4.25	1.48*	2.69	3.77	1.08*
Total	31.31	43.00	12.69*	29.16	38.95	9.79*

flexibility, originality, elaboration, commitment, and performance. The 1–5 scale rating of *not evident* (1) to *extremely evident* (5) was designed to measure each of the behaviors (Rubin, 1991). According to the 1990–1991 report of student progress in a preliminary evaluation (Metis, 1992), "student achievement was measured by a comparison of pretest (fall, 1990) and posttest (spring. 1991) performance on a locally developed teacher rating scale for behavioral characteristics." The preliminary findings were based on 75 cases with matched pretest and posttest rating scale data. The methodology and results as explained by Metis (1992) were as follows:

> Within each behavioral characteristic, a composite score was calculated for The Identified Intelligence and In General [areas]. The differences between pretests and posttests were tested for statistical significance. It was expected that students' rating scale scores would increase for each behavioral characteristic . . .
>
> Table 1 shows the results of the t-test analyses for the composite scores for each behavioral characteristic for both The Identified Intelligence and In General [areas] and for the total scores across characteristics for both The Identified Intelligence and In General columns. It can be seen from the table that statistically significant gains were achieved for each behavioral characteristic and for the total scores.

In addition to the formative information in Table 1, a video of a program in which the students participated was also made. Commenting on the video, one of the host principals indicated that "changes in self-confidence, communication skills, sophistication, and knowledge exhibited by fine students were due to their experiences in the program."

Parental and Student Evaluation

Although parental input was an important aspect of the review data, the evaluation of parental involvement and change was equally important. The grant activities included a required workshop for parents which addressed: (a) an introduction to multiple intelligence theory (MI); (b) MI—from theory to practice; (c) a parent's guide to nurturing MI at home; (d) the learning centered classroom; and (e) parents and teachers; partners in excellence. Parents filled out a resource survey which included a check list for areas of work or hobbies and their profession or trade.

In addition, newsletters to parents that included program highlights and ways in which parents could become active partners in the program were periodically prepared and sent out. My meeting with parents was one of the highlights of my interviews. Fathers and mothers were present and spoke frankly without prompting about the program. Their verbal and written responses indicated that this program had been an intellectual oasis for their children. Parents felt a sense of power. One parent indicated that she would advocate that all teachers have the type of training these teachers had received so that they could stimulate the development of whatever potential abilities the children of this district possessed. Parents felt that they had ownership of the program and were learning important ways to reinforce the classroom activities.

Statements such as the following communicated their personal feelings:

I think it is a great program. It has brought out creative and artistic talents in D. that I was not aware of. She likes to tell stories by drawing pictures and using words. K. has progressed greatly in reading. She reads better and enjoys it. I appreciate the many different things her teacher and the Javits Program have opened my daughter's eyes to.

I think the Javits Program is an excellent one. The program has helped because she has grown up in the way she words her sentences, her aptitude in math, her progress in general, is great. The program is a well rounded one. S. is now interested in all aspects of learning. Not only is the program excellent but the teacher is also. She is patient, caring, and she has this way of motivating the students—it's unbelievable.

I am very honored to have my son in the Javits Program. He is very excited about the things he has accomplished. Now, more than ever, he loves to do his homework. He also shares whatever he learns with his little sister and so she is also gaining from the program. I am happy to be a volunteer parent in the program, as it helps me to understand my son's homework and be of more help to him.

Similar quotes from students indicated the feeling of happiness and self-confidence parents and teachers had observed throughout the year.

I feel like I am someone special, but people don't take me as someone special, but I think I am very special. I have learned to express myself more freely at home and in school. I enjoyed learning from the artists. I learned I was gifted and I thank the Javits Program for helping me to realize my gift.

Teachers' Evaluation of Program

It is no wonder that students and parents are excited about the program because the teachers themselves are special. They discussed the things they had learned from the workshops and from the children. They have invested energy and time in the program and are concerned that it become a part of the regular funding in the district. Rooms were filled with exciting projects, and children were buzzing around and interacting with each other as they worked on special projects. Teachers feel that the entire teaching staff of District 18 should have the rewarding experience that they have had. The following poem is a tribute to a teacher from one of the students in the program. It captures the general feeling I observed during my visit.

My teacher is the best. She's smart, helpful and intelligent. She can read very well, teach us good things, give us lots of homework and cares for us like she is our mother. Loves us like a mother.

—Kendrea—May 27, 1993

CONCLUDING COMMENTS

The Javits 7+ program is innovative and the director and staff of the district are to be commended for the manner in which they have organized and operationalized this program. The grant has caused ripples which have had an effect on classrooms throughout the district. The fact that monies were secured from within a school's budget to participate in the program when money was not available through the grant is an indication of dedication to helping economically disadvantaged students work up to their potential.

I am sure that as the district gains experience with the program, the process of assessment will become more and more refined. Teachers will become more aware of characteristics and behaviors that are indicative of excellence in the various intelligences. As teachers work with students, they will become more proficient at enhancing those intelligences where strengths are exhibited. These strengths will then become the catalyst for developing the total child, especially in those areas in which he/she will be expected to compete.

Whether Gardner's model should be adopted by all teachers is certainly debatable; however, attention to all aspects of a child's abilities and the use of these abilities as a catalyst for the development of others has merit. This program was designed to help those students who had potential to overcome some hurdles inherent in their academic and societal experiences. Unfortunately, some students who were selected using this innovative approach were not able to continue in a program for the gifted due to inadequate test scores. Teachers in the program were concerned that the gains made by those students who were placed back in their regular classes would be lost. However, according to teachers working with the grant, other teachers of students who had been returned to the regular class indicated that the Javits 7+ students were head and shoulders above those students who had not been selected for the program. One thing is certain: the parents, teachers, students, and staff who have had an opportunity to work in this program have been irrevocably changed. We can hope that the ripples from this experience will continue to change educators' perspectives on intelligences and instructional strategies that can more effectively help students blossom.

REFERENCES

Gardner, H. (1983). *Frames of mind: The theory of multiple intelligences*. New York: Basic Books.

Metis Associates, Inc. (1992). *Year two student concerns*. New York: Community School District 18 - Jacob Javits Gifted and Talented Program.

Rubin, J. (1991). *Teacher's rating scale for behavioral characteristics of Javits program students*. New York: Community School District 18 Jacob Javits Gifted and Talented Program.

9

Perceived Factors Influencing the Academic Underachievement of Talented Students of Puerto Rican Descent

Eva I. Díaz

University of Connecticut

This qualitative investigation explored the self and environmental perceptions of six talented students of Puerto Rican descent who were underachieving in an urban high school in the northeastern section of the United States. Family, school, classroom, community, and personality issues were examined, as were the ways that these experiences contributed to their actual academic status. Participant observation, interviews, document review, and other supplementary techniques were used to gather data. The major finding of this study was that the absence of early appropriate academic experiences thwarted students' possibilities of developing their high

Editor's Note: From Díaz, E. I. (1998). Perceived factors influencing the academic underachievement of talented students of Puerto Rican descent. *Gifted Child Quarterly*, 42(2), 105-122. © 1998 National Association for Gifted Children. Reprinted with permission.

abilities or talents later in life. Other interactive factors influencing the students' academic life were also identified. A model explaining the phenomenon of underachievement among the students emerged, as did suggestions for meeting their needs.

During the last 35 years, underachievement among talented students has been an intriguing phenomenon for educational practitioners as well as researchers. Late in the 1950s and early in the 1960s, research on underachievement flourished, providing the foundation for the current body of knowledge on this subject. This growing body of knowledge reflects a variety of perspectives on how the construct of underachievement can be defined and on the causes of underachievement, the characteristics of underachieving students, and how students, teachers, parents, and others may contribute to its reversal.

An examination of the early research literature on underachievement indicates that most is based on research carried out with primarily White, middle class students, who are predominantly males. Therefore, a gap in research exists about the experiences of underachieving *talented children from culturally and* linguistically diverse backgrounds. From 1980 to the present, an increased awareness of the ethnic diversity of our society has led researchers to consider a variety of issues related to giftedness among culturally and linguistically diverse populations. For example, manifestations of gifted behaviors, barriers to and strategies for identification of giftedness, and implications for educational practice have been increasingly addressed in the literature. Nonetheless, research on the phenomenon of underachievement among talented students from culturally diverse backgrounds remains minimal and focuses primarily on African American students. Dramatic demographic shifts in the United States population, and especially in the student population, suggest that Hispanics will soon become the largest ethnic group, surpassing African Americans in the United States. Unfortunately, at the present time, no research exists on the phenomenon of underachievement among talented Hispanic students. As a result, research studies in this area are urgently needed.

From 1992 to 1995, a team of researchers carried out a 2½ year cross-cultural ethnographic study of the high school experiences of 35 culturally diverse, high ability students in an urban context (Reis, Hébert, Díaz, Maxfield, & Ratley, 1995). As part of this larger study, a selected group of six talented students of Puerto Rican descent were involved in a study exploring the phenomenon of underachievement (Díaz, 1994). This exploratory study investigated the views that six talented academically underachieving students of Puerto Rican descent had of their life experiences. Family, school, community, and personality issues were explored, as were the ways these experiences contributed to their academic status. In order to develop a holistic understanding of the perceived factors in the talented Puerto Rican students' lives which were particularly relevant to the phenomenon of their underachievement, this investigation used a naturalistic, qualitative case study approach. This type of research focuses on examining a particular phenomenon within its natural or real-life context, and assumes that the ways in which individuals perceive their life experiences influence their behaviors or actions (Bogden & Biklen, 1982). Sekuler and Blake (1985) stated that perceptions "guide people's actions in the world around them" (p. 1) and "behavior depends on what is perceived" (p. 6). In other words, during this investigation, students' interpretations (perceptions, subjective appraisals) of their experiences were emphasized. The ways in which they perceive and react to their life experiences provided vital information on how to better understand the phenomenon of underachievement and improve educational outcomes.

Putting the Research to Use

The findings of this study indicate that, in order to prevent academic underachievement among talented students of Puerto Rican descent, preventative and intervention efforts (e.g., early curricular enrichment and talent identification) at the early childhood and elementary levels are crucial. Proactive staff development and parental education opportunities involving teachers, counselors, administrators, students, parents or significant others, and community members must also be emphasized. An awareness of and sensitivity to the existence of talented students of Puerto Rican descent despite negative stereotypes would enable educators to provide more appropriate educational experiences as well as genuine personal support.

Runyan (1982) argued that a case study has an inherently greater suitability for "tasks such as describing an individual's experiences" and "developing idiographic interpretations of that experience" (p. 125). This research approach enabled the researcher to be sensitive to the students' experiences and realities, and to make interpretative sense of the phenomenon of underachievement among this selected group of talented students of Puerto Rican descent. This article (a) briefly reviews the literature in the areas of underachievement and Puerto Ricans in the United States, (b) describes the implementation of this investigation, (c) reports research findings, (d) proposes a theoretical model for understanding underachievement among the informants, and (e) suggests several implications for educators. The results of this investigation enhance previous work on the processes underlying academic underachievement by clarifying the developmental nature and the interactive dimensions and factors relevant to the phenomenon of academic underachievement. Moreover, for the first time, this investigation provides an in-depth exploration of underachievement processes particularly for a small group of talented students of Puerto Rican descent and suggests similarities to and differences from other paradigms of underachievement.

UNDERACHIEVEMENT

No current agreement can be found in the literature on a single definition of the construct of underachievement. However, the most acceptable and widely cited view of a gifted or talented student who underachieves in school is that of an individual whose performance, as judged by some measure of productivity (i.e., grades and achievement test scores), is significantly below his or her potential for achievement. A more general definition refers to gifted underachieving pupils as those students who have high academic potential, as measured by intelligence or achievement tests, but who are doing poorly in school, as evidenced by their underachieving behaviors (Delisle & Berger, 1990; Supplee, 1990). It appears that students who are underachieving academically possess high ability, but their actual performance only reaches low or average levels that are far from their real capacity. Unfortunately, the phenomenon of underachievement is widespread in our society. For instance, the National Commission on Excellence in Education (1984) reported that approximately 50% of gifted students' achievement levels did not conform to their abilities, and Richert (1991) went even further, noting that this report only accounted for those gifted students who were identified through intelligence tests but excluded those gifted students who were not identified as gifted because their IQs did not reach the *cut-off scores*. Nor is underachievement, as described here, the only risk for such students; it has been estimated that approximately 10% to 20% of high school dropouts are gifted students (National Commission on Excellence in Education).

The phenomenon of underachievement has been studied along a variety of continua including the degree of discrepancy, duration, scope, and intensity. Considering the duration continuum, underachievement can be classified as either constant or situational (Fine, 1967; Fliegler, 1957; Miller, 1961; Shaw & McCuen, 1960). A *temporary* or *situational* underachieving student is one whose academic performance temporarily declines below what is expected. On the other hand, a *constant* or *chronic* underachieving student shows a pattern of underachievement over a long time (Whitmore, 1980). Yet, no specific time of occurrence has been identified to distinguish between chronic and situational underachievement, making the distinction a blurry one (McCall, Evahn, & Kratzer, 1992).

Distinctions concerning the scope of underachievement include differentiating between *general* and *specific* underachievement. Whitmore (1980) divided underachievement into three parts: specific subject, particular area, and general. She argues that some students only underachieve in a single subject or ability area. A student might be exceptional in science, but perform no better in science classes than in other subject areas; or a student might perform well in algebra or foreign languages for what might be simply motivational reasons. Some students underachieve only in a particular content area, such as mathematics or language arts although anecdotal reports by investigators searching for young people who underachieve in one subject area suggest that specific underachievement may be unusual (McCall et al., 1992). Kessler (1963), Pecaut (1979), and Roth (1970) have described other types of underachievement and

Table 1   Characteristics of Gifted Students Underachieving in School

School Related Behaviors	Personality Traits
• dislike of school, negative attitudes towards school	• low self-esteem, low self-concept, low self-image
• selection of friends who have negative attitudes towards school	• lack of self-confidence
• test phobia	• need for power and control
• incomplete school work	• low perception of abilities
• verbally fluent but poor written work	• difficulty in peer relationships
• absence of academic skills, poor study habits	• belief of being disliked by peers
• difficulty working in groups	• lack self direction
• restless, inattentive	• rebellious, impulsive
• disorganized	• hostile (both inward and outward) reactive
• lack of concentration, high distractibility	• sense of external locus of control
• bored	• inclined to be excessively self-sufficient or too dependent
• dislike of repetitive tasks, drill and memorization	• failure to develop a sense of self-efficacy
• difficulty with analytical tasks which are detailed, computational or convergent problem solving tasks which require precise and analytical information processing	• excessively self critical, perfectionist
	• skilled at "faking bad"
	• less persistent, less assertive
	• acute sensitivity and perceptions related to self, others, and life in general
• pretension of not knowing the answers	• purposefully act unintelligent
• poor academic self-concept	• tendency to withdraw
• weak motivation for academic achievement	• autonomous spirit – unwillingness to conform, look for instant gratification
• friendly with older students	• feelings of helplessness, victimization, constant thoughts of worthlessness
• good at abstract thinking	• misuse freedom
• lively imagination	• avoidance of responsibility, unreliable
• inventive	
• strong interest in one special area	
• diligent and creative when pursuing own interests	
• highly withdrawn or disruptive in the classroom	
• avoidance of competition and new activities	

Note. Sources included Bandura, 1988; Bar-Tal, 1978; Bricklin & Bricklin, 1967; Clark, 1988; Coleman et al., 1966; Delisle, 1992; Dirkes, 1985; Ford 1992; Gallagher, 1985; Kerry, 1981; Losoney, 1977; Pendarvis, Howley, & Howley, 1990; Pirrozo, 1982; Redding, 1990; Rimm, 1984; Roth & Puri, 1967; Whitmore, 1980; Zilli , 1971.

underachievers. Finally, the intensity of underachievement may align in a continuum from *mild* to *severe*.

Research data (presented in Table 1) exist about the most frequently cited characteristics of gifted underachieving students. One must be very careful in

Table 2   Factors Leading to Underachievement Among Gifted Students

Home/Family	School	Personality
• excessive parental pressure or power • inconsistent parental attitudes and values • identification with a non-achieving parent • unhappy home climate due to parents' illness, parents' absence and poor parents' relationship • financial limitations • little support for independent behavior	• dull, unchallenging curriculum • poor instruction • anti-academic peer group • incompatibility of student's learning style and teacher's instructional style • low expectations • teachers and counselors' attitudes • highly competitive environment • anti-intellectual school atmosphere	• low self-concept • resistance to adult pressures • opposition • suppressed aggression • external locus of control • lack of effort to achieve • lack of academic skills • fear of ridicule or alienation • inappropriate coping skills • personal adjustment problems

Note: Sources included Abraham, 1981; Pirozzo, 1982; Rimm, 1984, 1986, 1991; Whitmore, 1980.

interpreting this information because a broad range of possible characteristics, causes, and explanations exist for this phenomenon. Not all gifted under-achieving children display each of the characteristics suggested by researchers.

Research also exists about the potential reasons for underachievement among gifted students. However, most researchers generally assume that one or two specific factors are fully responsible for the underachievement of gifted students. In fact, few investigations address a blend of variables. Gifted students seem to underachieve for various reasons, and the most frequently cited causes for the underachievement of gifted students are listed in Table 2.

PUERTO RICANS IN THE UNITED STATES

Today, Puerto Ricans comprise the second largest Hispanic subgroup in the United States following Mexican Americans. According to the United States Bureau of the Census (1995), the Hispanic population totaled about 26 million, i.e., approximately 10% of the entire United States population in 1994. Of those 26 million Hispanics living in the U.S., approximately 2.7 million, or 10.6%, were of Puerto Rican descent. In 1993, 52.5% of Puerto Ricans in the U.S. were females and 47.5% were males. At that time, nearly 50% of Puerto Ricans living on the U.S. mainland were born in Puerto Rico. The integration of Puerto Ricans to the mainland has taken place through conquest and immigration. In 1898, the United States invaded Puerto Rico and made it a U.S. territory. In 1917, Puerto Ricans were granted secondary U.S. citizenship, enabling them to travel to the United States without restriction. Although Puerto Rican immigration had existed since the 19th century, it was not until the 1940s that large numbers of Puerto Ricans immigrated to the United States for economic reasons.

In terms of geographic location, Puerto Ricans are highly concentrated in the urban areas of the northeastern U.S. For example, 50% of the Puerto Rican population in the continental United States lives in nine central cities (National Puerto Rican Coalition [NPRC], 1992). Nevertheless, Puerto Ricans are currently moving away from the greater New York area to smaller cities and to other states. Alvarez (1992a) reported that Puerto Ricans comprise the largest Hispanic subgroups not only in New York but also in Connecticut, Pennsylvania, and Massachusetts.

In 1994, approximately 78% of Puerto Rican males and 46% of Puerto Rican females were in the taxed labor force. Occupation figures during 1992 suggest gender differences in employment patterns. For example, more females than males were in technical, sales or administrative support positions as well as in managerial or specialized professional positions. On the other hand, more males than females were employed as operators, fabricators, or laborers. During the same year, the unemployment rate for Puerto Ricans was 12.3%, with a higher unemployment rate for males than females. This unemployment rate is the highest of all Hispanic subgroups.

Puerto Ricans have the lowest median household income ($18,999) of all Hispanic subgroups, that is, 42.4% less than for White non-Hispanics in 1992. The mean number of persons in Puerto Rican households is 3.33. Currently, Puerto Ricans also have the highest poverty rate in the nation with nearly 40% of the total Puerto Rican population below the poverty line. In 1993, 40.5% of Puerto Rican families were headed by females (no husband present). Furthermore, 60.3% of female-headed Puerto Rican families were considered poor. According to NPRC (1992), "Puerto Rican children have the unfortunate distinction of being the poorest in the nation" (p. 1).

Currently, close to 40% of the Puerto Rican population is under the age of 17. Puerto Rican and other Hispanic youths are the youngest population of the United States. Pallas, Natriello, and McDill (1988) predicted that, by the year 2020, Hispanic youth will comprise 25% of the U.S. youth population; that is, one in every four youngsters is expected to be Hispanic. It is also expected that as the general population ages, Hispanics will become the majority of the school population in many cities.

Many Hispanic, and especially Puerto Rican, students are considered educationally at risk. For instance, educational data on Hispanic students reflect a picture of low achievement levels, high dropout rates, poor school attendance rates, higher placements in special education and remedial tracks, higher enrollment in segregated schools, and under-representation in gifted programs (Alvarez, 1992b; Meléndez, 1986; National Center for Education Statistics, 1992; Passow, 1986; U.S. Bureau of the Census, 1995). Unfortunately, low achievement has been a major barrier to the advancement of Hispanics in the U.S. For example, a 1992 report by the National Center for Education Statistics, relating the 1988 National Education Longitudinal Study, indicated that Hispanic eighth graders failed to achieve the basic levels of performance on the reading and math achievement tests. This report also revealed that in the case of Puerto Ricans the situation was worse, since low achievement levels were registered not only in reading and mathematics but also in writing, science, and computer competencies.

Regarding dropout rates, the National Center for Education Statistics (1992) pointed out that about one-third of all Hispanics age 16 through 24 had not finished high school and were not enrolled in school. The status dropout rate of 43% for Hispanics ages 16 through 24 who were born outside of the 50 states and the District of Columbia was higher than the status dropout rates for first generation Hispanics (17%) or second generation or more (24%). The status dropout rates for Hispanics, taken as a group, ranged from two to five times those of whites and blacks. However, when dropout rates were computed separately for Hispanic subgroups, the rates for Mexican Americans and Puerto Ricans were three times the rates for non-Hispanics, while the rate for Cubans was about the same as the non-Hispanic rate (p. viii).

The same report indicated that the overall dropout rate for Hispanics was 35.3% in comparison to 8.9% for White non-Hispanic and 13.6% for Black non-Hispanic. In other words, Hispanics have the highest dropout rates (across all income levels) in the nation. Furthermore, status dropout rates for Hispanics from low income backgrounds was 47.9%. On the other hand, educational attainment figures for Puerto Ricans 25 years old and over indicated that 59.8% had finished four years of high school or more and only 8% had finished four years of college or more in 1993.

Walsh (1991) asserted that the nature of schooling for Puerto Ricans is contradictory. She found that a mismatch exists between the classroom or school environments and the daily reality of these students' lives. This mismatch usually fosters poor student attitudes and motivation which in turn promote low achievement levels. Moreover, these students are at risk of being labeled "emotionally disturbed," "behavior problems," and "bad students." Alvarez (1983) investigated the differential achievement of 98 inner-city Puerto Rican students and found that school was the major contributor to achievement among low-income Puerto Rican children. In other words, the impact of schools on the achievement levels of these students was higher than the impact of family background or personal traits.

Research on the experiences of talented Puerto Rican descent students is sparse. For instance, Soto (1986) and Hine (1991) explored the family environment and characteristics of high achieving Puerto Rican students. Nevertheless, research concentrating primarily on talented underachieving students of Puerto Rican descent is largely absent.

METHOD

The Site

This study was carried out in Middlefield (fictitious name used to maintain confidentiality and anonymity), a large city located in the northeastern part of the United States. Middlefield's population includes a wide variety of ethnic and cultural groups. However, the largest ethnic group in the city was Hispanic, and Puerto Ricans represented 70% of this Hispanic population.

The Middlefield public school district is the largest school system in the state, including some 33 schools serving nearly 27,000 students from grades K-12, approximately 92% of whom were of "minority" background. Hispanic students made up 45.2% of the total student population. South City High School was selected for this study. It served a student population of 1,658, primarily Hispanic and African American students. Hispanic students comprised approximately 65% of the total student population at this school, and Puerto Rican students represented more than 70% of the Hispanic student body at South City High School. The school was located in a school district in which Hispanic students displayed the lowest levels of academic performance according to 1991 state test results.

Informants

Based on the qualitative nature of this study, criterion-based sampling was employed. Criterion-based sampling involves establishing the informants' theoretical criteria necessary to participate in the investigation ahead of time and then identifying individuals who match the criteria (Goetz & LeCompte, 1984). Informants were selected on the basis of their potentially significant contributions to the findings of this investigation. The informants for this investigation were six academically talented students of Puerto Rican descent, three females and three males, who were underachieving academically, as evidenced by low grades, while attending South City High School. All six students were between the ages of 14 and 19 and had been enrolled in a gifted program or were previously achieving (elementary or middle school) at a superior level as evidenced by grades, standardized achievement test scores, teachers' observations, awards or honors among others.

The selection process of the informants for this investigation included an initial screening of informants based initially on guidance counselors' nominations. However, due to an absence of nominations, the researcher, in coordination with three guidance counselors, carried out a closer examination of some students' records in order to identify potential informants. Each nomination involved (a) identifying the student in accordance with the selection criteria; (b) contacting by phone the parents or guardians of the student; and (c) sending a packet including a letter to parents or guardians, an explanation of the study, consent forms, and a questionnaire to the parents or guardians of the student. Written and verbal communication with parents and students was carried out in the language of their preference, either in Spanish, English, or bilingually (Spanish and English). All documents used during this investigation were also available in Spanish and English. Finally, those students who returned the consent forms and the questionnaires were briefly interviewed by the researcher in order to clarify the purpose of the investigation, obtain a final decision regarding their commitment to participate, and guarantee anonymity to students, families, and all other informants involved in this investigation. If, during this interview, the student agreed to participate voluntarily, then the student became an informant for this investigation.

Demographic information about the informants and their families through the use of assumed names are provided in Tables 3 and 4, respectively.

Research Questions

The following questions guided the study:

1. What family experiences do talented Puerto Rican underachievers perceive as factors contributing to their underachievement?

2. What classroom or school experiences do talented Puerto Rican underachievers view as factors contributing to their underachievement?

3. What community or social experiences do talented Puerto Rican underachievers perceive as factors contributing to their underachievement?

4. What personal characteristics or circumstances do talented Puerto Rican underachievers perceive as factors contributing to their underachievement?

Data Collection

Multiple methods, strategies, and techniques were used to facilitate data collection. Interviews, participant observation, and document review were the main strategies in data gathering. During this investigation, the researcher spent 45 days of an academic year as an observer-participant and interviewer. Participant observation took place within the school setting, the immediate community, and at several students' homes. Interviews were the primary source of information providing access to the informants' perspectives. Through interviews, informants discussed their perceptions, knowledge, feelings, past and present experiences, thoughts and intentions related to the duality of being talented, academically underachieving students. Unstructured and semi-structured interviews were used according to the particular purpose of the interaction. Informants, students, parents, teachers, administrators, guidance counselors, other school personnel working with the students, community members, and friends were interviewed during this investigation. Interview data were collected on school, family, and community settings. Each informant was interviewed between five and eight times, ranging from 45 minutes to four hours each time. Their families were interviewed once and the interviews lasted from two to five hours. At least one parent and a sibling were present during the interviews.

The researcher also examined personal documents such as (a) informants' cumulative records including students' grade reports, test results, teachers' observations, disciplinary actions, academic awards, and so forth; and (b) informants'

Table 3 Informants: Demographic Information

Informant's Name	Gender	Birth Place	Age	Time in the U.S.	Time in the City	Grade	Test Percentiles Reading/Math/Language			Class Track	Class Rank	QPA
Marwin Pérez	M	US	15	15	4	9	90	93	98	G / A / H	*	0.0 F
Milton Escobar	M	PR	15	9	9	9	99	97	89	A / H	*	1.8 D-
Marcos Alicea	M	US	17	17	17	10	93	96	94	G / A	294/485	1.8 D-
Yvellise Santos	F	PR	15	5	5	9	99	93	*	G / A	*	6.8 B-
Rose Marie Ortiz	F	US	16	16	7	10	82	98	94	A	37/485	6.7 B-
Sandra Agosto	F	US	18	18	18	12	98	98	99	H	13/330	8.6 B

Note. *Indicates that information is missing. The test percentiles indicated here are on either the Metropolitan Achievement Test (MAT) or the Comprehensive Test of Basic Skills (CTBS), except for Yvellise Santos whose test percentiles were based on SABE, an achievement test in Spanish. G = general, A = academic, and H = Honors

Table 4   Informants' Families: Demographic Information

Informant's Name	Informant lived with	Parents' Marital Status	Parents' Birth Place		Parents' year In the U.S.		Parental Education		Parental Mother	Occupation Father
			Mother	Father	Mother	Father	Mother	Father		
Marwin Pérez	mother father brother	Married	US	PR	35	25	Less than HSD	Less than HSD	Home-maker	Auto Mechanic
Milton Escobar	mother's boyfriend brother sister mother	Divorced	PR	PR	9	0	HSD	HSD	Home-maker	*
Marcos Alicea	father brother mother	Married	PR	PR	30	32	HSD	HSD	Home-maker	Salesman (retired)
Yvellise Santos	father two sisters mother	Married	PR	PR	7	7	HSD	Less than HSD	Home-maker	Co-owner of an Auto Parts Shop
Rosa Marie Ortiz	brother sister mother	Divorced	C	PR	30	*	TCD	*	Nurse	Pastor
Sandra Agosto	mother father sister brother	Married	PR	PR	30	30	Less than HSD	HSD	Home-maker	Machine Operator

Note. *indicates that information is missing. US = United States, C = Colombia, PR = Puerto Rico, HSD = High School Diploma, and TCD = Technical College Diploma written work such as poems and notes on specific topics related to this investigation. Public documents including newspapers, magazines, flyers, memorandums, and so forth, were reviewed. In addition, supplementary techniques such as fieldnotes, tape recordings, photography, and projective techniques were part of this investigation.

Data Analysis

The qualitative analysis of data was ongoing throughout the investigation. Data collection and analysis occurred concurrently. Qualitative analysis involved coding the data, searching for patterns, relationships, and explanations for the existence of them, and developing categories. While collecting data, the researcher was inductively analyzing the data, formulating, and verifying hypothetical ideas or explanations. Strauss (1987) described induction as:

> the actions that lead to discovery of an hypothesis—that is having a hunch or an idea, then converting it into a hypothesis and assessing whether it might provisionally work as at least a partial condition for a type of event, act, relationship, strategy, etc. (p. 11)

The qualitative analysis of the data collected involved the use of the coding paradigm suggested by Strauss and Corbin (1990). During data collection and analysis, three major types of coding were used: open, axial, and selective coding (Strauss, 1987; Strauss & Corbin). Open coding involved conceptualizing the data. During data collection, the researcher coded the data unrestrictively, reading the transcribed interviews, fieldnotes, and documents approximately four to six times. Descriptive labels were given to particular incidents, events, or ideas. In addition, notes or memos including interpretative ideas were also written. Once the data collection and fieldwork were finished, the researcher revised, sorted, and reflected upon all the data. Further labeling or conceptualizing of the data was also done. Since four research questions guided this investigation, the following categories were specified a priori: family, school, community, and personal factors contributing to the academic underachievement of six talented students of Puerto Rican descent. Therefore, related concepts were grouped together in order to substantiate the previous categories. Once the established categories were substantiated by the data, a refined process of reflection upon the data led to identification of sub-categories. These sub-categories were described using sources such as in vivo codes or words used by the participants involved in this investigation, investigative codes or words formulated by the researcher of this investigation, and scholarly codes or constructs available through existing theories. For example, under the category of family factors, a sub-category was labeled as unhappy home climate that further involves various concepts. By this time, the grounded theory started to be more explicit and organized. Selective coding involved the analytical conceptualization of the central phenomenon emerging from the data. In other words, a core category was established. In this investigation, inappropriate early curricular experiences were identified as the central factor contributing to the actual academic underachievement of several talented students of Puerto Rican descent. All the other factors (categories and sub-categories) revolved around this core factor.

Reliability and Validity

For the purposes of this investigation, reliability or accuracy of the observations and trustworthiness were enhanced by the use of (a) tape recording and fieldnotes that allowed the researcher to examine and clarify information, assuring completeness and faithfulness to the informants' words; (b) photography to document and study specific situations or settings that required more than a single viewing; (c) triangulation among methods and sources, including observations of informants in various settings, interviews with informants, teachers, relatives and others, document review, and photography; (d) depth of detail, continuous cross-checking, and monitoring of the data; (e) debriefing sessions during investigation with co-workers at the National Research Center on the Gifted and Talented (NRC/GT) who were not involved in the research project as well as a peer researcher in a parallel project, in order to explore ideas, doubts and for personal support; and (f) a calendar of daily activities and a researcher's daily journal that had a cathartic purpose, helping the researcher to deal with her emotions during fieldwork. Sanjek (1990) indicated that "diaries record the ethnographer's personal reactions, frustrations and assessments of life and work in the field" (p. 108).

In order to enhance the validity or quality of the conclusions, the processes through which these were reached, and the credibility of the findings of this investigation, the researcher made (a) intensive direct observations and interviews until data saturation was reached or the information became redundant and did not offer useful reinforcement of information previously collected (Bogden & Biklen, 1982): (b) a detailed description of how the investigation was done, the efforts or precautions taken in ensuring the accuracy of the observations, and the evidence on which interpretations were made; and (c) arrangements to have a research partner play the role of "devil's advocate."

RESULTS

An examination of the self and environmental perceptions of six talented underachieving students of Puerto Rican descent revealed that a combination of external and internal factors was perceived as influencing students' academic performance. In order to summarize the findings of this investigation, a conceptual model was developed (See Figure 1). Each square within the main square represents a category and its subcategories. The arrow heads represent

Figure 1   Perceived factors negatively influencing the academic achievement of six talented students of Puerto Rican descent

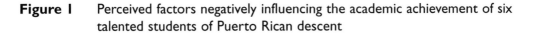

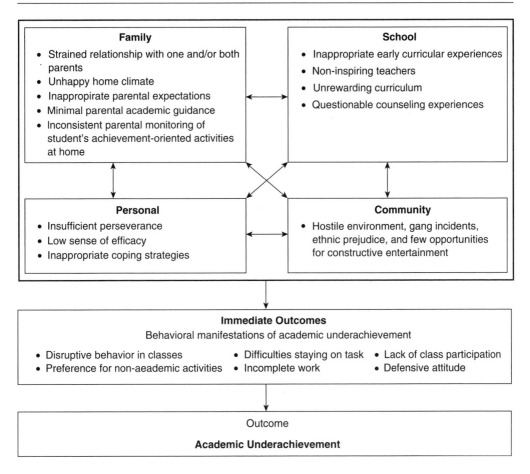

their interactive nature. The interactions of these categories family school, personal, and community) result in visible behavioral manifestations of academic underachievement which is represented by the rectangle entitled "Immediate Outcomes." Finally, the second rectangle represents the final outcome of academic underachievement in this population.

Grounded Theory

The most critical factor influencing the informants' actual academic performance was the absence of early appropriate academic experiences. All the other factors revolved around this fundamental element. In Figure 2, a model is presented to explain the phenomenon of underachievement among the six talented students of Puerto Rican descent who participated in this investigation. This model synthesizes the interactive dynamics underlying the phenomenon of

Figure 2   Model of academic underachievement for six talented students of Puerto Rican descent

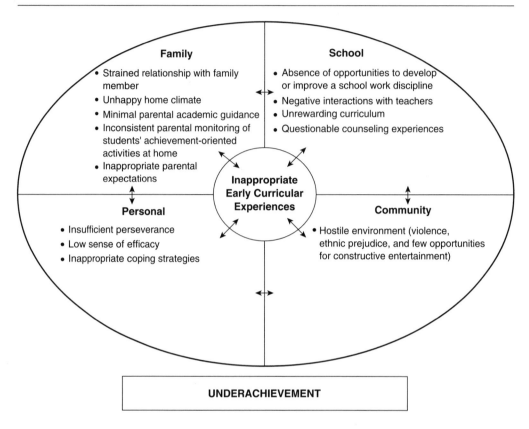

underachievement among the informants of this investigation. The subsidiary categories and their subcategories surround the core category, in this model. The interactions between and within categories and subcategories are represented by the arrow heads. The quandary provoked by the interaction of external and internal factors is represented by the inverted triangle which is oriented toward the rectangle representing the visible outcome of underachievement.

School experiences. At the core of this model are the early ill-suited academic experiences of these students (small circle in the center of the model). Inappropriate experiences or an absence of appropriate learning experiences during elementary school played a decisive part in the onset of these students' academic underachievement. First, low-challenge academic curricula during elementary school had a negative impact on the students' perceived need to expend effort and to develop sophisticated learning strategies and study habits. Second, although students were easily able to achieve perceived high levels of academic performance in their early school years, their high abilities were not properly nurtured. Consequently, their subsequent possibilities to achieve at levels that match their potential were diminished. In other words, the early absence of the nurturance of students' abilities hampered students' later capacity to demonstrate their abilities and talents during middle and high school years. For example, Milton indicated "breezing" through elementary school. Sandra and Marwin agreed their classes and academic tasks were sometimes "too easy." Sandra remembered that at one time, she had to do 10 compound words, and she ended up doing 110. She reported that during elementary school she used to go well beyond her assigned work. Marwin said, "Elementary school was fun. I always got As and Bs on my report cards. I ain't never studied. I studied when we were in class doing work and correcting it. I never really had to study at home."

Middle and early high school years represented a critical trial-and-error period involving a transition characterized by a demand for efforts and perseverance. Academic achievement required both effort and perseverance that had not been previously acquired or extensively practiced by these talented students. At first, when informants began facing new demanding academic experiences, they acknowledged their need to work harder. Those who by working harder and being persistent experienced some success in their new academic endeavors were able to fortify their sense of self-worth, believing that they were capable of handling the new challenges. These students were able to overcome immediate difficulties, although they later experienced some degree of stress when they encountered "difficult" work. Nevertheless, if they could complete the work, the likelihood of visible or chronic underachievement was lessened.

On the other hand, those students who made an effort by working harder and persevering in order to overcome the challenges faced in middle and high school, but who did not experience success, tended to devalue themselves. Informants perceived that their efforts were worthless and that they were not capable of meeting these new academic challenges. In other words, students experienced doubts about their own ability. Consequently, the visible onset of underachievement occurred when students encountered challenging work. For example, Milton's biology teacher explained that Milton was a "very verbal, enthusiastic, and articulate student" at the beginning of his freshman year, but by the end of the first marking period, he started to lose his homework and to contribute minimally in class. Milton discussed his demoralizing experience:

> I got sick of it. I got tired of her giving me all that work. I used to try hard. She'd give me fifty-sevens and sixties on worksheets, and on tests I'd score low sixties. And I was thinking, "I'm working my butt off for a D?" Why should I bust my behind, working in a class, just to earn a D or a credit?

Students struggled with perseverance, diligence, and effort during their middle and high school years. During this time, study skills and learning strategies also played a crucial role. For instance, the poorer the student's study skills or self-regulatory learning mechanisms, the higher the demand for effort and perseverance. Furthermore, the absence of appropriate opportunities to develop students' discipline to work in school complicated the problem. In this regard, informants believed that teachers assumed their students' work habits were already developed, and that it was not the school's or teachers' responsibility to provide students with opportunities to enhance their working habits. Rose Marie complained about her experience: "I would like to know how to study. They never taught me in school. They expected us to do it by ourselves."

At that time, obvious manifestations of motivational issues emerged. Students became pessimistic about their schooling experiences and expressed dissatisfaction, boredom, and laziness. Although students recognized that they had experienced good times during their middle and high school years, the negative incidents overshadowed the positive moments. Negative experiences during high school resulted from negative interactions with teachers and counselors, unrewarding curricular activities, scarcity of options for talent development, and questionable counseling experiences. For instance, informants perceived that uncaring teachers and teachers who did not know how to teach effectively had a negative impact on them. These teachers were described as being unable to establish a satisfactory level of rapport and empathy with the students. They were also unable to provide challenging and enjoyable teaching-learning experiences. This type of teacher utilized inflexible instructional methods and discouraged students' interest and involvement in class. In some cases, incompatible teachers' and students' personalities as well as teaching and learning styles resulted in both implicit and explicit manifestations of dissatisfaction by both teachers and students. Some teachers became openly or surreptitiously offensive, and some students displayed disruptive behaviors in the classroom or became passively rebellious. Rigid administrative and disciplinary rules also exacerbated students' sense of helplessness. For example, Rose Marie demonstrated superior ability in mathematics, but she was failing her honors geometry class. Although she had previously demonstrated outstanding talent in the areas of conceptual understandings, computational skills, and problem solving, she experienced difficulties in geometry. In addition to a limited background in geometry, Rose Marie claimed that her math teacher's style aggravated her problems. Her math teacher focused on rote memorization which Rose Marie found uninteresting, and she decided "just to sit there and do no work at all." She explained:

> I hated it. I don't like the teacher at all. He would stand in front of the table, and he would go through the problems in the book. I just don't like his method of teaching. At times, I didn't even pay attention to him. I didn't do my homework or anything. It's pointless to study for math. I have no interest. So that really is like giving up, I'd rather teach myself.

Sandra, who was interested in pursuing a career in pediatrics, enrolled in an optional honors biology course. She wanted to take the course, but her experiences in the classroom and her negative perceptions of the teacher's personality discouraged her. Apathy toward the class and the teacher became evident, and although she tried to drop this optional course, she was not allowed to. Sandra explained:

> I just took it because I wanted to take it. So far I got two Fs. I'm doing so crappy . . . [I'm] failing the class because I am bored to death and just not interested and the work is kind of hard. If something bores me, I just don't get interested in the class. A little encouragement will help but nothing [is given]. I need feedback. If he is not interested in me and my work that's the way I am going to be to him, too. I'm not going to do my work. He is just nothing, nobody important to me.

Marwin also expressed disappointment with some of his teachers' styles. He enjoyed cooperative work and open class discussions, but disliked lectures and various unsuccessful experiences such as in his geology class:

> He doesn't do nothing. He makes us watch movies all the time. I mean, movies are good to watch but it's like we are not learning nothing. He gives us dittos, and we watch a movie while we look at the dittos. I tried to get out but they said that they couldn't get me out. This is the class that I used to cut a lot.

Few options for talent development and no gifted programs were available for these students in their high school. In addition, efforts to provide enriching and motivating learning experiences within the regular curriculum were negligible according to these informants. Provisions for students in the regular classroom were at the discretion of already overloaded teachers. Under these circumstances, the individualization needed by these students was seldom provided. Learning seldom focused on students' strengths, and their abilities and talents continued to be neglected often because honors classes had been eliminated and all achievement levels had to be addressed in the same class. Sandra articulated this problem as follows:

> They can't challenge your talents. They sometimes put honors, academics, and general people in the same class so the teacher has to reteach certain things. That is not right because it slows down the people who are faster. If not, the teacher would be like "Oh, since you are faster, you guys can work on your own," but sometimes we can't do that. They might be hoping that general students will advance but what about us?

Personal, family, and community experiences. To complicate the picture, several out-of-school factors such as personal, family, and community difficulties related in a variety of ways to result in negative influences on the students' willingness to persevere and endure difficult times. These problems generated internal turmoil which further drained students' energies and affected their academic performance. For instance, age-appropriate, adolescent concerns occupied students' minds. Adolescence is a crucial transitional period in the physical, emotional, and intellectual development of all children. Students experienced new physiological needs, especially concerns about their physical appearance, image, and sexuality.

Regarding their emotional development or psychosocial needs, informants confronted issues such as independence or autonomy, pride in oneself, and acceptance of peers, especially during the first years of high school. During this time, participants engaged in keen self-reflection, aiming at self-awareness or the development of personal understandings. For instance, several dilemmas became evident for this particular group of students, including their struggle for independence while remaining connected to their families. Their ethnicity was also explored in encounters with discrimination or by a growing conflict between the home values and the values of the dominant society. Actually, some of the informants indicated feeling embarrassed about societal views of their ethnic group. Milton explained:

> People think they are better than you. I was with my friends in McDonald's. And there were people in there calling us "spics." They wanted us to leave. There were some dudes in there. They were a lot bigger than us, so we didn't fight. We left. I was embarrassed that people were calling me a "spic." A "spic" is like calling a Black person a "nigger."

Students' motivational difficulties to persevere in school were also affected by unsuccessful attempts to achieve (experience of failure) which damaged students' personal sense of efficacy and self-worth. Milton explained: "Look, I was working hard on a class, and I got a D. It made me feel bad. I mean, you feel low." Informants reported not only feeling lazy but also confused about their own level of ability and competence. They were uncertain about their capacity to compete with others and consistently said they were uncomfortable in competitive situations since they experience doubts about their capabilities to meet the demands of this type of situation. Milton, for instance, believed that his teachers and other people around him expected too much from him. He indicated that this situation put a lot of pressure on him, and made him wonder about his potential to fulfill those expectations.

Motivational barriers also arose because of difficulties in their families. For instance, when Sandra was in 10th grade, her sense of worth was so damaged by her family conflicts that she attempted suicide.

> I did it because I thought I was the cause to my family's problems. So I thought, yes, let me just get rid of myself and everybody will be happy. My mother will be happy and my mother won't be crying no more because of me, my mother won't be sick no more because of me. Also, because like if things would happen in my house, my father would

come to me, like, "Go calm your mother down." Like I would be the one that everybody will focus their attention on to keep the family together. It was too much pressure besides the fact that I was the only natural daughter. My mother would be like, "I gave birth to you." I'd say, "But I didn't ask to be born." It's like all that guilt. All of that just got to me.

Distressing community or social forces which fostered attitudes of resistance and defensiveness among the students also influenced their moods and daily actions. The participants in this study used ineffective coping strategies, including withdrawal through intensive and extensive reading for pleasure, disruptive behavior, procrastination, reaffirmation of street life, and attempted suicide by one of the informants. In many instances, these coping strategies protected student's perceived sense of self, which in turn, diminished the level of threat or dissonance being experienced. Rose Marie procrastinated in her school work. At the beginning, putting school work off provided immediate relief for Rose Marie, but as time passed, it became a powerful source of pressure and stress which further negatively affected her academic performance. Rose Marie compared her school work with her running experience. The first marking period (first lap) went smoothly for Rose Marie, but when classes started to be more demanding during the second marking period (second lap), she started putting school work off. By the third marking period (third lap), she was extremely behind on her school work and feeling overwhelmed and anxious about her academic status. Finally, during the fourth marking period (last lap), she made a frenzied effort to catch up on her school work, leaving her exhausted and sometimes unable to keep up:

> The first lap is okay. The second lap I start to feel short of breath. The third lap, it kills me. So I have to pick it up on the third lap. My coach yells at me "Pick it up, pick it up." I feel so guilty! And then the last lap is the best lap. Even if I feel awful, I go and finish it up. Can you see any similarity with my school work?

DISCUSSION

The results of this study provide a better understanding of the nature of underachievement as experienced by six talented students of Puerto Rican descent. No other study addressing this student population and the phenomenon of underachievement has been published. The results of this investigation also enhance previous work on the causes and processes underlying academic underachievement by clarifying the dimensions and multiplicity of factors relevant to the phenomenon of underachievement among a small group of talented students of Puerto Rican descent.

This investigation revealed that the factors involved in the academic underachievement of six talented students of Puerto Rican descent are similar to the reasons for underachievement among talented Anglo and African American students. However, specific cultural factors increased the complexity of the issues. For instance, in terms of family factors, this investigation reveals that talented but underachieving students of Puerto Rican descent often experience strained relationships with parents or siblings and an unhappy home climate. Minimal parental academic guidance or support, inconsistent parental monitoring of students' achievement-oriented activities at home, and inappropriate parental expectations also contribute to the underachievement of the participants of this investigation. Conflicting family relationships have also been mentioned in the literature as a contributor to the underachievement of gifted students from several cultural, linguistic, racial, and ethnic backgrounds. Clark (1983) indicated that conflict between family members occurs frequently for low achieving African American students. Other researchers such as Whitmore (1980) and Rimm (1984) have also identified poor parent-child relationships and unhappy home climates as contributors to the underachievement of talented Anglo students. However, the specific causal conditions for the conflicting family relationships are unique for each student and play a major role in determining the degree of impact upon student academic achievement. In this respect, incongruent family, cultural, and student values and beliefs may exacerbate the problem. For example, conflicting points of view between students and parents emerged in relation to Puerto Rican traditional cultural values regarding interdependence versus independence, "respeto" (respect) toward parental authority, and conceptions of virginity and appropriate dating practices, especially for females. These incongruent experiences (inconsistency in living in different cultural worlds) often arose as part of the students' bicultural development.

Minimal parental academic guidance or support, inconsistent parental monitoring of students' achievement-oriented activities at home, and inappropriate parental expectations have also been identified as contributors to the low achievement of gifted as well as non-gifted students (Clark, 1983; Rimm & Lowe, 1988; Whitmore, 1980). According to Dornbusch, Elworth, and Ritter (1989), appropriate academic encouragement helps develop internal motivation and improves academic performance. The parents of the participants expressed concern about their children's academic life, but felt helpless about their ability to contribute academic guidance and support. They encouraged their children to do well in school but their own limited academic background and knowledge of resources impeded the provision of further academic guidance or support. Under these circumstances, school support became even more important, and, if academic support was not provided either at home or at school, students faltered.

Five major school and classroom factors negatively influenced the academic performance of the students in this investigation. A lack of early exposure to appropriate academic or curricular experiences, an absence of opportunities to develop or improve a school work discipline, negative interactions with teachers, an unrewarding curriculum, and questionable counseling experiences constrain students' paths to success. Early identification and provision of appropriate educational services played a crucial role in the student's development of his or her high abilities. Unfortunately, schools frequently use inappropriate screening, identification, and selection procedures, especially when assessing students from diverse cultural, linguistic, and ethnic backgrounds. For these six talented students of Puerto Rican descent, the absence of early identification meant an unconscious or conscious denial of access to supportive experiences that would have enabled them not only to explore and nurture their high potential but also to procure overall better life conditions. Both early identification and access to appropriate learning and schooling experiences could be critical factors in counteracting a history of educational barriers (discrimination, low achievement and educational attainment levels) and economic exploitation.

These students and many other talented students in the United States describe their schooling experiences as boring, unrewarding in terms of personal meaning and interests, and unsatisfactory, leading them to experience other motivational difficulties which later foster low achievement levels. For instance, Colangelo, Kerr, Christensen, and Maxey (1993) found that White young males from affluent families who were underachieving in school were dissatisfied with their high school class instruction and guidance services. This investigation provides support for Ramsden, Martin, and Bowden's (1989) assertion that students in these circumstances only try to meet the minimal academic requirements. In addition, students do not experience a sense of excitement, nor intellectual engagement, in learning. Informants of this investigation also reported nonparticipation in extracurricular activities.

Certain educational practices also negatively affected underachieving students. For example, students who had lower than a C average were not allowed to enroll in sports or benefit from special summer programs in the school described in this study. In this aspect, Coleman (1995) and VanTassel-Baska (1989) found that participation in summer programs had motivational benefits for students. Once again, a rigid school policy denies these students access to opportunities to manage their underachievement. The absence of a qualitatively different or responsive educational context influenced these students' motivation to achieve academic excellence, reinforcing Alvarez's (1983) assertion that school is the major contributor to achievement among Puerto Rican children.

In terms of community or social factors, the participants in this investigation identified the hostile environment, including gang-related incidents, ethnic prejudice, and few opportunities for constructive entertainment, as a contributor to their academic underachievement. All the participants, except one, expressed a desire to escape from the city. Little research has addressed these specific concerns among academically talented students from diverse cultural backgrounds. In one recent study, Ford (1992) found similar social forces influencing the motivation and academic achievement of gifted African American students. In this study, peers and friends were perceived as having minimal influence on their academic lives. Only one informant indicated that her close friends supported or sustained her academic efforts. Nevertheless, having a small group of close or special friends was important to all the informants, primarily to satisfy their need for belonging.

Finally, regarding personal factors, insufficient perseverance, low sense of efficacy, and inappropriate coping strategies were identified as contributors to the underachievement of the talented students of Puerto Rican descent in this investigation. As mentioned before, these internal factors related to their learning experiences. Students' failure to succeed in school caused negative self judgments which subsequently influenced students' self perceptions of efficacy and competence. When students entered a cycle of these judgments, perceptions, and experiences, their motivation and academic performance were seriously restrained, leaving them vulnerable to external conditions, for example, an academic context that did not support their talents.

The findings of this investigation are similar to those of Willig, Harnisch, Hill, and Maehr (1983) who claimed that Hispanic students may experience some difficulty in recognizing their high abilities and talents. The participants of this investigation knew about their high abilities, but were not confident about the extent of their potential, and displayed a low sense of efficacy that further influenced their levels of perseverance and effort.

Stevenson, Chen, and Uttal (1990) concluded that something occurs after the elementary school years that destroys some children's enthusiasm and opportunities to succeed in high school and college. The findings of this investigation suggest that for the six talented students of Puerto Rican descent, the onset of underachievement or low achievement occurs earlier, in elementary grades. However, the visible manifestations of students' academic underachievement did not become evident until later in elementary school or even during middle or high school. For the participants of this investigation, underachievement was not a sudden phenomenon, but an ongoing process with various dimensions depending upon interactive situational variables. Their academic underachievement varied in intensity and behavioral manifestations.

Implications

To help talented students of Puerto Rican descent to develop their potential and lead them to fruitful lives, certain issues must be addressed. The results of this investigation indicate that to prevent or diminish the onset of academic underachievement among talented students of Puerto Rican descent, preventive and intervention efforts must be taken early on at the early childhood and elementary levels. Proactive measures must be emphasized. Educators, practitioners, administrators, and the public in general must recognize the existence of talented students of Puerto Rican descent despite the negative stereotypes of intellectual inferiority, low achievement, and laziness about Puerto Rican individuals that may exist. Furthermore, educators, counselors, administrators, parents, and community members must acknowledge that they play a crucial role in these students' academic development. Suitable educational provisions as well as genuine emotional and affective support must be available to these students. For these purposes, it is necessary to:

1. Provide staff development addressing issues related to the identification of talent potential in young children of Puerto Rican descent; to the design and provision of a high-end learning environment that not only provides challenging learning experiences but also attends to the affective needs of the students; and to the identification, prevention, or management of academic underachievement.

2. Develop comprehensive procedures for the screening, selection, and identification of talent potential among young students of Puerto Rican descent.

3. Provide relevant educational alternatives such as curriculum compacting, learning enrichment, individual learning, personal projects, gifted programs, and magnet schools capable of meeting the students' academic needs.

4. Incorporate alternative learning strategies (how to learn and study) in the curriculum. Opportunities to acquire learning and study strategies should be also offered through alternative means to students in need.

5. Have a talent development specialist available in schools. This person can serve as an advocate for talented students and a resource for teachers, counselors, and administrators.

6. Encourage guidance counselors to take immediate actions in the presence of not only underachievement among academically talented students but any student. Counselors are usually in a good position to access students' records and should, therefore, be able to identify patterns of underachievement. Counselors must pay careful attention to talented underachieving students to help them understand their problems, identify effective strategies to attain change in problematic areas, and locate other means for further help.

7. Provide opportunities for parental education about gifted education issues such as identification, nurturance, as well as academic and emotional support.

8. Establish significant partnerships with community, especially youth organizations. These partnerships, whether academically related or not, may provide opportunities for personal, social, and academic growth. Participation in out of school activities which attend to students' interests may not only sustain students' motivation to engage in learning experiences but also help them use their time more positively and creatively.

Intervention efforts must be introduced as soon as initial symptoms of underachievement emerge and must concentrate on helping students overcome the stumbling blocks in their way to high academic achievement. Since the causes of underachievement vary for each student, intervention should be individualized. Intervention efforts may include modifications in teaching practices; provision of special services such as counseling, tutoring and mentorships; and instruction on how to develop effective work habits.

All of the above have the potential to improve academic outcomes by changing students' self and environmental conditions which in turn will influence students' perceptions or meanings. Acknowledgment of students' interpretations and needs will facilitate the creation of more appropriate contexts for learning and achievement.

Limitations and Recommendations for Further Research

Although this investigation contributes to our understanding of underachievement, limitations preclude adequate identification of causal relationships and generalization to other groups of students. Results should not be applied to all Puerto Ricans or other Hispanics as if they are homogeneous groups. Nevertheless, the results of this investigation suggest that the proposed multidimensional model may be helpful in understanding the process of academic underachievement among talented students of Puerto Rican descent. These results are also expected to serve as a foundation for future development in this area. For instance, further investigation of other areas such as the construct of resilience in multi-ethnic and English language learners, and the influences of ethnicity, generational status, gender, class, and race are needed. Also, a study of these issues from the perspective of the politics of education, including deeper philosophical, cultural, political, and economic factors would be invaluable. In addition, a longitudinal study will advance expanding knowledge of these issues. This investigation offers insights into the factors contributing to the academic underachievement of six talented students of Puerto Rican descent. These insights represent new knowledge which can be used to develop working hypotheses.

REFERENCES

Abraham, W. (1981). Recognizing the gifted child. In B. S. Miller & M. Price (Eds.), *The gifted child, the family, and the community* (pp. 24–26). New York: Walker.

Alvarez, M. D. (1983). *Puerto Ricans and academic achievement: An explanatory study of person, home and school variables among high-risk bilingual first graders.* Unpublished doctoral dissertation, New York University, New York.

Alvarez, M. D. (1992a). Puerto Rican children on the mainland: Current perspectives. In A. N. Ambert & M. D. Alvarez (Eds.), *Puerto Rican children on the mainland: Interdisciplinary perspectives* (pp. 3–15). New York: Garland Publishing.

Alvarez, M. D. (1992b). Promoting the academic growth of Puerto Rican children. In A. N. Ambert & M. D. Alvarez (Eds.), *Puerto Rican children on the mainland: Interdisciplinary perspectives* (pp. 135–166). New York: Garland Publishing.

Bandura, A. (1988). Human agency in social cognitive theory. *American Psychologist, 44*(9), 1175–1184.

Bar-Tal, D. (1978). Attributional analysis of achievement-related behavior. *Review of Educational Research, 48*(2), 259–271.

Bogden, R. C., & Biklen, S. K. (1982). *Qualitative research for education: An introduction to theory and methods.* Boston, MA: Allyn & Bacon.

Bricklin, B., & Bricklin, P. M. (1967). *Bright child-poor grades: The psychology of under-achievement.* New York: Delacorte.

Clark, B. (1983). *Growing up gifted: Developing the potential of children at home and at school* (2nd ed.). Columbus, OH: Charles E. Merrill.

Clark, B. (1988). *Growing up gifted: Developing the potential of children at home and at school* (3rd ed.). Columbus, OH: Charles E. Merrill.

Colangelo, N. B., Kerr, B., Christensen, P., & Maxey, J. (1993). A comparison of gifted underachievers and gifted high achievers. *Gifted Child Quarterly, 37*(4), 155–160.

Coleman, L. J. (1995). The power of specialized educational environments in the development of giftedness: The need for research on social context. *Gifted Child Quarterly, 39*(3), 171–176.

Coleman, J., Campbell, E., Hobson, C., McPartland, J., Mood, A., Weinfeld, F., & York, R. (1966). *Equality of educational opportunity.* Washington, DC: Government Printing Office.

Delisle, J. (1992). *Guiding the social and emotional development of gifted youth: A practical guide for educators and counselors.* New York: Longman.

Delisle, J., & Berger, S. L. (1990). *Underachieving gifted students.* Virginia: The Council for Exceptional Children.

Díaz, E. I. (1994). *Underachievement among high ability Puerto Rican high school students: Perceptions of their life experiences.* Unpublished doctoral dissertation, Pennsylvania State University, University Park.

Dirkes, M. A. (1985). Anxiety in the gifted: Pluses and minuses. *Roeper Review, 8*(1), 13–15.

Dornbusch, S. M., Elworth, J. T., & Ritter, P. L. (1989). *Parental reaction to grades: A field test of over-justification approach.* Unpublished manuscript.

Fine, B. (1967). *Underachievers: How they can be helped.* New York: E. P. Dutton.

Fliegler, L. A. (1957). Understanding the underachieving gifted child. *Psychological Reports, 3*(4), 533–536.

Ford, D. Y. (1992). Determinants of underachievement as perceived by gifted, above-average and average Black students. *Roeper Review, 14*(3), 130–136.

Gallagher, J. (1985). *Teaching the gifted child* (2nd ed.). Boston, MA: Allyn & Bacon.

Goetz, J. P., & LeCompte, M. D. (1984). *Ethnography and qualitative design in educational research.* Orlando, FL: Academic Press.

Hine, C. (1991). *The home environment of gifted Puerto Rican children: Family factors which support high achievement.* Unpublished doctoral dissertation, University of Connecticut, Storrs.

Kerry, T, (1981). *Teaching bright pupils in mixed ability classes.* London: Macmillan.

Kessler, J. W. (1963). My son, the underachiever. *PTA Magazine, 58*, 12–14.

Losoney, L. (1977). *Turning people on: How to be an encouraging person.* Englewood Cliffs, NJ: Prentice-Hall.

McCall, R., Evahn, C., & Kratzer, L. (1992). *High school underachievers: What do they achieve as adults?* Newbury Park, CA: SAGE Publications.

Meléndez, D. (1986). Hispanic students: Still not achieving. *Thrust, 15*(4), 14–16.

Miller, L. M. (1961). *Guidance for the underachiever with superior ability.* Washington, DC: U.S. Government Printing Office. (No. DHEW Publication No. OE-25021)

National Center for Education Statistics. (1992). *Language characteristics and academic achievement: A look at Asian and Hispanic eighth graders in NELS 88.* Washington, DC: Author.

National Commission on Excellence in Education. (1984). *A nation at risk: The imperative for educational reform.* Washington, DC: U.S. Government Printing Office.

National Puerto Rican Coalition. (1992). *Policy brief: Puerto Rican poverty.* Washington, DC: Author.

Pallas, A. M., Natriello, G., & McDill, E. L. (1988, April). *Who falls behind? Defining the at-risk population: Current dimensions and future trends.* Paper presented at the American Educational Research Association, New Orleans, LA.

Passow, A. H. (1986). *Educating the disadvantaged: The task school districts face.* (EPIC Document Reproduction Service No. ED 267 138).

Pecaut, L. S. (1979). *Understanding and influencing student motivation.* Glenn Ellyn, IL: Institute for Motivational Development.

Pendarvis, E. D., Howley, A. A., & Howley, C. B. (1990). *The abilities of gifted children.* Englewood Cliffs, NJ: Prentice-Hall.

Pirozzo, R. (1982). Gifted underachievers. *Roeper Review, 4*(4), 18–21.

Ramsden, P., Martin, E., & Bowden, J. A. (1989). School environment and sixth form pupils' approaches to learning. *British Journal of Educational Psychology, 59*(2), 129–142.

Redding, R. E. (1990). Learning preferences and skill patterns among underachieving gifted adolescents. *Gifted Child Quarterly, 34*(2), 72–75.

Richert, E. S. (1991). Patterns of underachievement among gifted students. In M. Bireley & J. Genshaft (Eds.), *Understanding the gifted adolescent: Educational, developmental, and multicultural issues* (pp. 139–162). New York: Teachers College Press.

Rimm, S. B. (1984). Underachievement . . . or if God had meant gifted children to run our homes, she would have created them bigger. *Gifted Child Today, 31*, 26–29.

Rimm, S. B. (1986). *Underachievement syndrome: Causes and cures.* Watertown, WI: Apple Publishing Company.

Rimm, S, B. (1991). Underachievement and superachievement: Flipsides of the same psychological coin. In N. Colangelo & G. Davis (Eds.), *Handbook of gifted education* (pp. 328–344). Boston, MA: Allyn & Bacon.

Rimm, S., & Lowe, B. (1988). Family environments of underachieving gifted students. *Gifted Child Quarterly, 32*(4), 353–359.

Roth, R. M. (1970). *Underachieving gifted students and guidance.* Boston, MA: Houghton Mifflin.

Roth, R. M., & Purl, P. (1967). Direction of aggression and the nonachievement syndrome. *Journal of Counseling Psychology, 14*(3), 277–281.

Runyan, W. M. (1982). *Life histories and psychobiography.* New York: Oxford University Press.

Sanjek, R. (1990). A vocabulary for fieldnotes. In R. Sanjek (Ed.), *Fieldnotes: The makings of anthropology* (pp. 92–121). New York: Cornell University Press.

Sekuler, R., & Blake, R. (1985). *Perception.* New York: Alfred A. Knopf.

Shaw, M. C., & McCuen, J. T. (1960). The onset of academic underachievement in bright children. *Journal of Educational Psychology, 51*(3), 103–108.

Soto, L. D. (1986). *The relationship between the home environment and intrinsic versus extrinsic orientation of fifth and sixth grade Puerto Rican children.* Unpublished doctoral dissertation, Pennsylvania State University, University Park.

Stevenson, H. W., Chen, C., & Uttal, D. H. (1990). Beliefs and achievement: A study of Black, White and Hispanic children. *Child Development, 61*(4), 508–523.

Strauss, A. L. (1987). *Qualitative analysis for social scientists.* New York: Cambridge University Press.

Strauss, A. L., & Corbin, J. (1990). *Basics of qualitative research, grounded theory procedures and techniques.* Newbury Park, CA: Sage Publications.

Supplee, P. L. (1990). *Reaching the gifted underachiever: Program strategy and design.* New York: Teachers College Press.

U.S. Bureau of the Census. (1995, September). *Statistical abstract of the United States: The national data book* (115th ed.). Washington, DC: U.S. Government Printing Office.

VanTassel-Baska, J. (1989). The role of family in the success of disadvantaged gifted learners. *Journal for the Education of the Gifted, 13*(1), 22–36.

Walsh, C. E. (1991). *Pedagogy and the struggle for voice: Issues of language, power and schooling for Puerto Ricans.* New York: Bergin & Garvey.

Whitmore, J. R. (1980). *Giftedness, conflict, and underachievement.* Boston, MA: Allyn & Bacon.

Willig, A. C., Harnisch, D. L., Hill, K. T., & Maehr, M. L. (1983). Sociocultural and educational correlates of success-failure attributions and evaluation anxiety in the school setting for Black, Hispanic, and Anglo children. *American Educational Research Journal, 20*(3), 385–410.

Zilli, M. G. (1971). Reasons why the gifted adolescent underachieves and some of implications of guidance and counseling to this problem. *Gifted Child Quarterly, 15*(2), 279–292.

10

Economically Disadvantaged Students in a School for the Academically Gifted: A Postpositivist Inquiry into Individual and Family Adjustment

James H. Borland

Rachel Schnur

Lisa Wright

Teachers College, Columbia University

In this paper, we report the results of an inquiry into the effects of the placement of five economically disadvantaged minority students from

Editor's Note: From Borland, J. H., Schnur, R., & Wright, L. (2000). Economically disadvantaged students in a school for the academically gifted: A postpositivist inquiry into individual and family adjustment. *Gifted Child Quarterly*, 44(1), 13-32. © 2000 National Association for Gifted Children. Reprinted with permission.

central Harlem, who were identified in kindergarten as potentially academically gifted through nontraditional means, in a school for gifted students. Achievement and aptitude test data and qualitative data collected during the students' first year at the school support the conclusion that the students were appropriately placed and adjusted well academically, socially and emotionally. Follow-up data suggest that the students' academic careers have, in the six years since the original data were collected, for the most part progressed well. We present assertions that begin to explain why these students have succeeded academically despite being at-risk for educational disadvantage. These assertions concern the students themselves, their families, their school, and Project Synergy, through whose activities the students were identified as potentially gifted.

BACKGROUND OF THE PROBLEM

The underrepresentation of economically disadvantaged children and adolescents—especially those from racial and ethnic minority groups—in programs for gifted students is one of the most recalcitrant and troubling issues confronting educators of gifted students (see, for example, Borland & Wright, 1994; Office of Educational Research and Improvement, 1993). Although a review of the literature (e.g., Kearney & LeBlanc, 1993; Passow; 1989; Richert, 1987; VanTassel-Baska, Patton, & Prillaman, 1989) reveals a long-standing awareness of and concern over this issue within the field, its urgency and seriousness have been underscored in recent years by a renewed emphasis on equity in education, spurred in part by various movements to reform and restructure American education.

Putting the Research to Use

The underrepresentation of economically disadvantaged students, especially students who are members of racial and ethnic minorities, has been a persistent problem in the field of gifted education. This article reports on research that attempted to determine which factors contributed to the success of the placement in a school of gifted students of five inner-city African-American and Hispanic students identified as potentially gifted through nontraditional means.

One clear lesson of this investigation is that the potential for academic giftedness can be identified, nurtured, and helped to blossom in all groups and schools in our society. Innovative identification methods are required (see Borland & Wright, 1994), and some form of what we call a *transitional services* curriculum is needed to bridge the gap between potential and actual giftedness. Careful attention to placements is also essential in making the fit between students and the receiving school optimal and successful.

Probably most salient in this study is the role of the family. Interpreted in light of Ogbu's work on voluntary and involuntary minorities and caste (e.g., 1992), the findings related to the importance of family support for education suggest significant implications for gifted education. As educators, we need to understand the role the family plays in the realization of giftedness in children from traditionally underrepresented groups in our society, to understand some of the dynamics explicated by such researchers and theorists as Ogbu (e.g., 1992) and Fordham (e.g., 1988), and, armed with this knowledge, to provide whatever support we can for children and families.

Correlates of Educational Disadvantage

The problem of restricted educational opportunities and lower educational attainment among economically disadvantaged minority students relative to middle-class White students is, of course, not unique to the field of the education of the gifted. It is part of a larger national tragedy that, in the words of Natriello, McDill, and Pallas (1990), is "the result of long-term conditions that are not susceptible to short-term solutions" (p. 1). Natriello et al. listed five "key indicators associated with the educationally disadvantaged . . . correlated with poor performance in school" (p. 16). These are (a) being Black or Latino, (b) living in poverty, (c) living in a single-parent family, (d) having a poorly educated mother, and (e) having limited English proficiency. Considering that these conditions are part of the lives of an increasing number of children in this country, it becomes clear that the subtitle of the Natriello et al.'s book, *Racing Against Catastrophe*, is anything but hyperbole.

A Cultural-Ecological Perspective

Knowing that certain life conditions are correlated with educational disadvantage is informative, but not explanatory. In order to address the problem of disproportionate educational failure among economically disadvantaged students more effectively, we need to identify the sociological and psychological processes that shape the attitudes and behaviors underlying educational disadvantage and to understand how these develop and operate within specific sociocultural contexts. The work of the anthropologist John Ogbu (e.g., 1978, 1985, 1992) is useful in providing a framework for investigating the causes and mechanisms of educational disadvantage. What follows is a brief discussion of some ideas.

Voluntary and involuntary minorities. Since economic and educational disadvantage is visited disproportionately upon racial and ethnic minorities, understanding the nature and effects of minority status is essential to addressing its educational consequences. To this end, Ogbu makes a distinction between voluntary minorities, who come to this country by choice to seek economic opportunity or greater political freedom, and involuntary minorities, such as African Americans, who were originally brought to this country against their will, denied assimilation into the mainstream, and relegated largely to menial occupations.

Primary and secondary cultural differences. Although voluntary-minority children may initially experience school difficulties, they do not typically fail generation after generation as many involuntary-minority children do. Ogbu attributes some of this discrepancy in school success to the different ways the two groups differ from the cultural mainstream. According to Ogbu, voluntary minorities experience *primary cultural differences*—differences in language, religious practice, dress, child rearing—that existed before they came to the United States. These cause educational difficulties at first, but the problems rarely persist because voluntary minorities see primary cultural differences as barriers to overcome in order to adapt to and assimilate into the mainstream culture and achieve the goals that motivated their immigration in the first place. Maintaining these differences is contrary, not essential, to their identity and sense of self-worth.

Involuntary minorities experience primary cultural differences, but also what Ogbu called *secondary cultural differences*, which arise after arrival in this country when "members of a given population beg[i]n to participate in an institution controlled by members of another population, such as the schools controlled by the dominant group" (1992, p. 8). Secondary cultural differences arise in reaction to negative contacts with the dominant culture and serve as "coping mechanisms under 'oppressive conditions'" (Ogbu, 1992, p. 10). Whereas voluntary minorities see primary cultural differences as barriers to assimilation that must be overcome, involuntary minorities see secondary cultural differences as protectors of their very identity and "have no strong incentives to give up these differences as long as they believe they are still oppressed" (Ogbu, 1992, p. 10).

Cultural inversion. One possible form secondary cultural differences can take is cultural inversion, "the tendency . . . to regard certain forms of behavior, events, symbols, and meanings as inappropriate . . . because these are characteristic of White Americans" (Ogbu, 1992, p. 8). In response to oppression and denial of opportunities to assimilate into the mainstream culture, involuntary minorities may develop a subgroup identity based on values, attitudes, and behaviors that are directly oppositional to that of the White culture. Once this occurs, socializing children involves teaching behaviors and values discrepant from those of the mainstream culture, and sanctions are often applied to those who appear to embrace the values and behaviors perceived as being part of the mainstream culture, such as employing standard English or striving for academic achievement.

Socialization and caste. Ogbu (e.g., 1978, 1985) has argued that involuntary minorities occupy the lowest stratum of a caste system that grants them little chance for upward mobility. Inferior positions in the caste system require little education, and the rigidity of the system is maintained by disproportionately meager rewards for involuntary minorities who do acquire an education.

This leads to Ogbu's analysis of the so-called *failure-of-socialization* hypothesis. This hypothesis, with which Ogbu takes issue, represents an attempt to explain the disproportionate educational failure rate among involuntary-minority children by asserting that their parents socialize them less effectively than middle-class parents socialize their children, with the result being that these children become indifferent to and unlikely to achieve academic success. Ogbu challenged this hypothesis, arguing that the real difference is in the *content* or *objective*, not in the *manner*, of socialization. Writing about African-American involuntary minorities, Ogbu stated that, "black children's school behavior is not just a spillover of adult adjustive behavior; *it is a part of the training of black children for their survival in the American caste system*" (1985, p. 372). Further, he wrote,

> We should not expect blacks and whites to have the same socialization practices and experiences, because they are not being prepared for roles requiring the same kinds of competence. . . . When blacks differ from whites in . . . skills it is probably because their status positions require variant forms of the skills in question, not because parents have failed in their socialization duty. (1985, p. 374)

In other words, the fact that many involuntary-minority children do not appear to be socialized for success in the educational system does not imply a failure by their parents to prepare them for their roles in society. Just the opposite is the case: Considering their limited horizons and the rigidity of the caste system, these children are being socialized realistically for the future that awaits them. This, Ogbu has argued, is *successful*, not failed, socialization.

The impact on students' school attitudes and behavior is predictable. Nearly all children find certain aspects of schooling to be meaningless and boring. However, White children and children from voluntary-minority groups are socialized to endure the school routine because their parents know that real benefits can accrue to them if they do so. Ogbu believes that, for involuntary-minority children, however, there is likely to be little or no reward for brooking the tedium of the classroom, a fact not lost on parents who realistically instruct their children in the development of other, more adaptive skills.

The burden of acting White. This creates a dilemma for potentially gifted involuntary-minority students, which Fordham (1988, 1991; Fordham & Ogbu, 1986) referred to as the "burden of acting white."

Learning school curriculum and learning to follow the standard academic practices of the school are often equated by the minorities with . . . "acting white" while simultaneously giving up acting like a minority person. School learning is therefore consciously or unconsciously perceived as a subtractive process: a minority person who learns successfully in school or who follows the standard practices of the school is perceived as becoming acculturated into the white American frame of reference at the expense of the minorities' cultural frame of reference and collective welfare. (Fordham & Ogbu, 1986, pp. 182–183)

The quandary faced by gifted students from involuntary-minority groups can be a painful one: either adopt attitudes and behaviors that, although facilitative of school success, serve to alienate one from friends and culture, or maintain loyalty to friends and culture by sacrificing one's prospects for academic and vocational success. This is no small matter. Those who attempt to cross cultural boundaries may experience what Fordham and Ogbu (1986), borrowing from DeVos (1967), called "affective dissonance," the feeling that "they are . . . betraying their group and its cause" (p. 182; see also Fordham, 1988, 1991; Mickelson, 1990).

Research by Ford (1992, 1993, 1996) suggests that this is a significant problem for some bright involuntary-minority students. In her sample of 148 African-American fifth and sixth graders identified as gifted, above-average, or average in academic ability, 97 "reported exerting low levels of effort in school" (1992, p. 134). This included 38 of the 48 gifted students, despite the fact that this group endorsed what Ford called the "American achievement ideology."

Assimilation without accommodation. For involuntary-minority children both to succeed academically and to deal with the burden of acting White, they need more than what Ogbu (1992) called "primary strategies," such as positive academic attitudes, hard work, and perseverance that are essential for all academically successful students. Involuntary minority students must also adopt "secondary strategies," which "shield them from the peer pressures and other detracting forces of the community" (p. 11).

Some secondary strategies, such as emulation of Whites or "cultural passing," exact a significant psychological toll. Others, such as "encapsulation in peer group logic and activities . . . [refusing] to do the White man's thing or . . . [to] consider schooling important" (Ogbu, 1992, p. 11), come at the cost of wasted talent. More successful, with a smaller although not negligible price, is "accommodation without assimilation," adhering to school norms in school, but cultural norms at home and in the community. These secondary strategies, with respect to the goal of enabling involuntary-minority students to succeed academically, achieve various degrees of success at varying costs. Yet, under the conditions that obtain in this country today, Ogbu believes they are necessary for involuntary-minority students to achieve.

Ogbu's work suggests that there is a powerful array of forces, often misunderstood, that work to lower the academic achievement of involuntary-minority children. Fordham and Ogbu (1986), referring to African-American children, summarized these as follows:

> The low school performance of black children stems from the following factors: first, white people provide them with inferior schooling and treat them differently in school; second, by imposing a job ceiling, white people fail to reward them adequately for their educational accomplishments in adult life; and third, black Americans develop coping devices which further limit their striving for academic success. (p. 179)

Clearly, the underrepresentation of economically disadvantaged children, especially those from racial and ethnic minority groups, in programs for gifted students is a problem that, in Ford's (1992) words, is "complex and perplexing ... requiring movement away from traditional theories and paradigms, including those which hold that underachievement results only from a lack of motivation to achieve" (p. 134). Moreover, it is part of a larger problem—the failure of our educational system to educate economically disadvantaged and minority students—that is the product of persistent structural inequities in our society. For this reason, its amelioration is likely to be difficult and incremental. The research described in this paper derives from one such incremental approach.

Project Synergy

Project Synergy was a research and development project of the Department of Special Education and the Leta Hollingworth Center for the Study and Education of the Gifted at Teachers College, Columbia University. The project's goals were (a) to develop nontraditional ways to identify young, economically disadvantaged, potentially gifted students; (b) to work with identified children, their parents or guardians, and their teachers to encourage the development of the children's potential for academic giftedness; and (c) to secure appropriate academic placements for identified children. Working in P.S. 149/207 in central Harlem, and later in other schools, we identified, in each of six academic years starting in 1990–91, a cohort of 15 to 18 potentially academically gifted students. Few, perhaps none, would have been identified in schools that use traditional identification procedures.

Briefly, the identification process developed in Project Synergy is as follows (see Borland & Wright, 1994, for a more complete description of the identification process). Initial screening involved gathering data on all kindergarten students at P.S. 149/207 through observation of behavior in structured and free-play activities, open-ended teacher and parent referrals, draw-a-person tests scored for developmental levels of drawing, and curriculum-based assessment activities that yielded verbal and figural products. All data were placed in portfolios, one for each student, and, over the course of a two-day case-study meeting of the project team, about 40 of the 100 kindergartners were identified as possible candidates for services and placed in the candidate pool.

Students in the candidate pool then received individual assessment, including standardized measures such as the Peabody Picture Vocabulary Test (Dunn & Dunn, 1981), the Test of Early Mathematical Ability (Ginsburg & Baroody, 1990), and the Test of Early Reading Ability (Reid, Hresko, & Hammill, 1989). Nonstandardized assessment included dynamic assessment using a project-developed matrix task, a child interview, and an individualized curriculum-based assessment activity. A case-study approach carried out by the project team was then used to identify about 15 students who were invited to participate in project activities.

Once identified as potentially gifted, students attended "transitional services" classes in the summers following their kindergarten and first-grade years and on weekends during those academic years. The curriculum was diverse, but the primary emphasis was on developing basic skills in reading, writing, and mathematics; problem-solving skills; and positive school attitudes and behaviors. Workshops for parents and guardians were held concurrently with the transitional services classes. Again, the range of topics was broad, but the greatest emphasis was placed on helping parents understand the workings of the educational system and how to become effective advocates for their children. Near the end of the students' first-grade year, their progress was evaluated, and, in consultation with parents and guardians, appropriate placements for second grade were considered.

In September 1992, five students from the first Project Synergy cohort, who had been identified two years earlier in kindergarten as potentially academically gifted, entered the second grade of a New York City public school for gifted students[1]. The purpose of the inquiry reported here was to follow the students, their families, their classmates, and their teachers over the course of the students' first academic year in the school in order to determine whether the placements were successful. In addition, we sought to develop a set of assertions about the students' personal characteristics, their families, their school, and Project Synergy, that we hoped would begin to elucidate the factors that facilitated or frustrated the success of the students' placements. Our hope was that, by studying a small group of economically disadvantaged minority children who were both at-risk for educational disadvantage according to the criteria of Natriello et al. (1990) and potentially academically gifted according to the criteria of Project Synergy, we could gain some understanding of the complex web of psychosocial factors that affect such children's academic attainments.

The work of such researchers as Ogbu and Fordham has pointed toward an understanding of the forces that militate against academic success for economically disadvantaged involuntary-minority children. Ford's research has demonstrated how widespread the underachievement among gifted African-American students may be, and it has explored some of the causes and sequelae of this underachievement. We hope the present research will add to our understanding by shedding light on an instance where, as we ultimately concluded happened here, economically disadvantaged involuntary-minority students realize their potential for academic giftedness.

Table 1   Presence of "Disadvantaging Characteristics" That Contribute to Educational Disadvantage (Natriello et al., 1990) for the Five Students

"Disadvantaging Characteristic"	Darryl	Ramon	Child* Jenny	Rose	Chantal
Being Black or Latino/Latina	x	x	x	x	x
Living in poverty	x	x	x	x	x
Not living with both parents	x		x	x	x
Having a poorly educated mother				x	x
Having limited English proficiency		x**			

Note: *An X indicates the presence of the disadvantaging characteristic; **At the beginning of kindergarten

METHOD

Axiomatic and Methodological Base

This inquiry was, to a large extent, informed by the axioms and methods of postpositivist inquiry (Borland, 1990; Lincoln & Guba, 1985), although both qualitative and quantitative data were gathered. Our goal was to begin to understand the realities constructed by the students, their families, their classmates, and their teachers over the academic year. However, our strategy was opportunistic. To the extent that quantitative data and positivistic methods could assist us, we adopted them to help us determine whether the placements were successful and to provide a basis for triangulating the qualitative data that informed the assertions we developed. Moreover, we followed an emergent, rather than an a priori, design (Lincoln & Guba).

The Students and Their Families

The five students described in this paper were second graders when this inquiry was undertaken. The children (whose names have been changed) are Darryl, an African-American boy; Ramon, a Latino boy whose family immigrated from Ecuador; Jenny, a girl of African-American, Native-American, and Latino ancestry; Rose, whose father is African American and whose mother is Latina; and Chantal, whose family is African American from the Virgin Islands. All, except Ramon, live with single mothers, and all are economically disadvantaged.

According to the indicators proposed by Natriello et al. (1990), the children as a group are at-risk for "educational disadvantage," as Table 1 indicates. Four of the five indicators are present for two children; three are present for the other three.

Settings

P.S. 149/207. The students were identified as potentially gifted as kindergartners at Public School 149/207 in central Harlem, New York City. P.S. 149/207 serves a student population that is three-quarters African American and one-quarter Latino; over 99% are economically disadvantaged. Life in the neighborhood presents daunting challenges for the children and their families. Drug use is widespread, barely stopping at the schoolhouse door. On one of our first visits, one of our project team mentally drew a semicircle with a 10-foot radius on the sidewalk in front of the school's front door; within that area he counted over 30 discarded crack vials.

At the time we identified the students in this study, P.S. 149/207 was a "School Under Registration Review," meaning that, owing to a history of low student achievement, the school's performance was being monitored by the state, and it was threatened with decertification. The gravity of the situation is reflected in the fact that, out of 625 public elementary schools in New York City, P.S. 149/207 ranked 617th with respect to scores on the Degrees of Reading Power Test in AY 1992–93, with only 14.1% of its students reading on grade level. However, as the principal and teachers insisted, and our experience confirmed, there are children at P.S. 149/207 with the potential for academic giftedness.

The Lab School. The students were placed in the New York City Laboratory School for Gifted Education, a school that was, for a number of reasons, suited to the needs of the children and families involved in Project Synergy. First, the school serves a population of high-ability children that is diverse, not only racially and ethnically, but socioeconomically as well, with a range that extends from children of upper-middle-class professionals to children from families on public assistance. Second, the school has an admission process that utilizes professional judgment and eschews inflexible cut-off scores on standardized tests. Although applicants must submit IQ test scores, other data, including information supplied by parents and preschool teachers, as well as direct observation of applicants, is used in the selection process, which involves a committee decision done on a case-study basis. Third, the school's curriculum and instruction are less focused on accelerated skill acquisition than is the case at most other schools for gifted students. Thus, it was felt that, although Project Synergy students would receive the skill work they need, they would not find themselves as far behind their classmates at the point of admission as they might in other schools for gifted students. Finally, the school's director welcomed the opportunity to participate in the project, which smoothed the entry of the children and their families into the school.

Procedures

Data gathering began in September 1992 and ended in May 1993, with informal follow-up interviews in January 1994 and September 1998. The research team[2] met weekly from September 1992 through June 1993 to develop the emerging design of the inquiry; discuss the data; develop, refine, and modify assertions; discuss relevant literature; and develop a plan for the report. Initial data gathering, which consisted of observations and some interviews, was exploratory and did not focus on particular issues other than the general one of the adaptation of the students and their families to the new school. Tentative assertions began to emerge around the midpoint of the academic year. We then began to consider ways to test the assertions. Thereafter, data were collected relative to the assertions as they emerged and changed, with the goal of testing their validity by searching for disconfirming evidence.

Data Sources

Observation. Observing students in various settings was the primary method used to gather data. Observations, in the form of running records and focused observations, began in September and continued through the academic year. We observed students in their self-contained classrooms and special classes, on the playground, in the cafeteria, and at Teachers College. We observed parents in parent conferences, at the school's "curriculum night," as they brought their children to school or picked them up, and at workshops at Teachers College. We observed classmates and teachers in the self-contained classrooms, in the cafeteria, and on the playground. The observations culminated in each child being "shadowed" by a different researcher for an entire school day in the spring.

Interviews and focus groups. Interviews with the students, parents, and teachers were conducted by the research team in an open-ended fashion in the fall of 1992 and following a structured format in May 1993. The fall 1992 interviews were held at the Lab School, and the spring 1993 interviews were held at Teachers College. The length of the interviews ranged from approximately 15 minutes (in the case of teachers, some of whom, owing to their schedules, needed to be seen more than once in both the fall and the spring) to over an hour (parent interviews were, on average, longer and more wide-ranging than the other interviews). The May interview schedules were developed with the aim of gathering information relative to the emerging assertions, although considerable latitude was given to the interviewers to follow any interesting or potentially fruitful paths the respondents' statements might suggest. Brief follow-up interviews with the students' third-grade teachers were held early in 1994. Parents were contacted by telephone in September 1998 to obtain information about the children's current placements.

Focus groups (Krueger, 1994) were held with the five students in the winter and again in the spring of 1993 (on the same day the individual interviews were conducted). Three additional focus groups were held with randomly selected classmates from the three classrooms into which the five students had been placed. Focus group sessions with Synergy students were about one hour in length; focus group sessions with their classmates ran for about half that time.

Sociometric data. Sociograms were constructed in the classrooms in October 1992 and again in May 1993.

Psychometric data. The Kaufman Test of Educational Achievement (KTEA) (Kaufman & Kaufman, 1985), an individual achievement test, and the Stanford-Binet IV (Thorndike, Hagen, & Sattler, 1986) were administered to the five identified students, the KTEA in January and February of 1993 and the Stanford-Binet in May 1993. One child, referred to here as Chantal, also was given the WISC-III (Wechsler, 1991) in June 1993 as part of a full psycho-educational assessment prompted by a suspicion that she had a learning disability.

Additional testing took place in May 1993. This included administration of (a) The Children's Personality Questionnaire (CPQ) (Porter & Cattell, 1975), a scale assessing 18 personality dimensions (14 first-order factors and 4 second-order factors); (b) depending on the child's age, either the Pictorial Scale of Perceived Competence and Social Acceptance for Young Children (Harter, 1985) or the Perceived Competence Scale for Children (Harter & Pike, 1983), self-esteem measures with four and six dimensions respectively; and (c) the Nowicki-Strickland Locus of Control Scale for Children (Nowicki & Strickland, 1973). As mentioned above, Chantal also received a full psycho-educational assessment at the Teachers College Child Study Center.

Numerous data had already been gathered before this investigation began as the students were being identified as potentially gifted in 1991 and over the next year and a half as they participated in transitional services classes. These consisted of observations, data from dynamic assessments, and standardized test data from the Peabody Picture Vocabulary Test (PPVT) (Dunn & Dunn, 1981), the Test of Early Mathematics Ability (TEMA) (Ginsburg & Baroody, 1990), and the Test of Early Reading Ability (TERA) (Reid, Hresko, & Hammill, 1989).

Data Analysis

Quantitative data were analyzed for descriptive and, in the case of Chantal, clinical purposes and were usually not aggregated. Qualitative data were analyzed according to an approximation of the constant comparative method (Glaser & Strauss, 1967), incorporating suggestions from Lincoln and Guba (1985). Throughout, as tentative assertions emerged and were modified, we formulated ways to gather information that might disconfirm the assertions. For example, once an assertion was suggested, we would discuss what statements might be made and behaviors observed if the assertion were actually false. We then searched for such disconfirming evidence in the data we had gathered to that point, and we developed questions for future interviews and focus groups and focused our remaining observations to see if disconfirming evidence could be generated. The absence of disconfirming evidence, or a very high ratio of confirming to disconfirming evidence, led us to accept an assertion.

RESULTS RELATED TO THE SUCCESS OF THE PLACEMENTS

The results will be presented in two parts. In this section, we will present data, largely quantitative, that support one of our major conclusions that the placements

Table 2   Percentile Ranks on the Subtests and Composites of the Kaufman Test of Educational Achievement for the Five Students

	Percentiles				
Subtest or Composite	Darryl	Ramon	Jenny	Rose	Chantal
Reading Decoding	99.0	99.7	98.0	90.0	5.0
Spelling	99.9	99.0	96.0	34.0	12.0
Reading Comprehension	99.0	96.0	87.0	45.0	4.0
Math Computation	98.0	66.0	66.0	13.0	9.0
Math Applications	91.0	37.0	45.0	47.0	37.0
Reading Composite	99.0	99.0	97.0	70.0	4.0
Math Composite	96.0	50.0	55.0	21.0	18.0
Battery Composite	99.6	98.0	94.0	47.0	5.0

were successful, academically and otherwise. In the next section, we will present assertions we developed in attempting to understand the factors that contributed to the successful placements, and we will provide some examples of the evidence we believe supports the assertions.

Academic Achievement

Table 2 presents the results of the Kaufman Test of Educational Achievement, which was administered at about the midpoint of the students' first year at the Lab School.

The KTEA results suggest satisfactory academic adjustment and progress, especially in light of the deficiencies in the students' previous schooling and the demands of adjusting to a school with much higher expectations and a high-achieving student body. The median KTEA Math Composite percentile for the five students was 50; the median Reading Composite percentile was 97. The total Battery Composite median percentile was 94, with three students above the 90th percentile, one above the 99th.

Of the remaining two students, one scored in the bottom quartile in mathematics,[3] although her reading composite was well above average. The fifth student, Chantal, scored in the bottom quartile in mathematics and extremely low in reading, consistent with our suspicion, which grew throughout the course of the year, that she had a learning disability.[4] It is interesting that the two students with the lowest scores on the KTEA, Rose and Chantal, were the two students who had four of the at-risk factors for educational disadvantage identified by Natriello et al. (1990).

General Ability

Table 3 shows the results from the Stanford-Binet IV and earlier PPVT results. All Binet composite IQs were above the population mean, three were at least one standard deviation above the mean, and one was more than two standard

Table 3   Subtest and Composite Scaled Scores on the Stanford-Binet Intelligence Scale (4th Ed.) and 1991 and 1992 Peabody Picture Vocabulary Test Standard Scores for the Five Students

Test ot Subtest	Scaled Scores				
	Darryl	Ramon	Jenny	Rose	Chantal
Stanford-Binet (M = 100, SD = 16)					
Verbal Reasoning	136	104	112	126	121
Visual Reasoning	137	130	104	105	103
Quantitative Reasoning	136	112	100	110	96
Short Term Memory	122	111	102	112	95
Test Composite	139	117	106	116	104
Peabody (M = 100, SD = 15)					
May 1991	102	40	87	105	95
April 1992	107	68	90	109	94

deviations above the mean. These scores are very encouraging in light of the students' PPVT scores from one and two years before and the fact that Binet IV scores tend to be significantly lower than Binet L-M scores for students who score in the upper range of the distribution (Silverman & Kearney, 1992). These results suggest that the students were appropriately placed in a school for academically gifted students that, because it has no IQ cut-off for admission and a diverse population, serves students whose IQs range over the top one-third of the IQ distribution.

Social Acceptance

Sociograms constructed in the fall and the spring indicated that, although none of these students was the most popular in his or her class, none was socially isolated. This was confirmed by observations, which revealed that the students played and associated freely with their classmates; by interviews with the students and their teachers; by the focus groups with the students' classmates; by the interviews with the students themselves; and by the students' scores on the Social Acceptance Subscale of the Perceived Competence Scale for Children.

Emotional Adjustment

Results of the Children's Personality Questionnaire were mostly within the average range on the 18 primary and second-order factors, including the Anxiety scale. An analysis of scores that fall more than one point outside the average range suggests that Ramon is somewhat distant and apprehensive; Jenny is accommodating and sensitive; Rose is detached and light-hearted; and

Chantal is both calm and tender-minded. Although they hardly capture the multidimensional complexity of the students, these profiles are consistent with our impressions.

Darryl's profile is the most intriguing in that (a) his scores fell outside our expanded average range on 7 of the 14 first-order factors, and (b) his profile is contradictory. To simplify, the pattern of scores incorporates calm, ingenuousness, self-assurance, and cooperation with what the CPQ manual refers to as "undisciplined self-conflict . . . follows own urges, careless of social rules" (Porter & Cattell, 1975, p. 10). Darryl is the student who has experienced the most academic success, which he naturally finds rewarding, and this may explain the scatter in his CPQ profile. As he was responding to the items, the tester had the impression that he was striving to provide the "correct answer," as opposed to the artless responses provided by the other students. It is possible that, in attempting to say what he thought we wanted to hear, Darryl responded in a way that made his profile meaningless if taken at face value. It is also possible that this profile truly reflects the emotional turmoil caused by "the burden of acting white" (Fordham, 1991) and the need to use secondary strategies for academic success (Ogbu, 1992). CPQ data are shown in Table 4.

On the Pictorial Scale of Perceived Competence and Social Acceptance for Young Children and the Perceived Competence Scale for Children, all scores were within the normal range (See Table 5). Of interest are the normal scores on the Scholastic Competence Subscale, the Social Acceptance Subscale, and the Global Self-Worth Subscale of the first measure (administered to Ramon, Jenny, and Chantal, who were slightly younger and whose ages matched the appropriate age range for this measure) and on the Cognitive Competence and Peer Acceptance Subscales of the second measure (administered to Darryl and Rose, who were slightly older and were too old for the Pictorial Scale).

The Nowicki-Strickland data are interesting in light of findings that under-achievers (Whitmore, 1980), including African-American underachievers (Ford, 1993), tend to have an external locus of control. Since this instrument is normed on students from grades 3 through 12, third-grade norms were used. Nowicki and Strickland (1973) reported that the third-grade means are 17.97 for males ($SD = 4.67$) and 17.38 for females ($SD = 3.06$), with lower scores reflecting an internal locus of control. Scores decrease more or less monotonically with age.

Darryl's score of 18 was at the mean for third-grade males, whereas Ramon's score of 15 was almost two-thirds of a standard deviation below the mean, indicating an internal orientation. Chantal's score of 23 was about 1.8 standard deviations above the mean for females, indicating a pronounced external orientation, whereas Jenny and Rose, each of whom scored 20, scored about 0.8 standard deviations above the mean for females, indicating a less pronounced external orientation.

There are clear sex differences within this small group, even allowing for sex-specific norms. Moreover, the two children with the most internal orientation had the highest composite achievement scores on the KTEA. These findings are highly tentative in light of the size of the sample, and there is a possibility

Table 4   Children's Personality Questionnaire Profiles of the Five Students

Dimension		Darryl	Ramon	Score* Jenny	Rose	Chantal
A:	Cool/Warm	5	3	5	2	6
B:	Concrete Thinking/Abstract Thinking	6	5	4	5	4
C:	Affected by feelings/Emotionally Stable	6	5	5	5	*8*
D:	Phlegmatic/Excitable	2	6	4	6	*3*
E:	Obedient/Dominant	2	6	2	7	5
F:	Sober/Enthusiastic	6	4	4	8	4
G:	Expedient/Conscientious	*8*	7	4	6	4
H:	Shy/Bold	6	7	4	6	5
I:	Tough-minded/Tender-minded	6	7	*10*	5	9
J:	Vigorous/Guarded	5	6	5	3	6
N:	Forthright/Shrewd	*1*	5	4	6	5
O:	Self-assured/Apprehensive	2	9	5	6	5
Q_3:	Undisciplined self-conflict/ Controlled	*8*	5	5	4	6
Q_4:	Relaxed/Tense	*3*	5	6	6	2
	Extroversion	5.0	4.1	4.5	5.7	5.1
	Anxiety	4.0	5.5	5.6	6.0	4.6
	Tough poise	4.8	6.0	4.3	6.7	4.7
	Independence	4.7	5.8	4.0	5.0	5.1

Scores of 5 and 6 are in the average range. Scores from 1 to 4 indicate a tendency toward the first descriptor in the dimension name (e.g., Cool), the lower the stronger. Scores from 7 to 10 indicate a tendency toward the second descriptor in the dimension name (e.g., Warm), the higher the stronger. Scores on the four second-order factors have the same range, with high scores indicating a tendency toward the named trait (e.g., Extraversion). Scores more than one point beyond the average range are in bold italics.

of a sex-achievement confound, despite the separate norms for boys and girls. At best, the data provide mild support for Ford's findings and suggest the possible value of more systematic investigations in this area.

Follow-up Data

1994 data. In February 1994, we returned briefly to the Lab School to speak with the students' third-grade teachers. That year, Darryl, Ramon, Jenny, and Rose were in the same classroom. According to their teacher, all were doing at least acceptable work, although Rose was a bit below the class average and Darryl, ordinarily the strongest student, was, in the teacher's view, "not living up to his potential." Chantal was, according to her teacher (who was Rose's teacher the previous year), showing "flashes of brilliance" and improvements in reading, although she was still below grade level in this area. She appeared to be stronger in mathematics.

The teachers also reported that the students were well integrated into the classroom socially. Jenny had strong leadership skills, her teacher said, and

Table 5   Scores on the Pictorial Scale of Perceived Competence and Social Acceptance for Young Children and the Perceived Competence Scale for Children for the Five Students

Score	Darryl*	Ramon**	Jenny**	Rose*	Chantal**
Cognitive Competence	4.00			3.83	
Peer Acceptance	3.17			3.83	
Physical Competence	3.83			3.17	
Maternal Acceptance	3.33			3.33	
Scholastic Competence		3.17	3.17		2.17
Social Acceptance		2.33	3.17		3.83
Athletic Competence		2.33	2.83		2.33
Physical Appearance		2.33	3.50		4.00
Behavioral Conduct		3.17	3.33		3.33
Global Self-Worth		3.67	4.00		3.50

Note. Scale 1–4: 1-negative, 4-positive; *Scores on the Pictorial Scale of Perceived Competence and Social Acceptance for Young Children; **Scores on the Perceived Competence Scale for Children

Rose was so social that it interfered with her schoolwork. Rose was also frequently late, and Chantal was absent more than most students, although she always returned with a note from her mother. The teachers viewed the children as emotionally stable. For the most part, these conversations confirmed our impressions from one year earlier.

1998 data. More than four years later, in October 1998, we gathered data on four of the children, who were now in eighth grade. We were unable to locate Rose, who had been the most transient of the group and who had lived with her mother for a while in a homeless shelter prior to her identification by Project Synergy.

Darryl attends, on full scholarship, a small, private, ethnically diverse school that has a commitment to working with able students. The headmistress of the school described him as "a solid kid, very motivated" who "works his heart out." In addition to being successful academically, Darryl is active in the school's sports program, plays in the brass band, and acts in school dramatic productions. He is applying to high schools, including boarding schools.

Chantal and Ramon attend the same parochial school in New York City. Although Chantal's reading is still merely "OK," according to the school's director, her mathematics achievement on standardized tests is above the 90th percentile nationally. Her Iowa Test of Basic Skills percentiles were 93 for mathematics computation, 80 for language usage, and 11 for spelling. The school's director reported that Chantal is popular with the other girls and has a circle of close friends. As she did while in Project Synergy, Chantal talks about a career in medicine.

Ramon was described by the director of his school as "one of the top eighth graders," a student with "a good attitude" a "solid customer." His academic performance was described as strong across all subjects. Like the others, Ramon is in the process of applying to high schools, and his school's director guessed that he would end up in one of the city's academically selective Catholic high schools.

Jenny attended the private school now attended by Darryl for one year and then transferred to an innovative public middle school with a science and technology focus. According to her mother, Jenny is doing "exceptionally well," an opinion supported by her attendance at a recent breakfast for honor roll students and their families. Jenny has a number of friends, takes after-school dance classes, and plays basketball. She aspires to one of the city's elite high schools and to a career in either medicine or law.

Summary

On the basis of the qualitative and quantitative data available to us, we conclude that the five students were well-placed in the Laboratory School for Gifted Education in that (a) they made better academic progress than could have been expected at their previous school, (b) they were integrated socially into the life of the school, and (c) they appeared to be experiencing no adverse emotional reactions to the new placement. In addition, during the interviews, each child reported being happier at the new school. Six years later, the four children whom we could locate were doing well academically and socially and had high educational and professional aspirations.

ASSERTIONS REGARDING FACTORS RELATED TO THE SUCCESS OF THE PLACEMENTS

Why did these students, who were at-risk for educational disadvantage and whose potential giftedness in kindergarten was discovered only through the use of nontraditional measures, develop academically and personally to the point where they could succeed in second-grade classrooms in a school for gifted students? On the basis of our inquiry, we have developed some assertions that we believe begin to answer this question. These concern the children themselves, their families, their school, and the intervention of Project Synergy, and together they begin to limn the interactions of psychosocial forces and systems that can, under favorable conditions, confound the prediction inherent in the label "at-risk."

Assertions Concerning the Students Themselves

Table 6 lists five assertions concerning the students themselves that we believe illuminate aspects of the students' make-up that have contributed to their success at the Lab School.

Assertion 1: The identification of the students as potentially gifted was valid. Support for this assertion is presented in the previous section.

Assertion 2: The students are goal-directed, aspire to success, see the instrumentality of academic achievement, and have age-appropriate understandings of the requirements for vocational success. The students endorse what Ford (1992) called the "American achievement ideology": they aspire to higher socioeconomic status and see education as a means to that end. This is contrary to the effects described by Ogbu (1978, 1985) of socialization for life in a caste system. Moreover, their concepts of what is required to achieve their goals are realistic and age-appropriate. Ramon wants to become a painter and, when asked what he would have to do to realize this ambition, he replied that he would have to work hard, do a lot of painting, and attend college. Chantal believes that to become a doctor, she has to go to medical school and "study hard."

Assertion 3: The students are emotionally stable and socially adept. Support for this assertion is presented in the previous section.

Assertion 4: The students see themselves as special. This, we suspect, is not the norm for children living in poverty in central Harlem who attend the New York City public schools. Darryl, for example, referred to his being special by virtue of giftedness deriving from a "power that goes . . . through my brain." Ramon, who appeared not to speak English when we first encountered him in a bilingual kindergarten classroom, and who therefore had one of the indicators of at-risk status for educational disadvantage listed by Natriello et al. (1990), asserted that he was special because he could speak two languages.

The girls responded that they knew they were special because of what their parents told them or did (which is consistent with their more external locus of control). Rose, however, also went on to describe herself as special as follows: "I'm sweet, I'm kind, I'm polite, and I always help somebody who is in trouble."

Assertion 5: The students are eldest, only, or "functional only" children. This assertion concerns the benefits of being the eldest, an only, or a "functional only child" (one whose next oldest sibling is at least seven years older). Darryl and Rose are eldest, Jenny an only child, and Ramon and Chantal have siblings who are much older. Research on gifted individuals going back to Yoder (1894) reveals that only children and firstborns are over-represented among the gifted. Owing to the confusion over the causes of this finding (e.g., Steelman, 1985), the present assertion is more descriptive than explanatory. Favorable birth order may have contributed to a sense of being special, although none of the students mentioned this in their interviews.

Summary. We believe that the students' success at the Lab School derives in part from certain personal characteristics, including high academic aptitude, emotional

Table 6   Assertions Concerning the Students Themselves

1. The identification of the students as potentially gifted was valid.
2. The students are goal-directed, aspire to success, see the instrumentality of academic achievement, and have age-appropriate understandings of the requirements for vocational success.
3. The students are emotionally stable and socially adept.
4. The students see themselves as special.
5. The students are eldest, only, or "functional only" children.

security, a sense of themselves as special, ambition, and awareness that school success is necessary for meeting goals.

Assertions Concerning the Families

Table 7 lists assertions regarding the students' families that we think illuminate major factors in the students' success.

Assertion 1: The parents do not believe in a totally intractable caste system. Unlike the involuntary minority parents described by Ogbu (1978, 1985), the four single mothers and one mother currently living with her husband do not believe in a totally inflexible caste system to whose bottom rungs their children will inevitably be consigned. This came through unequivocally in the interviews and is reflected in their children's participation in Project Synergy and in the parents' steady attendance at the parent seminars.

Assertion 2: Parents believe that academic success can lead to upward mobility, and they socialize their children accordingly. Related to the first assertion, the parents view education as the means by which their children can rise in society. The parents' view of the benefits of education came through clearly in the parent interviews when they were asked about their ambitions for their children. This belief has affected how they socialize their children, and, consequently, the students hold the same view.

Rose's mother, for example, indicated that she would like to see her daughter become a doctor or a lawyer, and she asserted that this would be possible "if she puts her mind to it" and gets a good education. Ramon's mother would like him to become an engineer, like others in her family. Chantal's mother stated, "She wants to be a doctor . . . and I think if she continues, that's where she's going to go." Darryl's mother's ambitions for her son were anything but limited: "I want him to be anything he wants to be. I want him—I would like him to be somebody very important, like a President . . . of the United States of America." Jenny's mother discussed this issue in light of the possibility that her daughter might encounter sexual bias in the future:

> Well, you know, we had this talk two days ago because she keeps telling me, "I want to get a house," and "I want to have children," and I told

Table 7   Assertions Concerning the Families

1. The parents do not believe in a totally intractable caste system.
2. Parents believe that academic success can lead to upward mobility and socialize their children accordingly.
3. The parents create a home environment in which the prevailing norms resemble middle-class norms, lessening the pressure on the children for "assimilation without accommodation."
4. The parents are unwilling to attribute all disappointments to racism or are willing to ignore some instances of racism for their children's sake.
5. The parents recognize and encourage their children's giftedness.
6. There are positive role models for the children in the home, including parents.
7. The parents are willing to take risks.
8. There is no overt family pathology. The families, although headed by a single mother in four of five cases, are stable and provide love and support for the children.

her there's other things out there instead of staying home and taking care of children. Now there are those who don't feel it's wrong that the woman stays home. I guess I have mixed feelings about her, but I want her to know that's not the only thing out there for her because she is a little girl. She can go out there and do something else, she can be in the business world and whatever she wants to do, but she has to get that education to put her there.

Assertion 3: The parents create a home environment in which the prevailing norms resemble middle-class norms, lessening the pressure on the children for "assimilation without accommodation." Unlike the situation described by Ogbu (1992), in which life for involuntary minority families is characterized by secondary cultural differences and cultural inversion, the values subscribed to by the families of these students are, for want of a better term, "middle class." Children are socialized to value education and remain in school, and achievement requires less accommodation without assimilation" because school and home values are consonant.

There is considerable evidence that the parents support these norms, beginning with the fact that the parents accepted a place in Project Synergy for their children and remained with the project for six years. In addition, the parents stress the importance of speaking standard English and of school success, two areas cited by Ogbu as areas in which cultural inversion can frequently be manifested. While they attended the Lab School, Ramon and Chantal had older siblings in college, and the mothers of Darryl and Jenny attended a community college during the same period with the goal of starting middle-class careers. The parents also attended parent-teacher conferences and were otherwise involved in school activities.

To an extent, Rose's family is an exception. Rose and her mother spent some time in a shelter for the homeless. Rose's mother was less involved in activities at the Lab School than were the other mothers, and Rose's frequent lateness was a concern. It is illuminating, however, that during Rose's first year in the Lab School, her mother moved the family to the Bronx, some distance from the Lab School, and enrolled Rose in the school in the new neighborhood. Rose was very unhappy, and the school was obviously inferior to the Lab School, so her mother re-enrolled her in the Lab School and managed the logistics required to get her daughter to school. Thus, although spending time in a homeless shelter is not an experience typical of middle-class families, the mother's drive toward self-sufficiency and efforts to secure a good education for her daughter were.

Assertion 4: The parents are unwilling to attribute all disappointments to racism or are willing to ignore some instances of racism for their children's sake. As members of minority groups, the parents could not be unaware of, or immune to, the effects of racism. However, like the achieving students in Ford's (1992) study, the parents either believed that the effects of racism were lessening, that racism was a burden but not an absolute barrier, or that, although it was the source of considerable injustice, racism was no excuse for personal failure.

For example, when asked if she thought being a member of a minority group would make it difficult for Darryl to succeed, his mother replied, "I hope not. I hope that by the time he gets of age, all this racial stuff will be gone, under the covers. I just hope." Similarly, Ramon's mother asserted, "I don't think he's going to have any problems. I don't believe in that discrimination. I think if you are really prepared for the future and you try to progress, nobody's going to stop you." Jenny's mother acknowledged the burdens of both racism and sexism but, she still expressed confidence in her daughter's future, saying,

> I think it might make it somewhat difficult because, not only being a minority, because of color, but being a female in this country does not help much either. But I guess if you just put your mind to it, you can block out everything else and get to the point where you need to be.

Assertion 5: The parents recognize and encourage their children's giftedness. Support for this assertion is found in the fact that the students were enrolled in Project Synergy and the Lab School, and in the parent interviews. Jenny's mother first started thinking that her daughter had high academic potential when her kindergarten teacher suggested this was the case. Darryl's mother noticed that, unlike other children in his Head Start program, he had memorized his address and telephone number. Ramon's prekindergarten teacher in Ecuador called his mother's attention to his ability, although the mother had already concluded that her son, like her older daughter, was highly capable. Rose's mother noticed that Rose had special abilities at age one, and Chantal's mother stated that Chantal was special from birth:

> Really, from the time she was born . . . she was so different from all the other children. When [Chantal] was a baby, she never cried really. . . . And

then, as she started to grow, she was so quick to grasp. If you said anything, if you talked in riddles, she would pick up on what you said.

Assertion 6: There are positive role models for the children in the home, including parents. Darryl's mother attended college, as did Jenny's mother. In addition to her mother, Jenny had the example and encouragement of an aunt, her mother's sister, who lived with the family for some time and was, while Jenny was at the Lab School, a law student at the University of Virginia. Prior to that, Jenny attended her aunt's college graduation ceremony, which made quite an impression on her. Jenny's mother quoted her as saying, "I'm going to go to school and finish school, and I'm going to have that graduation like Auntie had." Rose, in her interview, mentioned cousins who were either attending or had graduated from college and who had told Rose that college had been a positive experience. Ramon's sister was in college in 1992–93, and he has uncles in Ecuador who are engineers. During that same year, Chantal had two sisters in college and a brother who planned to attend the following year.

Assertion 7: The parents are willing to take risks. The parents are risktakers, specifically with respect to their willingness to leave a familiar and comfortable situation for the sake of their children. Although P.S. 149/207 may not seem to be a comfortable environment, for the families who live within its catchment area, it is close, familiar, and, with respect to New York City standards of public school safety, secure. More than a few parents who send their children to this school are, for a variety of reasons, wary of the educational system and the prospect of venturing beyond P.S. 149/207. In many cases their children are big fish in a small pond, and a larger pond full of large fish does not strike all parents as a congenial environment for their children. Not parents, even those whose children are potentially gifted, have the level of aspiration for their children described above; many seem more resigned to the caste system Ogbu (1978, 1985) described, and they socialize their children accordingly.

It is easy to underestimate the courage and confidence required for the parents even to attend an orientation meeting for Project Synergy at a university whose location on Morningside Heights overlooking Harlem has symbolic, as well as geological, significance. To participate in the project and attend the parent workshops, to violate, to some extent, the cultural norms Ogbu and Fordham described (Fordham, 1988, 1991; Fordham & Ogbu, 1986; Ogbu, 1992), thus bearing the "burden of acting white," to presume to exercise their rights of school choice despite the disapproval of the principal of their children's first school, to venture to a new and different school in a new and different neighborhood—all these require a willingness to take risks on their children's behalf.

Risk taking shows up in other aspects of family life. Two of the single mothers, Darryl's and Jenny's, attended college while raising children. Two families, Ramon's and Chantal's, immigrated to this country (or to the mainland, in Chantal's case) after the birth of the children. Rose and her mother endured life in a homeless shelter, during which time the mother was pregnant with Rose's younger sister. We are convinced that the parents' dauntless, persistent dedication to their children's welfare has been a major factor in the children's realizing their giftedness.

Assertion 8: There is no overt family pathology. The families are stable and provide love and support for the children. Despite the fact that in four of five cases the family is headed by a single mother living in poverty, these are secure, supportive families that are not dysfunctional. This is obvious for Ramon, whose family is intact. Jenny's mother has a long-standing relationship with a man who is involved in raising Jenny and who was often the only man at Project Synergy meetings and parties. Rose's mother also has a serious relationship with a man, the father of Rose's sister, and Rose was able to stay in his apartment, which is fairly close to the Lab School, after her unhappy experience in the Bronx. Chantal's older siblings, who were her care givers at times, constitute an important part of her extended family.

In the case of all four of the single mothers, the father is completely removed from the family, which may contribute to the stability of the remaining family members.

Summary. We strongly believe that the children's families have been an important factor in the children's academic success. As researchers working with other populations (e.g., Feldman, 1991, with child prodigies; Bloom, 1985, with talented young people) have shown, ability is not sufficient for the realization of potential. Strong, consistent family support is also needed. What was true for the middle-class families studied by Feldman and Bloom appears to be true for these families, as well.

Assertions Concerning the Students' School

We generated one assertion with seven parts concerning the school into which the five students transferred (see Table 8). The assertion is that the Lab School is an optimal placement for the students for the following reasons: (a) the school is racially, ethnically, and—of great importance—socioeconomically diverse; (b) the school has a flexible, inclusive definition of giftedness; (c) the school has a flexible admission process; (d) there is a range of achievement levels among the students at the school; (e) the school's curriculum is less oriented toward the sequential acquisition of skills than is typical of schools for academically gifted students; (f) the school nevertheless expects and receives high levels of achievement from its students, and thus provides the academic challenge the students require; and (g) the school's director wanted Project Synergy students in the school.

Thus, there was consistency between the nontraditional identification procedures used by Project Synergy and the selection process employed by the Lab School. Moreover, adjustment to the new school was facilitated by the fact of the school's diversity and its curriculum, which expected less in the way of

Table 8   Assertions Concerning the Students' School

I. The Laboratory School for Gifted Education is an optimal placement for the students because:

    a. The school is racially, ethnically, and socioeconomically diverse.

    b. The school has a flexible, inclusive definition of giftedness.

    c. The school has a flexible admission process.

    d. There is a range of achievement levels among the students at the school.

    e. The school's curriculum is less oriented toward the sequential acquisition of skills than is typical of schools for academically gifted students.

    f. The school nevertheless expects and receives high levels of achievement from its students and thus provides the academic stimulation the five students require.

    g. The school's director is committed to having students from Project Synergy in the school.

developed skills than might have been expected in other schools. Nonetheless, the expectation for achievement and the level of instruction were appropriate to the students' needs.

Assertions Concerning Project Synergy

Finally, we are proposing three assertions concerning the intervention provided by Project Synergy, as shown in Table 9.

Assertion 1: The project helped the parents and the students themselves to view the students as special, in part because project personnel held high expectations for the students and their families. Although the parents stated that, in some cases, they saw their children as different from a very early age, we saw these opinions strengthen as the families participated in the project. In an interview with CNN news, for example, Darryl's mother stated that, although she always viewed Darryl as smart, she never saw him as potentially gifted until he was identified by Project Synergy.

One of the first workshops for parents was on the topic of seeing their children as special. As our parent-service coordinator reported, this was not just a matter of strengthening this belief but, in many cases, of planting it in the parents' minds in the first place. Like many bright children, these children are frequently more demanding than other children, and often parents interpreted this simply as trouble making.

A strong conviction on the part of project personnel that these children had the potential for academic giftedness, we believe, in part motivated parents and the students themselves to think that way. We began the project with only one a priori assumption: that potentially gifted children could be found in any school in the country. After observing and assessing these children for a period of months prior to substantive intervention, we had no doubt that their potential was considerable. It is possible that our expectations for the children affected the attitudes and behaviors of the parents and the children.

Assertion 2: The project helped the students develop appropriate academic skills and attitudes. Achievement test data discussed above substantiate this assertion, and we discount the possibility that the students' skill acquisition was the result of their previous school (basic skill work in this school was desultory and largely ineffective) or maturation (acquisition of basic academic skills obviously does not take place as a function of biological maturation, but rather through education) instead of the transitional services classes and tutoring they received through the project.

Assertion 3: The project provided parents with the knowledge and support necessary to become effective advocates for their children, including the emotional support needed to make the move to a more challenging school outside the families' neighborhood. We believe the fact that the parents exercised their right to choose a new school for their children is, in large part, attributable to the intervention of the project. More than any other topic, the parent workshops focused on helping parents understand how the educational system works and what their rights are in this system. We saw gains in the parents' confidence and assertiveness as their knowledge grew. The project was the catalyst that allowed these bright, ambitious, risk-taking parents to act on behalf of their potentially gifted children.

DISCUSSION

Identifying Giftedness Among Economically Disadvantaged Children

We began this paper with a discussion of the problem of underrepresentation of economically disadvantaged children, especially minority children, in programs for gifted students. Although we do not want to suggest that there are easy solutions, we think our experiences with Project Synergy provide some hope. During the years in which we worked at the school, P.S. 149/207 had one of the lowest records of academic achievement in New York City. Nonetheless, five students, approximately 5% of its 1990–91 kindergarten class, were admitted to and succeeded in a school for academically gifted students. This statistic, we believe, confirms our contention that giftedness, or its potential, is present in every school in the country if we have the will, the energy, or, admittedly in our case, the grant money to find it.

Even without significant additional funds, schools can do more to identify giftedness among economically disadvantaged students than they are doing now (see Borland & Wright, 1994). To do so will require the adoption of nontraditional identification procedures utilizing such approaches as observation, dynamic assessment (e.g., Lidz, 1987), portfolio assessment (Wright & Borland, 1993), and focusing on best performance (Roedell, Jackson, & Robinson, 1980).

It will also require an understanding that giftedness manifests itself in different ways in different settings, and that, in order to understand these manifestations, one must understand the setting. As Armour-Thomas (1992) has argued, cognitive potential and cultural experience cannot be understood apart from each other. Part of the problem discussed at the beginning of this paper stems, we suspect, from failing to realize that the potential for conventional academic giftedness may, in its nascent forms, reveal itself differently in various subcultures within our society.

Confronting the Larger Problem

Although identification is part of the problem, it is important to realize that it is not the entire problem. We need to develop methods for identifying giftedness that are sensitive to its expression in culturally diverse settings. But, even if this were to be accomplished, all would not be well because racism and other forms of prejudice and class bias are neither absent from our society nor benign in their effects. A child born into poverty, especially a child of color, will find it more difficult to develop the cognitive abilities for which he or she has the potential than will a White child born into a middle-class home. Poverty and racism, although they diminish us all as a society, do singular damage to the most vulnerable, especially children, who are their direct victims. To believe otherwise is to ignore the evidence, of is our most appalling collective failure.

If one believes that the potential for giftedness exists in roughly equal proportions in all groups in our society and that social forces are undermining its development in some groups, it becomes clear that some form of intervention is needed, not just better identification, if the problem of inequity in programs for gifted students is to be resolved. In Project Synergy, our work with children involved three phases: (a) site-specific identification focusing on potential giftedness, (b) transitional services designed to help students move from being potentially gifted to being manifestly gifted, and (c) placement of students, when they are ready, in classes for gifted students.

It is the second phase, transitional services, that we think is needed along with better identification procedures. Achieving these goals requires that we acknowledge that, as a group, economically disadvantaged children, despite being born with equal potential, can suffer delays as a result of the inequitable allocation of resources in this country (e.g., Kozol, 1991). Moreover, it requires that we acknowledge that we need to intervene before these children can be placed in programs for gifted students. This, then, is the task as we see it: First, identify potential giftedness; second, intervene to develop the strengths that are present in more or less latent form.

Why Bright At-Risk Students Succeed

The potential for giftedness among economically disadvantaged children is, thankfully, not always extinguished, as the examples of the five students who

Table 9   Assertions Concerning Project Synergy

1. The project helped the parents and the students themselves view the students as special, in part because project personnel held high expectations for the students and their families.
2. The project helped the students develop appropriate academic skills and attitudes.
3. The project provided parents with the knowledge and support necessary to become effective advocates for their children, including the emotional support needed to make the move to a more challenging school outside the families' neighborhood.

participated in this inquiry demonstrate. What made the difference in this case? Why have these children, who exhibited enough indicators of at-risk status for educational disadvantage to suggest serious danger, succeeded where others have failed? We believe the explanation can be found in the mix of psychological and social forces and factors that are enumerated in the assertions presented above.

According to Tannenbaum (1983), manifest giftedness is a psychosocial phenomenon resulting from the interaction of an individual's general and specific cognitive abilities, nonintellective psychological factors, and environmental factors, with chance often playing an important, if unpredictable, role. A similar psychosocial perspective can be derived from an integration of the assertions we have developed, with roles being assigned to (a) the students' cognitive ability, emotional stability, achievement motivation, and belief in their exceptionality; (b) the families' faith in the possibility of merit-based advancement, belief in the value of education, middle-class values, willingness to take risks, and stability; (c) the school's philosophy and practice, which are compatible with the students' educational profiles and needs; and (d) the intervention of Project Synergy, a program with an approach that is psychosocial and that, to an extent, represents an element of chance in the lives of these children and their families.

We believe that the family is the crucial element in this mix. The family is also central in Ogbu's work, but in a much different manner and with strikingly different results. The secondary cultural differences described by Ogbu, especially as manifested in cultural inversion, are much less in evidence in the families of the five children in this study. Absent, too, is the fatalistic belief in a rigid, unbending caste system and the socialization for indifference to school learning that accompanies such a belief.

These students would be more likely to feel affective dissonance (DeVos, 1967) by repudiating middle-class aspirations and failing in school than by succumbing to the lure of the street. School success does not seem to carry the "burden of acting white." Ford (1993) found something similar. She wrote,

> Gifted Black achievers are less concerned with peer pressure. If given the choice between peers and success, they would choose (or have chosen) success. On the other hand, gifted underachievers . . . worry more about being called "nerds," "geek," "teacher's pet," and "acting white." (p. 83)

It is difficult to determine the extent to which Project Synergy was a cause or catalyst, or whether the students would have made it on their own. We suspect that the argument that bright students will make it on their own is as fallacious for potentially gifted economically disadvantaged students as educators of the gifted (see Office of Educational Research and Improvement, 1993) argue it is for gifted students from the middle class. The intervention must have had an effect. Nevertheless, these were students and families who were receptive to intervention, who had done much of the hard work already. In that sense, Project Synergy merely gave a boost to those who were already prepared.

That, however, is the case with academic giftedness among students who are not economically disadvantaged. The interaction of individual abilities with family and environmental support results in educational achievement that, in turn, requires an appropriate response from the educational system. This interaction is one expression of the fact of individual differences, one whose expression is suppressed among those living in poverty under the yoke of racism.

Support for Ogbu's Theories

The factors that, according to Ogbu, lead to the academic failure of many involuntary minority children were not present in the situations of the children in this study. That, in itself, does not lend solid support to his theories. The assertion that X leads to Y is not supported when it is found that not-X does not lead to Y (e.g., if we claim that red hair causes tuberculosis, finding 1,000 blondes and brunettes without tuberculosis does nothing to support our theory). Nonetheless, some mild support for his contentions can be found here.

The students under study here and their families were, on the surface at least, at-risk both according to the work of Natriello et al. (1990) and Ogbu's (e.g., 1992) characterization of involuntary minorities living in poverty. That the children, with the support of their families, were able to achieve academically is plausibly attributable to the absence of the critical psychosocial factors, especially cultural inversion and the belief in a rigid caste system structured along racial lines, that Ogbu sees as operating in the lives of poor involuntary minority families. More research with economically disadvantaged gifted students grounded in Ogbu's theoretical framework could result in findings of significant value, and we urge others to engage in such inquiry.

Implications for Practice

The question of what to do looms large here. Although we believe that the intervention of Project Synergy made a difference in the lives of these families, we also need to acknowledge that we identified the children who, although in an environment not conducive to their academic progress, were more likely to succeed than most of their peers. Family structures and parental attitudes supportive of school success were already in place, albeit in a form that required support from the project. It is quite likely, however, that other children with the potential, now or in the past, to achieve academic giftedness did not develop even the most rudimentary signs of that potential due to the absence of a supportive family.

Intervention at the stage of development appropriate to nurture the potential of all children would be a daunting enterprise, one that seems to belong to another, more hopeful and courageous era. Widespread infant intervention programs of the sort that would encourage and empower parents living in poverty to provide their children with the support and structure necessary to achieve in school is unlikely to become a reality in these times, Head Start notwithstanding.

We probably need to tend to our small corner of the educational field in ways that will lead to more equitable programs for gifted students. First of all, we need to widen our search for gifted students to places like P.S. 149/207. As we believed going into this project, there are potentially gifted students in every school, something that is demonstrated by the successful placement of 5% of this school's 1990–91 kindergarten class in a school for gifted students.

Second, we need to adopt nontraditional, rigorously validated identification methods that are more sensitive to expressions of potential giftedness in environments outside the mainstream, in which this field has usually operated. Our work (see Borland & Wright, 1994) and that of others working in Javits-funded projects needs wider dissemination and testing.

Third, the notion of potential giftedness as employed in Project Synergy and the implementation of transitional services designed to help able but lagging students realize their potential should be considered for wider application. We suspect that there are many students living in poverty and attending schools where expectations for their academic achievement are minimal who have the innate capacity to achieve academic giftedness. Identifying these students is only part of the task. We believe that placing them in traditional gifted programs without adequate preparation, without accelerating their learning so they can make up for time lost, would, in most cases lead to failure. Structured, well-thought-out intervention designed to bring students from the status of potentially academically gifted to academically gifted is needed and ought to be a priority in our field.

The Larger Question of Equity

We are dealing with a problem that is part of a larger problem, whose human dimensions are reflected in the fact that we ended up working with 5% of a class of students, all of whom had educational needs. One cannot help thinking, as we frequently did, of the other 95%. However, as stated above, progress will of necessity be incremental, and, as educators whose field of study is the educational needs of students of high ability, this is where we hope to add our increment.

We think there is real damage done to bright children who depend on publicly funded education where there is no response to their special needs. Children from more affluent families can always buy an appropriate education.

Poorer children cannot, and they suffer accordingly, as Kozol (1991) has made painfully clear. Indifference to, hostility toward, or low funding for special education for gifted students will only promote equity of a limited and pernicious kind: It will insure that no gifted or potentially gifted children whose families cannot afford to pay will rise above the mean unless they can do so in spite of the educational system that putatively exists to serve them.

Achieving equity in programs for gifted students, if it can be accomplished, will not solve all of society's problems, only the problem of inequity in programs for gifted students. But, that is the kind of incremental progress we refer to above. And, perhaps the greater good can be served, as well. W. E. B. DuBois (1903/1970) spoke of the "Talented Tenth," the academically most capable whose abilities could enrich not only their lives, but the communities in which they live, as the hope of African Americans. That is an elitist notion not much in favor today, and it is important to consider the pressing needs of the remaining nine-tenths. Nonetheless, it is difficult to conceive of an equitable society in which certain groups, defined by their socioeconomic status, their race, or their ethnicity, are not able to achieve full educational provision for those among them with the greatest potential for learning and producing knowledge.

NOTES

1. There was constant attrition from the time the first cohort of 18 children was identified in the spring of 1991 to the time the five children described in this article entered the special school in the fall of 1992. Initially, parents of 15 of the 18 identified children agreed to have their children participate in the program; 12 of these children remained by the end of the summer 1991 transitional services session. Of these 12 children, 2 were not invited to participate in the fall 1991 classes due to severe behavioral problems, and three more children left the program during AY 1991–92, either because their families moved from New York City or because the parent lost custody of the child to the Child Welfare Bureau. Of the remaining seven children, two were deemed not ready for placement outside P.S. 149/207. One has subsequently been placed in a parochial school.

2. The research was designed by the first and third author, and data were gathered and analyzed by the authors and a number of their graduate students, including the second author, who was a graduate student at the time. The first and third authors were the principal investigators for Project Synergy. Some of the students involved in this investigation were also members of the Project Synergy team.

3. Mathematics was a particularly weak curricular area in the students' previous school. Moreover, the sequential acquisition of basic mathematical skills was not emphasized at the Lab School. It is therefore not that surprising that, compared to national norms, two of the five students had Math Composites below the mean. However, this was not a noticeable liability on a day-to-day basis in the classroom, where mathematical reasoning, rather than computation and application, was stressed.

4. Chantal unfortunately did an effective job of masking her disability until she arrived at the Lab School. Her oral verbal reasoning and expression skills were strong

(see her Binet Verbal Reasoning score in Table 3). We regarded her as one of the brightest students in Project Synergy. Her performance in kindergarten and first grade, comparable to that of other students at P.S. 149/207, was not such that it would warrant suspicion. Her first-grade score on the Test of Early Reading Ability was at the 66th percentile, and her Peabody Picture Vocabulary Test scaled score was 94. Even Chantal's second-grade teacher at the Lab School was skeptical with respect to whether she had a learning disability and appeared not to notice that she was, for all practical purposes, illiterate. Chantal was given a full psychoeducational assessment at the Teachers College Child Study Center in the spring of 1993, which confirmed her learning disability. We explored the possibility of placement in a public school program for gifted learning-disabled students. However, Chantal's mother did not want her daughter to be classified as a special-education student or to be part of the New York City special-educational system.

REFERENCES

Armour-Thomas, E. (1992). Intellectual assessment of children from culturally diverse backgrounds. *School Psychology Review, 21*, 552–565.

Bloom, B. S. (Ed.). (1985). *Developing talent in young people.* New York: Ballantine.

Borland, J. H. (1990). Postpositivistic inquiry: Implications of the "new philosophy of science" for the field of the education of the gifted. *Gifted Child Quarterly, 34*, 161–167.

Borland, J. H., & Wright, L. (1994). Identifying young, potentially gifted, economically disadvantaged students. *Gifted Child Quarterly, 38*, 164–171.

DeVos, G. A. (1967). Essential elements of caste: Psychological determinants in structural theory. In G. A. DeVos & H. Wagatsuma (Eds.), *Japan's invisible race: Caste in culture and personality* (pp. 332–384). Berkeley, CA: University of California Press.

DuBois, W. E. B. (1970). The talented tenth. In *The Negro problem* (pp. 31–76). New York: AMS Press. (Original work published 1903)

Dunn, L. M., & Dunn, L. M. (1981). *Peabody Picture Vocabulary Test—Revised.* Circle Pines, MN: American Guidance Service.

Feldman, D. H. (1991). *Nature's gambit: Child prodigies and the development of human potential.* New York: Teachers College Press.

Ford, D. Y. (1992). Determinants of underachievement as perceived by gifted, above-average and average Black students. *Roeper Review, 14*, 130–136.

Ford, D. Y. (1993). An investigation of the paradox of underachievement among gifted Black students. *Roeper Review, 16*, 78–84.

Ford, D. Y. (1996). *Reversing underachievement among gifted Black students.* New York: Teachers College Press.

Fordham, S. (1988). Racelessness as a strategy in Black students' school success: Pragmatic strategy or pyrrhic victory? *Harvard Educational Review, 58*(1), 54–84.

Fordham, S. (1991). Peer proofing academic competition among Black adolescents: "Acting White: Black American style." In C. E. Sleeter (Ed.), *Empowerment through multicultural education* (pp. 69–93). Albany, NY: State University of New York Press.

Fordham, S., & Ogbu, J. U. (1986). Black students' school success: Coping with the burden of "acting white." *The Urban Review, 18*, 176–206.

Ginsburg, H. P., & Baroody, A. (1990). *Test of early mathematics ability* (2nd ed.). Austin, TX: PRO-ED.

Glaser, B. G., & Strauss, A. L. (1967). *The discovery of grounded theory: Strategies for qualitative research.* New York: Aldine de Gruyter.

Harter, S. (1985). *Perceived competence scale for children.* Denver, CO: University of Denver.

Harter, S., & Pike, R. (1983). *The pictorial scale of perceived competence and social acceptance for young children.* Denver, CO: University of Denver.

Kaufman, A. S., & Kaufman, N. L. (1985). *Kaufman test of educational achievement.* Circle Pines, MN: American Guidance Service.

Kearney, K., & LeBlanc, J. (1993). Forgotten pioneers in the study of gifted African Americans. *Roeper Review, 15,* 192–199.

Kozol, J. (1991). *Savage Inequalities.* New York: Crown.

Krueger, R. A. (1994). *Focus groups: A practical guide for applied research* (2nd ed.). Thousand Oaks, CA: Sage.

Lidz, C. S. (Ed.). (1987). *Dynamic assessment: An interactional approach to evaluating learning potential.* New York: Guilford.

Lincoln, Y. S., & Guba, E. G. (1985). *Naturalistic inquiry.* Beverly Hills, CA: Sage.

Mickelson, R. A. (1990). The attitude-achievement paradox among Black adolescents. *Sociology of Education, 63,* 44–61.

Natriello, G., McDill, E. L., & Pallas, A. M. (1990). *Schooling disadvantaged children: Racing against catastrophe.* New York: Teachers College Press.

Nowicki, S., & Strickland, B. R. (1973). Nowicki-Strickland Locus of Control Scale for Children. *Journal of Consulting and Clinical Psychology, 40,* 148–154.

Office of Educational Research and Improvement, U. S. Department of Education. (1993). *National excellence: A case for developing America's talent.* Washington, DC: U.S. Government Printing Office.

Ogbu, J. U. (1978). *Minority education and caste: The American system in cross-cultural perspective.* New York: Academic Press.

Ogbu, J. U. (1985). Minority education and caste. In N. R. Yetman (Ed.), *Majority and minority* (4th ed., pp. 370–383). Boston: Allyn & Bacon.

Ogbu, J. U. (1992). Understanding cultural diversity and learning. *Educational Researcher, 21*(8), 5–14.

Passow, A. H. (1989). Needed research and development in educating high ability children. *Roeper Review, 11,* 223–229.

Porter, R. B., & Cattell, R. B. (1975). *Handbook for the children's personality questionnaire.* Champaign, IL: Institute for Personality and Ability Testing.

Reid, D. K., Hresko, W. P., & Hammill, D. D. (1989). *Test of early reading ability.* (2nd ed.). Rockville, MD: PRO-ED.

Richert, E. S. (1987). Rampant problems and promising practices in the identification of disadvantaged gifted students. *Gifted Child Quarterly, 31,* 149–154.

Roedell, W. C., Jackson, N. E., & Robinson, H. B. (1980). *Gifted young children. Perspectives on gifted and talented education.* New York: Teachers College Press.

Silverman, L. K., & Kearney, K. (1992). The case for the Stanford-Binet L-M as a supplemental test. *Roeper Review, 15,* 34–37.

Steelman, L. C. (1985). A tale of two variables: A review of the intellectual consequences of sibship size and birth order. *Review of Educational Research, 55,* 353–386.

Tannenbaum, A. J. (1983). *Gifted children: Psychological and educational perspectives.* New York: Macmillan.

Thorndike, R. L., Hagen, E. P., & Sattler, J. M. (1986). *The Stanford-Binet intelligence scale* (4th ed.). Chicago: Riverside.

VanTassel-Baska, J., Patton, J., & Prillaman, D. (1989). Disadvantaged gifted learners: At risk for educational attention. *Focus on Exceptional Children, 22*(3), 1–15.

Wechsler, D. (1991). *The Wechsler intelligence scale for children* (3rd ed.). San Antonio, TX: Psychological Corporation.

Whitmore, J. R. (1980). *Giftedness, conflict, and underachievement.* Boston: Allyn & Bacon.

Wright, L., & Borland, J. H. (1993). Using portfolios to identify young, potentially gifted, economically disadvantaged students. *Roeper Review, 15,* 205–210.

Yoder, A. H. (1894). The story of the boyhood of great men. *Pedagogical Seminary, 3,* 134–156.

Index

Note: References to tables or figures are indicated by *italic type* and the addition of *"t"* or *"f"* respectively.